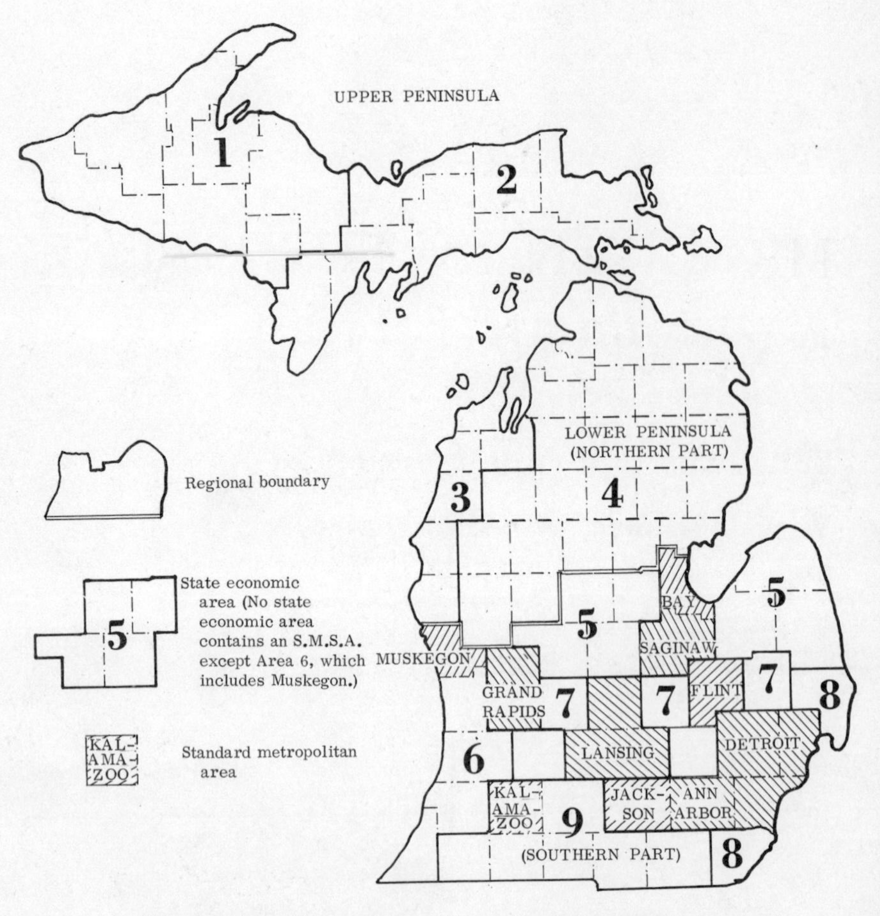

State of Michigan Showing Regional Boundaries, State Economic Areas and Standard Metropolitan Statistical Areas. (Source: *U.S. Census of Population*: 1960.)

Michigan Business Studies
Volume XVI Number 4

MICHIGAN IN THE 1970's
An Economic Forecast

Edited and with an Introduction by

William Haber, W. Allen Spivey, and Martin R. Warshaw

Bureau of Business Research
Graduate School of Business Administration
The University of Michigan
Ann Arbor, Michigan

PHOTOLITHOPRINTED BY CUSHING - MALLOY, INC.
ANN ARBOR, MICHIGAN, UNITED STATES OF AMERICA
1965

PREFACE

The development of the Michigan economy has been a subject of serious concern for many years, particularly since 1956, when it became clear that, after a period of remarkable growth, the state's economic environment was undergoing dramatic changes. Michigan, after several decades as one of the busiest states in the nation, was beginning to show signs of economic trouble.

Our employment levels were adversely influenced by several persistent developments. One was the geographic decentralization of automotive assembly plants. Another was the changing military requirements of the United States. These developments were not related to any specific internal weakness in the Michigan economy. The first was a natural response by the automobile industry to shifts in population and markets and to changing transportation costs. The second was caused by the relocation of military contracts and jobs in areas which met the requirements of the missile age for substantial development in electronics. There were, of course, other causes of Michigan's problems. One was related to our industry mix, to the lack of diversification in our manufacturing industry. The extent of efficiency-improving investment also had some temporary downward influence on our employment levels. In addition, one must mention certain psychological and political factors which, while difficult to measure, appeared to affect the climate for industry and the state's image and to exert some influence upon location decisions by industry.

These developments were examined in some detail in 1959 in *The Michigan Economy: Its Potentials and Its Problems*, a volume published by the W. E. Upjohn Institute for Employment Research.[1] In 1960 the institute published another volume of

[1]William Haber, Eugene C. McKean, and Harold C. Taylor, *The Michigan Economy: Its Potentials and Its Problems* (Kalamazoo, Mich.: W. E. Upjohn Institute for Employment Research, 1959).

studies, undertaken at the request of the Committee on Michigan's Economic Future and entitled *Taxes and Economic Growth in Michigan.*[2]

The economic situation in our state has improved materially since these volumes were published. The process of decentralization of the automobile industry appears to have been largely completed; the departure from the state of about 400,000 persons between 1958 and 1962--among whom were workers and their families who had migrated to Michigan before 1958—eased our unemployment problems by reducing the size of the labor force. This reduction, coupled with the automotive boom of the past three years, has given us exceptionally low levels of involuntary unemployment since 1962. In addition, the improved fiscal situation in the state, taken together with political and psychological factors, has definitely changed both the climate for industry and the state's image. There is no universal agreement that these noneconomic factors are of critical importance; in any event, they cannot easily be measured. It is clear, however, that beliefs or perceptions which are widely held by the business community do influence policy decisions. In recent years these perceptions have tended to be favorable.

It would be naive and even dangerous to believe that the exceptionally favorable economic situation of the past few years will continue indefinitely, or even into the immediate future. There are basic problems in the state's economy, problems which have been only temporarily eased by the unprecedented national prosperity, by the substantial migration from Michigan before 1962, and by the unusually good years for the automobile industry. Some of these problems are complex and deep-seated; they cannot be wished away. To identify and analyze them requires long and careful study. Their correction will call for a co-operative program that includes the best efforts of our government, our industrial and labor leadership, and our educational institutions. Basically, the problems of Michigan's

[2]Paul W. McCracken (ed.), *Taxes and Economic Growth in Michigan* (Kalamazoo, Mich.: W. E. Upjohn Institute for Employment Research, 1960).

economy still are intimately related to a swiftly rising population and changing labor force requirements. They require an objective demographic analysis. They also call for an examination of the qualitative characteristics of our labor force and of the technological changes which are perennial in Michigan's advanced industry. The present report does not presume to provide answers to these problems. Its goal is quite modest. Our purpose is to outline the general direction of the problems and trends as we see them and to provide quantitative estimates of important economic variables into the 1970's. Our hope is that these studies will lead to the more detailed and intensive research analysis that is required before a practical program can be formulated.

In the preparation of this volume the editors have received the co-operation and assistance of many persons. We are especially indebted to the men who undertook the basic analysis—Sidney Sonenblum, James J. O'Leary, David Goldberg, Lowell D. Ashby, Wilbur R. Thompson, and Louis A. Ferman. These authors have been most helpful from the outset; they participated actively in seminar-conferences in Ann Arbor and responded most expeditiously to suggestions. It has been a pleasure to work closely in the planning and editing of this book with Professors W. Allen Spivey and Martin R. Warshaw of the Graduate School of Business Administration. The editors deeply appreciate the help of Norman Barcus, director of research and statistics of the Michigan Employment Security Commission, who brought his seasoned judgment on economic trends in Michigan to a reading of parts of the manuscript. Thanks are also due to his colleague, Samuel C. Stearn.

We are indebted to the Bureau of Business Research and particularly to its director, Professor Alfred W. Swinyard, for undertaking the publication of this report and for the care and thoroughness with which the editorial tasks were accomplished. For this, we are especially grateful to the editors—Mrs. William R. Steinhoff, Mrs. Hubert English, and Mr. John Drew O'Neill.

William Haber

Ann Arbor, Michigan
November, 1964

ABOUT THE AUTHORS

WILLIAM HABER has been professor of economics at the University of Michigan since 1936 and is at present dean of the College of Literature, Science, and the Arts. His field of specialization is labor economics, particularly social security, manpower, and labor relations. He has served as special assistant to the Director of the Budget, as director of planning for the War Manpower Commission, and as a member of the Michigan Unemployment Compensation Commission and the Federal Advisory Commission on Social Security. During the past fifteen years he has been chairman, and later a member, of the Federal Advisory Council on Employment Security of the Department of Labor. He also serves on the Public Advisory Committee of the Area Redevelopment Administration in the Department of Commerce. A member of the National Academy of Arbitrators, he has arbitrated labor-management disputes for over twenty years. His writings include books on industrial relations, labor productivity, social security, and technological change.

W. ALLEN SPIVEY is professor of statistics in the Graduate School of Business Administration at the University of Michigan, where he has taught since 1957. He was formerly on the faculty of the University of North Carolina, where he earned his doctorate, and he has served as visiting professor at Harvard University. His main interest is the application of mathematics to business problems, especially mathematical programming, but he has also done research and writing on regional economic analysis. His publications include *Linear Programming: An Introduction; Linear Programming and the Theory of the Firm* (with Kenneth Boulding); and "Gains in Real Per Capita Personal Income: A Method of Analysis" (with L. D. Ashby), which appeared in the *Southern Economic Journal* (October, 1957).

MARTIN R. WARSHAW is associate professor of marketing in the Graduate School of Business Administration at the University of Michigan. A graduate of Columbia College, he received his doctorate from the University of Michigan. He had several years of experience as a Michigan businessman before entering the teaching profession. His interest in research centers in marketing management, with special reference to industrial marketing, marketing logistics, and the regional location of industry. Author of *Effective Selling through Wholesalers* and a frequent consultant to business firms, he is president-elect of the Detroit chapter of the American Marketing Association.

SIDNEY SONENBLUM, director of the Center for Economic Projections of the National Planning Association, is currently on leave from that post to direct a research program in regional economic analysis at the Institute of Government and Public Affairs of the University of California at Los Angeles. He was educated at New York University and Columbia University, where he earned his doctorate. Among his studies of economic and demographic growth potentials of the United States and its various regions are *The Local Impact of Foreign Trade* and *Long-Range Projections for Economic Growth*.

JAMES J. O'LEARY is vice-president and director of research of the Life Insurance Association of America. In this capacity he administers a broad research program on the functioning of the American capital markets. He was educated at Wesleyan and Duke Universities and taught economics at both institutions until joining the Life Insurance Association of America as director of economic research in 1947. He is a member of many professional societies and has served as consultant to the United States Treasury, the Federal Reserve Board, the President's Council of Economic Advisors, and the federal housing agencies.

DAVID GOLDBERG is associate professor of sociology and program director of the Institute of Public Administration at the University of Michigan, where he earned his doctorate in 1958. He has been associated with the University of Michigan Institute of Social Research in its Detroit Area and American

Family studies since 1954 and is engaged in research on population and family problems. His publications include "Another Look at the Indianapolis Fertility Data," in the *Milbank Memorial Fund Quarterly* (January, 1960), and "The Fertility of Two-Generation Urbanites," in *Population Studies* (1958).

LOWELL D. ASHBY is Assistant Chief, Regional Economics Division, Office of Business Economics, U. S. Department of Commerce. His research activities in regional economic analysis include a study of the economy of North Carolina. He has been professor of economics at the University of North Carolina, and in his present position with the Office of Business Economics he is engaged in research on regional change, with special emphasis on employment shift analysis. His publications include "Regional Change in a National Setting," *Staff Working Paper in Economics and Statistics, No. 7,* published by the Office of Business Economics; and "Economic Orientations to Urbanization" and "Industrial Development Trends and Economic Potential," which appear in *Urban Growth Dynamics in a Regional Cluster of Cities* (edited by F. Stuart Chapin, Jr. and Shirley F. Weiss).

WILBUR R. THOMPSON is on leave from his position as professor of economics at Wayne State University and is at present engaged in research for Resources for the Future, Incorporated, of Washington, D. C. He was educated at Wayne State University and the University of Michigan, where he received his doctorate in economics, and has taught at Wayne since 1950. His chief research interests have been urban economics and the economic problems of the state and the region. He has served as research director of a Michigan pilot study on forecasting state economic development and as research associate at Resources for the Future, Incorporated. He is the author of *A Preface to Urban Economics: Toward a Conceptual Framework for Study and Research, Preliminary* and "Urban-Regional Economic Analysis: Concepts, Measurement, and Data," published in the *Proceedings of the Social Statistic Section of the American Statistical Association* (1962).

LOUIS A. FERMAN is a sociologist on the research staff of the Institute of Labor and Industrial Relations, University of Michigan–Wayne State University. A graduate of Brown University, he received his doctorate in sociology from Cornell. His main research interests are the structure and functioning of the labor market, adjustments to job displacement, and problems of minority group employment. His publications include *Too Old to Work: Too Young to Retire; A Case Study of a Permanent Plant Shutdown* (with H. L. Sheppard and Seymour Faber) and *The Impact of Technological Change: The American Experience* (with William Haber and James R. Hudson).

CONTENTS

TABLES

Number *Page*

TABLES

TABLES

FIGURES

I

INTRODUCTION

William Haber, W. Allen Spivey,
and Martin R. Warshaw

Overview

For over one hundred years, with few interruptions, Michigan has been among the fastest growing states in the Union. A great deal of this growth, especially that which has taken place since the early 1930's, has resulted from the rapid expansion of the automotive industry and the subsequent high degree of utilization of the resources of this industry and the labor force of the state to meet ever-growing levels of consumer and military demand.

The population growth which has occurred in Michigan in the first half of this century has been largely a reflection of migration into Michigan from other states. The availability of good-paying jobs, associated with the production of durable goods, and the existence of attractive living conditions have served in the past as magnets drawing new residents from other parts of the nation and the world.

After the close of World War II economic forces began accumulating on the national level which were ultimately to influence local economic conditions in Michigan significantly. The effects of these forces were temporarily submerged and to some extent delayed by the military build-up occasioned by the Korean war and by the continued high level of demand for automobiles which characterized the immediate post-Korean war economy.

Inevitably, however, after the adjustments from a wartime to a peacetime economy had been completed, the economic forces, which in the past had been sufficiently isolated from each other so that the state's economy could somehow accommodate them, began to coalesce and to exert a profound influence during the latter half of the 1950's. To many observers of the national as well as the Michigan scene it appeared that a sudden change had occurred in the economic environment. In reality, the change was the result of a combustion of events that had been smoldering for some time.

By 1956-57, changes in the state's economic environment were sufficiently clear—and disturbing—to indicate the beginning of a new era for Michigan. Simply stated, Michigan in the mid-1950's had begun an economic change of life. The causes were numerous and varied in the intensity of their impact within the state. They included, among others: (1) the geographic decentralization of the automotive industry, (2) changes in the quantity and the type of goods being procured by the military, (3) the impact of technology and automation upon manpower requirements, and (4) changes in the quantitative, qualitative, and locational characteristics of the labor force.

The impact of these economic changes was seen in decreasing growth rates in specific industrial sectors within the state's economy. But the effects were of unequal magnitudes, damaging most heavily mining (especially in the Upper Peninsula), agriculture, and durable goods manufacturing. To make matters worse, changes in growth rates of selected industrial sectors—especially downward changes—caused extreme dislocations in certain segments of the labor force.

Since 1957 many adjustments to differential rates of economic and demographic change both at the national and state levels have occurred in Michigan. The most significant adjustment was a massive outflow of people from the state. From 1956 through 1962 over 400,000 more persons left the state than entered it. The net out-migration counterbalanced a net in-migration of almost equal size which had occurred in the period 1950-56. This exodus reduced the size of the state's labor force significantly; thus when business conditions improved from 1961 onwards, the unemployment rate dropped more rapidly and to lower levels than would have been the case had these people not left the state. Indeed, the departure of almost half a million people from the state in the latter part of the 1950's is, in our opinion, nearly as important a factor in Michigan's current low unemployment rate as the several good automobile years since 1960. Even with the outflow of people, the state's adjustment has been difficult. The current strength in automotive manufacturing eases the pain but cannot completely cure the patient. The reasons for this situation are clear.

First, the state is unbalanced with respect to the spatial distribution of population and related economic wealth. For example, Michigan encompasses 83 counties covering over 50,000 square miles; yet almost 50 per cent of the state's population lives within the Detroit Standard Metropolitan Statistical Area (S.M.S.A.),[1] which consists of Wayne, Oakland, and Macomb Counties. An additional 25 per cent of the state's population resides in 9 other metropolitan areas located in the southern portion of the Lower Peninsula; thus about 75 per cent of the state's population resides in 10 urban area clusters. Nonmetropolitan areas in the southern portion of the Lower Peninsula account for approximately 18 per cent of the state's inhabitants, with the remaining 7 to 8 per cent of the population scattered over the tremendous land areas of the northern part of the Lower Peninsula and the Upper Peninsula.

Second, the state's industry mix is heavily biased toward the manufacture of durable goods. Currently, for example, manufacturing accounts for more than 40 per cent of Michigan's nonagricultural employment, as compared with less than 30 per cent in the United States. Of even greater significance is the fact that in Michigan "durable goods, such as automobiles, machinery, and household appliances, account for 33 per cent of our nonfarm employment and 80 per cent of our manufacturing employment, by contrast with corresponding national figures of 17 and 43 per cent."[2]

[1]A standard metropolitan area consists of a central city of 50,000 or more and the county containing that central city. When adjacent counties appear to be economically integrated with the central city county, they may be included in the metropolitan area. The central cities of Michigan's ten standard metropolitan areas are: Ann Arbor, Bay City, Detroit (three counties), Flint, Grand Rapids, Jackson, Kalamazoo, Lansing (three counties), Muskegon, and Saginaw.

[2]Thomas Roumell, Statement before the Select Subcommittee on Labor of the Committee on Education and Labor, U. S. House of Representatives, August 10, 1964, p. 5.

The demand for durable goods is sensitive to changes in consumer expectations, in income levels, and in the willingness of consumers to incur installment debt. For these and other reasons, the purchase of durable goods can be postponed. Therefore, in periods of economic uncertainty or downturn, purchases of durable goods can fall more rapidly than those of other kinds of goods. On the other hand, when consumers are optimistic in periods of expansion, purchases of durables can rise rapidly, partly because of new demands being generated and partly because purchases are being made which were previously postponed. These factors in turn can cause wide fluctuations in production and employment in durable goods industries. Since Michigan is heavily endowed with these industries, it is not surprising that employment and unemployment in the state are subject to rather severe fluctuations. Figure I-1 shows the unemployment rates for Michigan, the United States, and Illinois for the years 1956-63. The volatility of Michigan's unemployment rate is clearly revealed, but we see an additional feature: not only did unemployment fluctuate widely; it remained *above* the national rate until 1963.

The heavy concentration of people in the southern portion of the Lower Peninsula—and especially in the Detroit urban area—and the direct dependence of almost a third of the employed labor force upon durable goods production, and an even larger proportion when indirect employment effects are considered, mean that even a small change in national consumption patterns, production methods, or the location of manufacturing activity can have a profound impact upon the lives of people in Michigan.

How successfully can a large, important industrial state adjust to economic change? The answer to this question is of vital importance because Michigan has been sharing national growth opportunities with other states to a larger and larger extent. Moreover, despite the migrations from the state, Michigan's population has grown enormously as a result of the increasing numbers of people who have been born in the state since the mid-1940's. These people live here today and will enter the state's labor force in large numbers beginning in 1965. Specifically, in Chapter IV below, a total population

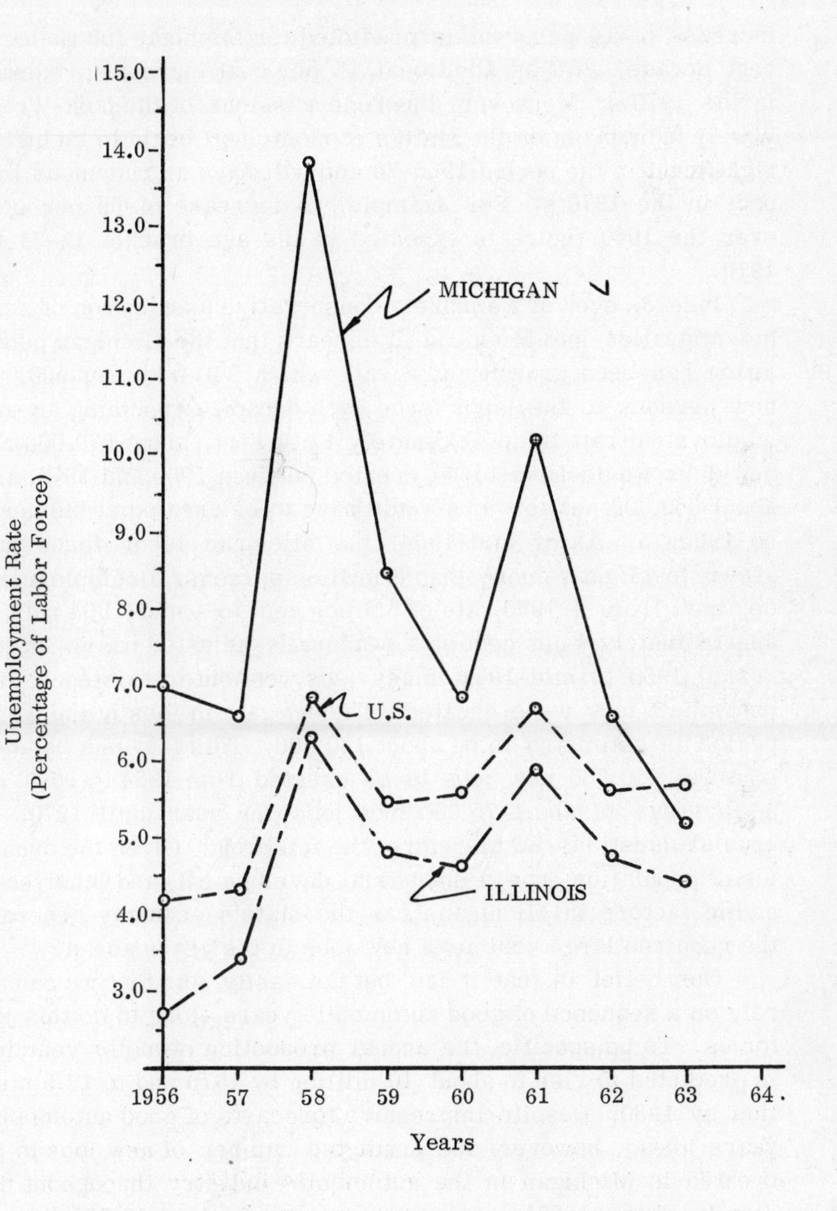

Fig. I-1. Unemployment Estimates for Michigan, Illinois, and the U.S., 1956-63, as a Percentage of the Labor Force. (Source: Michigan Employment Security Commission and the Illinois Department of Labor.)

increase of 14 per cent is predicted for Michigan for the current decade, with an additional 15 per cent increase predicted in the 1970's. Moreover, the repercussions of the post-World War II baby boom on the state's economy will begin to be highly significant in the period 1965-70 and will have an enormous impact in the 1970's. For example, an increase of 59 per cent over the 1960 figure is expected in the age bracket 15-24 by 1970.

Indeed, even if we make a conservative assumption of zero net migration into Michigan, it appears that the Michigan population has been growing at a rate which will add over 500,000 new persons to the labor force each decade. Assuming an unemployment rate of approximately 4 per cent, about 570,000 net new jobs would have to be created between 1960 and 1970, and about 860,000 net new jobs would have to be created in the period 1960-75. As of mid-1964, the Michigan labor force had grown to slightly more than 3 million persons. Unemployment declined from a 1960 rate of 6.9 per cent to a mid-1964 rate of approximately 4 per cent on a seasonally adjusted basis. In the period 1960 to mid-1964, many jobs went out of existence, and many new jobs were created. The *net* gain in jobs in the same period is estimated to be about 120,000. This leaves a balance of about 450,000 new jobs to be created from 1964 to 1970, or an average of about 75,000 new jobs per year until 1970. A crucial questions is, therefore, the following: Given the dynamics of population growth, industrial development, and other economic factors in Michigan, can the state's economy generate the required large volume of new jobs in the years ahead?

Our belief is that it can, but not easily, and that we cannot rely on a sequence of good automobile years alone to do this job for us. To be specific, the annual production of motor vehicles is predicted to rise to about 10 million by 1970 and to 12.5 million by 1980. Despite impressive forecasts of good automobile years ahead, however, the predicted number of new jobs to be created in Michigan in the automobile industry throughout the decade of the 1960's varies from a low of minus 10,000 (i.e., a loss of 10,000 jobs) to a high of 77,000, depending upon productivity and industry share assumptions (see Table IV-19). The moderately optimistic forecast made below is that new jobs from this source will number about 40,000 for the period 1960-70. Faced with the need for over 570,000 new jobs in the state between 1960 and 1970, we see that the direct employment created here by the manufacture of automobiles will account for at most 13 per cent of the required number of new jobs for the decade 1960-70 (if the high of 77,000 new jobs is realized) and more probably only 7 per cent (if the moderately optimistic estimate of 40,000 new jobs materializes).

The creation of new jobs in the automobile industry has the effect of multiplying new jobs in supporting industries (which include other manufacturing activities involved in supplying the automobile industry as well as the many service functions required to support the workers engaged in manufacturing). Unfortunately, no data are available by means of which an accurate estimate of this multiplier effect can be made. It is pointed out below that a reasonable but nevertheless rough estimate is that no more than two other jobs in supporting activities are created by the addition of one new job in the automobile industry. Relating this to the requirement of 570,000 new jobs in the period 1960-70, we estimate that with an expectation of 40,000 new jobs in automobile manufacturing, about 80,000 new jobs in supporting activities would be created, giving a total of about 120,000 net new jobs generated in Michigan during the decade as a result of a sequence of very good automobile years in the nation. This total is about 20 per cent of the new jobs required in the state between 1960 and 1970. Hence we concur with the statement made by David Goldberg in Chapter IV that "any tendency of state leaders to think that, because the picture of the automobile industry appears secure, they can relax in their efforts to attract new industry represents poor judgment."

Many of our estimates are based on an underlying assumption of zero or near-zero net migration through the mid-1970's. If, as Michigan's economy develops, in-migration to the state increases substantially, a further dampening influence on the state's economy will exist because the labor force will grow by an amount greater than we predict, and we will probably have more unemployment for a specified level of new job creation. To put it another way, with a positive net in-migration we would need even more than the estimated 860,000 new jobs during the period 1960-75. The state's past history indicates that improving economic conditions in Michigan have accelerated rates of in-migration. So, in a basic sense, our new job estimates are conservative, and it might be necessary for the state's economy to create even more new jobs than we estimate in order to maintain unemployment rates at current levels. Moreover, there is every reason to expect that population growth resulting from in-migration would intensify our training, retraining, and education problems.

To say that the state's economy is on an upward trend is by no means to say that the more than 860,000 jobs required will be created between 1960 and 1975. The provision of new jobs now and in the future, given technological developments and automation, is and will be a more difficult undertaking than the task would have been fifteen years ago. Jobs will require more training, the exercise of greater responsibility, higher skill levels, and so on. The creation of 860,000 new jobs in the state during the fifteen years between 1960 and 1975, on the other hand, is not impossible. We are neither prophets of doom nor are we highly optimistic.

Some Comments and Recommendations

What will be required to give Michigan the growth increments in new jobs that it will need? In our opinion the following will be necessary:

- Michigan's nonautomotive durable goods industries must grow at faster rates than they have in the past. Specifically, Michigan will have to increase its share of national employment in the faster growing industries such as electrical machinery manufacturing.
- Michigan must maintain its historically large shares of national employment in the manufacture of automobiles, other transportation equipment, nonelectrical machinery, and fabricated metals. These industries must, of course, maintain their activities at levels consistent with the forecasts of economic growth which have been made for the nation.
- Employment in nondurable goods industries in Michigan

must continue to grow at least as well as in the past. Service industries, and finance, insurance, and recreation activities, must grow at faster rates. Finance and insurance are especially significant as sources of employment expansion in urban areas, particularly in the Detroit area.

- Michigan must produce a supply of well-trained manpower to meet the demands created by the advancing technology of the 1960's and 1970's.

The point is simply this: the state's economy will grow in the years ahead, but an adequate amount of growth to generate about 860,000 new jobs in the state by 1975 will require significant expansion in the private sector of Michigan's economy as well as vigorous action in the public sector.

Although agencies, institutions, and individuals in Michigan obviously cannot influence all of the more important factors involved in each of the growth requirements stated above, what kinds of action can be taken? The following recommendations and comments cover, in our opinion, the more important issues which can be influenced by activities within the state.

1. A healthy business climate in Michigan is necessary if capital investments in job-creating activities by industry are to take place in the magnitudes necessary to avoid higher rates of unemployment in the future. Fundamental to such a climate are confident relations among business, government, and labor. Adequate profit levels and the maintenance of stable management-labor relations are positive forces in stimulating investment outlays which create more jobs.

2. Education, training, and retraining programs sponsored both by industry and government—federal and state—must be significantly enlarged in scope and more adequately financed. This is particularly needed because the advancing technology will create a demand for new skills and render many existing skills obsolete.

3. It is becoming increasingly clear, given the nature of the emerging technology with the education requirements and skill levels this implies, that job creation is also closely related to the education of persons in the labor force and to research and development activities in the private sector. In this respect the state's educational system constitutes one of its

most important resources, and the expanding role of universities in industrial development research activities (as is characterized by the Institute of Science and Technology at the University of Michigan) is also of considerable importance to the state's future growth prospects. Time and time again our contributors emphasize that, given the accelerating rate of change, education becomes the prime vehicle by which people may improve their adaptive capacity. According to Ashby, "the retention of people with high levels of educational endowment offers the greatest hope for the economic health of a state or a region."[3]

The people of the state must recognize that the changes—demographic, technological, and occupational—which are swiftly engulfing Michigan will necessitate expenditures for higher education of a magnitude significantly larger than those of the past.

4. It is of vital importance that economic opportunities sufficiently attractive to better educated people be created in the state in order to improve its record of retention of the most productive segment of society. Unfortunately, data illustrating the effects of exchange migration in the recent past between the East North Central region (which includes Michigan) and other parts of the nation support the contention that this region, in general, has been faring badly. Table IV-5 indicates that between 1955 and 1960 the East North Central region exported persons of higher educational attainment (as measured by the median number of years of education completed) than it imported in six out of eight interregional exchanges. Although corresponding data on exchange migration are not available on the state level, there is no evidence to suggest that Michigan's experience is any better than that of the region of which it is a part. In fact, since Michigan has a relatively well-developed educational system, the state's migration exchange is probably more unfavorable than that for the region as a whole. We may well be educating people efficiently while at the same time our lack of sufficiently varied economic opportunities results in the

[3]See p. 193.

export to other states of persons with higher median levels of education than those of persons coming into the state.

5. The implications of the advancing technology with respect to non-whites in Michigan must be more fully understood. Technological developments will result in a smaller proportion of job opportunities for semiskilled and unskilled workers, and in increased opportunities for employment in the professional and technical categories and for highly skilled blue-collar workers. This means essentially that the state's non-white workers will bear more of the impact of the changing technology than will white workers, since most of the state's non-white workers are engaged in lower-skilled blue-collar and service employment (see Table VII-8).

Moreover, the differential in education between whites and non-whites which has existed for years in the past will continue to be a strong impediment in the future to the full utilization of the Negro labor force. Even with more opportunities available to Negroes in the years ahead, there may be no sizable increase in Negro employment. Unfortunately, too few Negroes will possess the education and training that will be required in the labor market of the latter half of the 1960's and the 1970's. It is a sad fact that years are required to upgrade educational levels. Therefore, no time should be lost in assisting as many Negroes as possible to board the educational escalator to the new jobs of the 1970's. Vigorous and imaginative action is required now in dealing on a broad front with these problems of non-whites.

6. The Michigan Department of Economic Expansion, in co-operation with the Institute of Science and Technology of the University of Michigan and similar units in other Michigan colleges and universities, should facilitate a continuing review of important factors in the economic growth of the state. These include at least the following: transportation, water, conditions of doing business in Michigan as compared with other states, and the economic impact of taxation. Study of the role of local industrial development programs should also be encouraged, giving appropriate consideration to the adequacy of the provision of equity capital to Michigan firms as well as other financial inducements for new businesses. Finally, the Department

of Economic Expansion should encourage more thorough research into Michigan's problems—problems of the kind that are considered in this book and which are worthy of still further investigation.

It is our hope that the forecasts in this book—both optimistic and pessimistic—will have a constructive influence in the future. If our pessimistic forecasts should lead to policies which set in motion forces that prove our forecasts to be wrong, we shall consider ourselves fortunate indeed.

Summary of Salient Points

It is not our intention to try to convey even in brief all that is offered in the sections to follow. Indeed, this would be impossible to do adequately, since each chapter contains a great store of information and analysis which justifies detailed study. However, since the chapters will have the greatest value for specialists and since the layman may not be inclined to devote to them the detailed reading they deserve, we have provided in this introduction a summary of some of the salient points of the material presented in the remainder of the book. It is our hope that those who seek a detailed exposition of the material which follows in the introductory statement will turn to the chapters themselves for the more complete story.

The national economy in the mid-1970's

In Chapter II Sidney Sonenblum examines the future of the national economy from several standpoints. He develops a "present policy projection" which is based on the assumption that no fundamental changes in current policies or attitudes will occur between now and the 1970's. Secondly, he advances a "target projection" which sets its sights on goals believed attainable providing there are certain changes in government policy and public attitudes. And thirdly, he submits a "judgment projection" which reflects a probable, rather than an optimal, course of economic developments.

Despite the difficulty of grappling with so many imponderables, this chapter presents a judgment projection which foresees an increased rate of national economic growth in the years ahead: specifically, a 4.6 per cent annual increase in gross national product in the period 1962-73. This can be contrasted with a growth of about 3 per cent per year in the period 1946-62.

There are several areas in which current economic policy is inadequate for achieving full employment growth in the nation. Growth in consumer demand must be stimulated, probably through appropriate tax policy, including tax reduction. Increased government expenditures are compatible with cuts in tax rates and can help reach the goal of full employment without producing domestic inflation or aggravating balance of payments difficulties.

Improved educational programs will be required to meet the growing demand for professionals. This will involve more education for younger people and an expansion of retraining programs for older workers. The manpower demand for *civilian* employment is projected to be about 84 million in 1973, and "there are conservatively 30 million persons (ignoring reentrants) for whom education, training, and retraining must be provided in the coming decade if these people are to have the talents and skills needed to fill the new job opportunities." Even assuming an increase in job training programs, productivity will not increase so rapidly as to create a basic conflict between labor supply and demand.

The projected total labor force in the United States by 1973 is 90.1 million, resulting in 35 million "new faces" among job seekers between 1962 and 1973. Demand for employees is projected to increase by 16.5 million between 1962 and 1973 in an economy where total output will increase by $350 billion in the same period. This increase in employment would be twice the growth of the last eleven years, and "would not only create jobs for most of the new labor force entrants but would also reduce the unemployment rate to 4 per cent."

The most significant growth will be among white-collar workers, who will make up 16 per cent of the labor force by 1973, compared with 12 per cent in 1962. An increase of two million in the number of blue-collar workers by 1972 is also projected.

> The aggregate growth projection fails to reveal some significant aspects of the age, sex, and color composition of the labor force. Because of the aging process we can expect the age brackets up to 24 to make up about half the total increase to 1967; after 1967 the age groups over 25 begin to dominate the total labor force growth. If jobs are not quickly found for those in these younger groups they will fail to gain the experience needed for their later years when they are usually at the most productive stage in their lives and have greater responsibilities. (Chap. II, p. 59.)

Women have dominated the nation's labor force growth since 1947. About 60 per cent of the labor force growth between 1947 and 1957, and again between 1957 and 1962, was accounted for by women. Nearly half of the increase can be found among married women between the ages of 25 and 54. These projections show continued growth in the number of women in the labor force. However, women will account for less than 40 per cent of the increase in the coming decade.

Non-whites represent about 11 per cent of the civilian labor force and are expected to account for a slightly larger share in the future. Non-whites represent one-tenth of the labor force, but they currently account for over two-tenths of the unemployed.

> This implies a serious adjustment problem for the future, particularly since half the growth of the non-white labor force in the coming five years (as compared with a quarter of the white labor force growth) is projected to be in the 25-54 brackets—those age groups which are potentially most productive and which have the greatest family responsibilities (Chap. II, p. 60.)

Disposable income will reach a per capita level of $2,600 by 1973, and gross national product (GNP) will rise from a 1962 level of $552 billion to $905 billion by 1973 (as measured in 1962 prices). It is projected that almost twice as many consumer units (essentially families) will be in the $7,500 to $15,000 pre-tax income bracket as there were in 1962, and this group is expected to earn over 40 per cent of total income. The number of consumer units earning over $15,000 is expected to more than double, and such units are expected to earn about 35 per cent of total income. The number of consumer units earning less than $7,500 is expected to be below the 1962 number, and this group will earn about 20 per cent of total income.

Turning to government expenditures of all kinds—federal, state, and local—the projection sees a substantial increase to $283 billion in 1973 from a 1962 total of $160 billion. These expenditures will represent 31 per cent of the GNP in 1973, as compared to 24 per cent in 1962. State and local expenditures in the nation will grow at a faster pace than federal outlays. The total of government revenue is projected to increase somewhat more slowly than government expenditures. Implied in this projection is a cut in both personal and corporate effective tax rates.

National security requirements will continue to be important in the decade ahead, but more than half the projected federal expenditures in 1973 will not be related to defense. Continued economic growth will require substantial government expenditures for such programs as urban renewal, water resource development, air pollution control, transport facilities, and research and education.

Outlays for veterans, old age and survivors' insurance, interest, grants-in-aid to states and localities, subsidies, water development, air transport facilities, research and development, and hospital construction will all show increases.

Both output and productivity will increase more rapidly than in the past. Output is projected to grow most rapidly in durables manufacturing, finance and insurance, communications, public utilities, and services. Relatively rapid productivity improvements are seen in agriculture, mining, manufacturing, transportation, communication, and public utilities.

The period 1962-73 will witness a slight redistribution of population toward the southwestern and the far western states away from the Middle Atlantic, Great Lakes, plains, and southeastern states. The move towards urban areas will continue. By 1973, 80 per cent of the national population will be urbanized, and employment redistribution is expected to follow the same pattern as that for population.

The growth projections made by Sonenblum clearly require a sizable increase in the supply of capital in the years ahead. James O'Leary in Chapter III analyzes the sources and uses of capital in the United States since 1948 and makes projections about the nation's supply of capital funds for 1973. His conclusion is that the national economy will generate sufficient quantities of capital to sustain the economic expansion predicted by Sonenblum.

Population growth in Michigan[4]

During the past hundred years, with minor exceptions, Michigan's rate of population increase has been greater than that of the nation. The net balance of migration into Michigan from other states has been the primary factor causing Michigan's population to expand at a rate in excess of the national rate for a long period of time. The growth of the automobile industry undoubtedly influenced the exceptional migration to the state between 1910 and 1930, a period in which three out of five persons added to the population of the state were migrants. In the decade 1940-50, Michigan was still experiencing a heavy in-migration; its total of 329,000 net migrants was exceeded only by California, Florida, and Washington. In the decade 1950-60, Michigan ranked tenth among the states in net migration. Although the ratio of migration to population growth has declined considerably since the peak period 1910-30, there has always been a net balance of in-migrants to the state when the figures are viewed at ten-year intervals.

When the decade 1950-60 is broken down into yearly intervals, the demographic patterns indicate that a fundamental change has occurred in Michigan's population trends. For example, in each year from 1950 to 1956 there was a net balance of in-migrants to Michigan from other states (Table IV-2). About 400,000 more people came to the state during that period than left it. The production build-up associated with the Korean

[4]Chapter IV, by David Goldberg.

war was largely responsible for this massive influx.[5] However, by 1956-57 economic opportunities in Michigan had diminished to such an extent that the state had an excess supply of labor. Beginning with 1956, people began leaving the state in greater numbers, and this net out-migration of population continued in every year through 1962, the last year for which data are available. The net movement out of the state amounted to about 400,000 persons, or the same number that had entered the state during the first interval examined, 1950-56.

Dividing the decade 1950-60 in half at the year 1955 sheds some light on the qualitative aspects of the inflow and outflow of Michigan's population. We find, for example, that during the first five-year period three out of five net in-migrants were white. During the recession period of 1955-60 white people were leaving the state in large numbers, while small numbers of non-whites were coming in (Table IV-3). Although poorer economic conditions in Michigan clearly did not result in a return of non-whites to the South, they did appear to reduce the stream of southern migration headed for Michigan. For the decade as a whole, however, 83 per cent of net in-migration was non-white, compared to about 65 per cent in the 1940-50 decade.

The net outward movement of more than 180,000 whites from Michigan between 1955-60, mainly to the western states and Florida, has had a disturbing impact upon the skill level of the Michigan population. Looking at only one aspect of this problem, educational levels, analysis indicates that the East North Central States (a regional classification which includes Michigan) lost more educational talent in the interchange of migrants with other regions than any other of the state groupings.

The increasing proportion in Michigan of persons with less education—a result of exchange migration with other states—will no doubt intensify problems of unemployment, training, and

[5]In-migration between 1954 and 1956 was essentially a lag or carry-over from the peak war production year of 1953 and its unusually low unemployment level of 2.1 per cent (see Goldberg, Chapter IV, p. 123).

retraining in the future. If the loss to Michigan of people with higher education levels continues, there will be an unfavorable repercussion on the state's economy in the long run, and it may be difficult to offset this loss in the future. Figure I-2 shows the subregions of the United States as defined by the U. S. Bureau of the Census. Michigan, as was noted earlier, is part of the East North Central region. In Chapter IV, where the interregional exchange of people by educational levels is examined, it is pointed out that the median educational level of out-migrants from the East North Central region to every other region in the country exceeds that of the median of in-migrants from each region in six out of eight cases. Moreover, from 1955 to 1960 Michigan lost white migrants to all other regions in the United States and gained non-white migrants of lower education levels from the South.

Looking at net migration in locational terms makes it evident that the movement of people to the state over the past two decades has been almost entirely a result of the ability of the state's ten metropolitan areas to attract migrants.[6] Between 1940 and 1955 these areas experienced a net in-migration of over 600,000 persons while, in addition, over 100,000 persons were added to the highly urban nonmetropolitan areas of the southern Lower Peninsula. During this period the Upper Peninsula had a continuous net out-migration. For the period 1955-60 all sections of the state lost migrants to other areas, although about 85 per cent of the state's total net loss was from the Detroit metropolitan area.

Given the industrial profiles of most of the state's metropolitan areas and that of Detroit in particular, the probability is small that Michigan will approach the population growth rates of the 1940's or even of the 1950's. Although the nonmetropolitan areas appear to be holding their own with respect to net migration, the ten metropolitan areas which account for 75 per cent of state's population were lagging in rates of net migration during the past decade.[7]

[6]See Tables IV-7A and IV-7B.

[7]The ten Michigan metropolitan areas had rates of net migration of 3.6 per cent of population as compared with the East North Central States' 5.1 per cent and the national rate for metropolitan areas of 9.2 per cent.

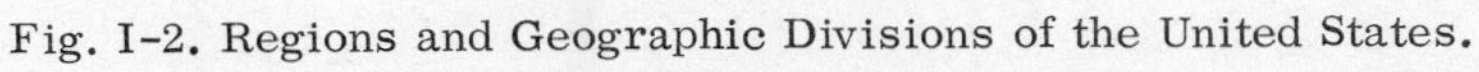
Fig. I-2. Regions and Geographic Divisions of the United States.

The future population of Michigan. Using the projections derived from studies of the national trends and adjusting these projections for the Michigan population, it appears that there will be 1.8 million births in Michigan in the 1960 decade and 2.2 million between 1970 and 1980.[8] The combined effects of the mortality, fertility, and migration assumptions made by David Goldberg in Chapter IV result in a prediction of a total population increase for Michigan of 14 per cent for the current decade and an additional 15 per cent increase during the 1970's (Table IV-8). By 1965 the state will have approximately 8.4 million persons; by 1970, 8.9 million; by 1975, 9.5 million; and by 1980, 10.2 million.[9]

It is important to note that the projections of the Michigan population indicate different rates of growth for various age groups. These may be summarized as follows:

(1) The number of pre-school children (up to age 4) is expected to decline slightly from 970,000 in 1960 to 867,000 in 1970 and then rise rapidly to 1,143,000 by 1980. This latter increase is caused by a larger number of parents rather than by an increase in family size.

(2) The population aged 5-14, which includes the elementary school population, is expected to increase from 1.623 million persons in 1960 to a 1965 level of 1.842 million and then remain stable at about that level to 1980.

(3) The population segment aged 15-24 will exhibit the largest change, increasing from 1 million persons in 1960 to more than 1.8 million in 1975. In percentage terms, the increase in population in this age bracket will be about 59 per cent from 1960 to 1970 and 80 per cent from 1960 to 1975. This increase is not speculative, since the people have been born already.

(4) The age segment 25-64, which encompasses the bulk of the labor force, will increase at the rate of 5 per cent between 1960 and 1970, a much lower rate than the 14 per cent rise anticipated for the total population. After 1970, growth rates in

[8]See Chapter IV, p. 135.

[9]*Ibid.*, p. 136, and Table IV-8.

this segment will increase as persons born in the 1940's enter this age bracket.

(5) Persons 65 and over are expected to represent an increasing portion of the population during the period 1960-80. In 1960, 626,000 persons, or 8 per cent of the state's population, were in this group. Projections indicate that by 1965 there will be 700,000 persons, or 8.4 per cent of the state's population, in the 65-and-over category. Figures for 1970 are 778,000, or 8.7 per cent of the state's population; for 1975, 847,000, or 8.9 per cent; and for 1980, 928,000, or 9 per cent. These projections may be too high if persons over 65 decide to leave the state in increasing numbers, as is indicated by recent evidence.

As has been noted previously, the continuing concentration of population in the state, by all age groups, will occur in the metropolitan areas at the expense of the Upper Peninsula and the northern portion of the Lower Peninsula. Detailed population projections through 1980 by counties are provided in the Appendix to Chapter IV, on pages 166-68. Table I-1 presents percentage changes in population by counties for the periods 1960-70 and 1960-75. Counties are grouped according to the magnitude and direction of change. Table I-2 presents similar information for the state's ten metropolitan areas.

The Michigan labor force

Projections of the Michigan labor force are closely associated with those of population. Labor force size is predicted by multiplying the projected size of various segments of the population by associated estimates of the extent of each segment's participation in the labor force.[10]

Michigan labor force participation rates, although they compare favorably with national rates in total, differ from the

[10] Participation in the labor force by segment is usually measured by calculating a labor force participation rate for that segment where the rate equals the percentage of persons in the segment who are seeking employment.

Table I-1

PERCENTAGE CHANGE IN POPULATION OF MICHIGAN COUNTIES, 1960–70 AND 1960–75

County	Percentage Change 1960–70	Percentage Change 1960–75
Fast growth*		
Genesee	20.4	32.1
Ingham	26.4	41.3
Iosco	38.1	53.3
Kalamazoo	22.0	27.3
Livingston	30.7	42.8
Macomb	64.9	104.5
Midland	31.6	44.0
Monroe	21.7	30.6
Oakland	31.2	46.9
Ottawa	22.0	30.9
Washtenaw	32.0	51.6
Medium growth		
Alpena	17.0	24.7
Berrien	18.0	25.7
Cass	19.4	27.7
Eaton	13.1	19.0
Isabella	11.2	16.6
Jackson	11.4	16.8
Kent	14.8	21.3
Muskegon	12.5	18.2
Roscommon	11.1	16.7
Saginaw	13.2	19.8
Van Buren	12.6	18.4
Slow growth		
Allegan	10.9	16.1
Barry	10.6	15.6
Bay	10.3	15.4
Branch	5.4	9.5
Calhoun	4.7	8.1
Chippewa	2.0	4.7

*Fast growth is taken to be a percentage change of 20 per cent or more for 1960–70; medium growth is 10 per cent to 19.99 per cent for the same period; slow growth is 0 per cent to 9.99 per cent; and negative change, is of course, any percentage change less than zero.

Table I-1 *(cont.)*

County	Percentage Change 1960–70	Percentage Change 1960–75
Slow growth *(cont.)*		
Clare	3.9	6.5
Clinton	10.9	16.2
Crawford	8.6	12.7
Gladwin	4.0	7.7
Grand Traverse	6.6	10.5
Gratiot	0.8	3.2
Ionia	3.0	6.0
Lapeer	6.6	10.7
Lenawee	10.0	14.5
Mackinac	6.9	10.6
Marquette	7.4	11.7
Mason	2.9	1.5
Mecosta	0.7	3.1
Montcalm	5.3	9.2
Newaygo	1.8	4.7
Oscoda	1.5	1.5
Otsego	7.4	11.3
Presque Isle	0.6	2.9
St. Clair	6.5	10.5
St. Joseph	10.1	15.0
Shiawassee	6.1	9.6
Tuscola	3.2	6.2
Wayne	10.7	5.7
Negative change		
Alcona	- 3.8	0.8
Alger	-15.7	-16.8
Antrim	-11.3	-13.2
Arenac	- 6.7	- 7.7
Baraga	-18.9	-21.7
Benzie	-13.2	-15.8
Charlevoix	- 9.1	- 9.1
Cheboygan	- 3.1	- 2.4
Delta	- 5.2	- 4.7
Dickinson	-11.8	-12.6
Emmet	-11.3	-13.2
Gogebic	-17.9	-19.6

Table I-1 *(cont.)*

County	Percentage Change 1960–70	Percentage Change 1960–75
Negative change *(cont.)*		
Hillsdale	- 7.0	1.0
Houghton	-18.1	-19.8
Huron	- 6.5	- 5.9
Iron	-11.6	-11.6
Kalkaska	-15.6	-15.6
Keweenaw	-25.5	-29.7
Lake	- 8.2	- 8.2
Leelanau	- 2.4	1.3
Luce	-13.1	-13.1
Manistee	- 6.5	- 6.0
Menominee	-10.9	-11.7
Missaukee	-17.5	-17.5
Montmorency	- 0.5	1.7
Oceana	- 6.2	- 5.7
Ogemaw	- 5.0	- 5.0
Ontonagon	- 6.5	- 6.5
Osceola	- 9.5	-10.3
Sanilac	- 4.4	- 3.8
Schoolcraft	-10.6	- 9.5
Wexford	-10.1	-10.1

Source: Table IV-Appendix 2, pp. 167-68.

national pattern when broken down by sex. Michigan males aged 25-64 have slightly higher participation rates, whereas the participation rates of Michigan females are considerably lower than the national average.[11] In the future it is expected that changes in labor force participation in Michigan will follow national trends: decreasing levels for men under 25 and over 55, and increasing levels for women 25 and over.

The total Michigan labor force is expected to increase from 3.0 million in 1960 to 3.2 million in 1965, 3.5 million in 1970, 3.8 million in 1975, and 4.1 million in 1980. Total growth will be unequally distributed, with nearly 62 per cent of the la-

[11] Tables IV-10 and IV-11.

Table I-2

PERCENTAGE CHANGE IN POPULATION IN STANDARD METROPOLITAN AREAS IN MICHIGAN, 1960-70 AND 1960-75

Metropolitan Area*	Percentage Change 1960-70	Percentage Change 1960-75
Ann Arbor	32.0	51.6
Bay City	10.3	15.4
Detroit	15.1	24.6
Flint	20.4	32.1
Grand Rapids	15.0	21.3
Jackson	11.4	16.8
Kalamazoo	22.0	27.3
Lansing	22.2	35.5
Muskegon	12.5	18.2
Saginaw	13.2	19.8

*For definition of Standard Metropolitan Statistical Area, see footnote 1, p. 3. (Source: Table IV-Appendix 2, pp. 167-68.)

bor force increase between 1960 and 1970 concentrated in the age group 14-24. The shock wave produced by this entry of young people to the labor force will be most acutely felt in 1965, when 40,000 more 18-year-olds will enter the labor force than entered it in the preceeding year.

A decennial growth of 500,000 persons in Michigan's labor force is not unusual, considering the history of the state in past years. However, since the rate of growth on the demand side has slowed down since 1953, the state must find new sources of growth if it is to fulfill the employment needs of a growing population.

We might speculate at this point on some of the implications of this projection with respect to new job formation. The labor force consists of the sum of the number employed plus the number unemployed. In 1960 the unemployment rate in Michigan was 6.9 per cent. If the labor force grows by 500,000 during the period 1960-70, and if we have a 4 per cent unemployment rate in 1970, the estimated number of new jobs required in Michigan during this period can be calculated as follows: First, 4 per cent of the 500,000 increment would be unemployed; so 480,000 new jobs would have to be found in this part of the 1970 labor force. Second, the unemployment rate for the remainder of the 1970 labor force would also have to be reduced from the 1960 rate of 6.9 per cent to 4 per cent, a reduction of 2.9 per cent. Applying this to the remainder of the labor force of 2.9 million gives a little less than 90,000 jobs. Thus a 1970 unemployment rate of 4 per cent implies a requirement of 480,000 plus 90,000, or 570,000 new jobs by the end of the 1960-70 period. A similar calculation for a 1970 unemployment rate of 5 per cent leads to the requirement of 535,000 new jobs between 1960 and 1970.

Problems of Michigan's industry mix

In Chapter V, Lowell Ashby examines the economy of Michigan in terms of its industry mix. Although the automobile industry has dominated the state's economy for many years, Michigan's growth in this industry began to lag as early as 1940. Today motor vehicle manufacture is only one layer of the Michigan economy and not the entire cake. The state is an important producer of other transportation equipment, machinery, metals, chemicals, rubber, and petroleum products. However, all of these industries are closely bound to the auto industry, and they react to fluctuations in motor vehicle production and employment.

It is unlikely that the auto industry will be displaced from its position of importance in Michigan. The automobile is part of the American way of life. Barring a disastrous national emergency, automobile use will continue to grow; and Michigan, with its huge capital investment in this industry, should continue in its role of the nation's leading auto producer.

Still, it is evident that the more than 500,000 new jobs the state of Michigan requires during the period 1960-70 cannot be derived from the motor vehicle industry alone. Consequently, the entire industrial spectrum will require attention if the employment problem is to be solved. To support this belief, Ashby cites Sonenblum's projections for Michigan and the nation, which indicate that Michigan is not maintaining its share of the national total employment in the 1960's and that the shortfall is something more than 100,000 jobs.

Will employment expand in Michigan as rapidly as in the nation at large in the industries where Michigan has its major commitment? Ashby replies that Michigan will do well if it can generally maintain its share of present industry involvements. But to meet its employment objectives Michigan must grow as rapidly as the nation in this period of expanding economy.

Inasmuch as entrepreneurial activity is an important factor in economic growth, it may happen, as it once did in the early days of the motor vehicle industry, that Michigan's economy will receive the impetus it needs from some technical or entrepreneurial genius from whom may come an entirely new industry. Economic historians have pointed out the differences that existed in 1870 between Chicago and Pittsburgh. The latter was even at that early date known as a "big man's frontier," with the steel industry already enjoying a monopoly of the city's skills and talent. Chicago, on the other hand, was a "little man's frontier," where the small firm could find skills and talent and financial backing as it attempted to get an economic foothold. The fact that Chicago's growth has far outstripped that of Pittsburgh is an implied warning against Detroit's becoming a "big man's frontier."

The frontier of the sixties and seventies will be the frontier of knowledge.

> New opportunities today are created by ideas which serve an ever-changing technology, rather than by movement to undeveloped regions. Limitations to movement are not only geographic but also educational. Given the accelerating rate of change, education becomes the prime vehicle by which people may improve their adaptive capacity. Therefore the retention of people with high levels of educational endowment offers the greatest hope for the economic health of a state or region. (Chap. V, p. 193.)

It therefore follows that "an area's educational institutions may be its most effective means of enabling the population to adapt to change. The importance of the state's educational system, not merely for growth but for better development of human resources, is re-emphasized by the acceleration in the rate of change." This condition will be even more intense as competition among states and regions intensifies.

The future of the Detroit Metropolitan Area[12]

Traditional urban regional growth analysis attempts to predict the future size and shape of an urban economy from the anticipated size and shape of its export sector. There are a number of reasons why this approach is not suited to a prediction of the growth of the Detroit economy.

First, the leading Detroit industry—automotive manufacturing—is a mature one and one that has recently been decentralizing. A moderately optimistic projection of employment for the local automobile industry would show it remaining constant during the next two decades. To predict a constant local export base and therefore a constant size for Detroit would contradict the clear trend toward concentration of an ever-larger share of the national population in urban areas. This does not mean that the auto industry will not be Detroit's principal employer for decades to come, only that it will probably not provide the significant marginal changes that will be the key to local development.

Second, the golden age of manufacturing seems to have run its course today, in other metropolitan areas perhaps more than in Detroit. This is not to imply that manufacturing will decline as precipitously as has agriculture during the past decade. Still, manufacturing in general and production employment in particular do not seem to hold the key to the pattern of employment growth in the age of automation.

Third, the large metropolitan area has developed what appears to be a life of its own, and its growth pattern is far more complex than can be explained by magnifying the growth patterns of its principal export industries.

Following this line of reasoning, a second approach to an analysis of Detroit's growth is to view the city as a potential

[12]Chapter VI, by Wilbur R. Thompson.

metropolis and to seek out some regularities in the growth behavior of other large metropolitan areas to which Detroit might conform.

Evidence is at hand that Detroit is rapidly settling into a pattern already established by such metropolitan centers as New York and Chicago. In 1940, for example, the export base of the Detroit area economy embraced very little outside the automobile industry, with 90 per cent of the net export employment of the area's economy in motor vehicle manufacturing. Today that figure has dropped to 75 per cent.

There are trends to indicate that Detroit is becoming both a metropolis and an automobile city. As a city grows, its role changes from producer to creator. Rather than simply disgorging volumes of standardized products, Detroit has been and must continue to be the center of automotive technique and design. But Detroit must become something more than just a center of automotive technology; it must emulate New York and Boston and Chicago by finding its very reason for being in invention and innovation that strike out in many and diverse directions.

The history of New York is a case in point. In the post-Civil War period its flour mills, tanneries, meat packing plants, textile mills, and foundries moved to the West. They were replaced by products less sensitive to transport, such as garments and cigars, and by office work. Today New York is losing the garment industry and much of its printing industry, but its growth does not falter. Chicago, Boston, and other metropolitan centers have gone through a similar cycle.

> Because it is almost inevitable that a substantial amount of decentralization will occur with the maturing of local growth industries, the big city should spend less time worrying about losing a share of some existing industry and more time working to cultivate new replacement industries. The city that aspires to be a true metropolis should pattern its actions on the executive image, delegating tasks readily as they become routine and keeping itself free to take on the new and sophisticated work in which it has a comparative advantage over smaller places. (Chap. VI, p. 229.)

The creation of new products and processes is almost certain to use more labor than the routine work of running standard manufacturing operations, especially in this age of automation. The big city's forte should be creative activity—technical discussion, experimentation, setting up pilot plants, laboratory research, market survey activities, consulting, patenting, and financing.

A true metropolis must be fully as much a center of business and technical services as of consumer and personal services. Detroit in the future is seen as a major professional and service center in such areas as finance, education, and wholesale trade. The opportunity in this direction is even greater because of Detroit's past underdevelopment in the service area.

Thompson advances what he calls a "reluctant projection" of the Detroit area economy in 1975. Employment by that time will rise to 1,700,000, requiring roughly 371,000 additional jobs over the total in 1960.[13] Manufacturing will account roughly for only one quarter, or 86,000, of these additional jobs. Professional services will add 78,000 jobs, while the wholesale and retail trades are projected to add another 62,500 jobs by 1975. Other large increases will be provided by public administration, up 26,700 jobs, and finance, insurance, and real estate, with a combined employment increase of 23,800.

Projected gains for service industry employment should provide hope to "the beleaguered central city." Service industries represent more promising sources of new employment at central city sites than do manufacturing enterprises.

Thompson foresees "a Detroit area large enough to offer the advantages which ensure its competitive position. As a metropolis it will therefore share, if no longer exceed, the general nationwide level of well-being and will grow steadily and

[13]This prediction is based on the assumption that unemployment in Detroit will remain at the same rate in 1975 as it was in 1960 (6.9 per cent of the labor force). If unemployment in Detroit were to be reduced to 4 per cent, about 435,000 new jobs would have to be created by 1975 as against 1960. A goal of 5 per cent unemployed would require slightly over 417,000 new jobs by 1975.

exhibit greater cyclical stability." But all this will take planning and will require the Detroit area to address itself to the growing problem of welfare and the development of human resources. "Detroiters will have the money; they must also have the will."

The Michigan labor market in the 1970's[14]

National patterns of employment, labor force participation, and unemployment have their counterparts in the Michigan labor market. However, national trends do not affect all communities or segments of the Michigan labor force in the same way. In the Upper Peninsula, for example, the major problem is the aging of the labor force because of the out-migration of younger workers who could not find work when mining declined; but in southeastern Michigan the problem is concerned with adjustments to a marked shift from commodity to noncommodity employment.

The employment shifts which have occurred are discussed in detail in Chapter V, but what of their effects on the occupational distributions and the manpower needs of the Michigan labor market in the 1970's? Over the years the most striking change has been the growth of white-collar employment; 32 per cent of the labor force was so engaged in 1940, 36 per cent in 1950, and 40 per cent in 1960. It is anticipated by Louis Ferman that this growth will continue into the next decade at about the same rate as for the period 1950-60, when professional and technical employment increased by 54.7 per cent and clerical and sales employment increased by 25.9 per cent (Table VII-7).

Among blue-collar workers, a sizable increase is foreseen only in service employment. In 1950-60 such employment increased by 30 per cent, and the same rate of growth is predicted for 1960-70. Although total blue-collar employment will probably increase slightly, this increase will be almost entirely in craft and maintenance employment. While there will be a

[14] Chapter VII, by Louis A. Ferman.

slight decrease in operative and kindred occupations because of changing technology, there will be sharp declines in the number of persons engaged in nonfarm labor (20 per cent) and in farm labor (45 per cent) during the 1960-70 period.

One of the major forces influencing the nature of jobs in the decade ahead is the advance of technology. This advance will cause, among other things, the displacement of men by machines in established processes as well as by entirely new production methods which require less human participation. Because of these changes a smaller proportion of total job opportunities will be in the categories of semiskilled and unskilled employment. On the other hand, there will be increasing opportunities for employment in the professional and technical categories and for highly skilled blue-collar workers.

Labor force participation. The labor force participation rate in Michigan has increased steadily over the past three decades and compares favorably with national participation rates. Given participation rates of 52.7 per cent in 1940, 53.8 per cent in 1950, and 55.0 per cent in 1960, it is estimated that 56.7 per cent of Michigan's population over 14 years old will be in the labor market by 1970. This would be the highest participation rate in Michigan for any peacetime period since 1900.

Growth in labor force participation is not distributed uniformly through all segments of the population. Because of variations in the demographic structure of the population, the availability of employment, and the requirements for employment, some groups are participating more now than ever before, while other groups are participating less.

The most striking long-term trend in the Michigan labor market is the increased participation by women and the concurrent decline in the participation of men. Although the trend has been evident since 1940, when 23.3 per cent of women over 14 were in the Michigan labor force, an acceleration of the rate of female participation increased the participation of females to 32.7 per cent by 1960. During this same period male participation dropped from 80.5 per cent to 78.3 per cent.[15]

[15]Table VII-5.

Causal factors for the growth in female employment rates appear to be related to the changes in Michigan's industry mix which give greater emphasis to nondurable manufacturing activities in which women can participate and to the growth of employment opportunities in clerical work, sales, service, nursing, teaching, social work, etc., which have been traditionally female.

Of course, the decline in durable goods employment opportunities may have caused the Michigan rates of male participation (which were higher than national) to decline toward the United States average. The data (Table VII-5) suggest, however, that although that may have been the case, an examination of the total male rate shows a modest downward trend for males aged 25-44 and more drastic reductions in the percentage of participation of males aged 14-24, and 65 and older.

The older workers appear subject to age discrimination, and their chances for re-employment are slight if they retire or lose their jobs. It is the younger group, however, that is really the key to the labor force problems of the 1970's. Because of the high birth rates of the postwar years, an increasing number of younger workers will enter the Michigan labor force in the next decade. *This increase in young workers is so substantial as to be the major factor shaping Michigan's labor market of the 1970's.*

The primary problem facing young males in the decade ahead will be to find employment in a labor market where educational and training requirements for jobs will be higher and where the new job opportunities in sales, clerical, and service work will favor females.

The racial factor is also an important consideration in a labor force analysis. In Michigan the rate of participation of white males over 14 years of age is higher than for non-whites. Although the total male participation rate declined between 1950 and 1960, the decline for non-white males was 2.5 times greater than for white males (see Table VII-6). The most striking declines were in the 14-19 age group and the group over 60.

For a growing number of young persons reaching the age level 14-19, and especially for non-whites, the increasing competition for jobs and the higher skill levels required undoubtedly result in withdrawals from the labor market. This is also true for older workers and especially non-white older workers who face both age and race discrimination.

The pattern is different for non-white females, whose participation rates have been increasing faster than those for white females.

The structure of unemployment in Michigan

Changes in employment opportunities, technology, and labor force participation will shape unemployment patterns in the 1970's. To a large extent the structure of unemployment in Michigan has followed regional and national patterns. There are, however, three areas in which the state faces peculiar circumstances which aggravate the problem of unemployment. These are: (1) Michigan's industrial mix, heavily concentrated in durable goods production, will undergo more rapid change than the national economy as a whole, and this will cause considerable revision in the requirements for employment; (2) the annual influx of young persons into the labor market, as previously noted, will be at a higher rate than the national rate; and (3) the opportunities for education and training in Michigan do not appear to be able to keep pace with the needs of the local labor market and the number of persons who require training.

The Negro in the labor market. A further look into Michigan's employment-unemployment profile in terms of race throws considerable light on the nature of the problems that must be faced through the mid-1970's.

United States Census data indicate that 95 per cent of the state's non-white labor force is located in the three-county Detroit metropolitan area. In addition, as of 1960, most of the state's non-white workers were engaged in lower-skilled blue-collar and service employment (Table VII-8). Among employed males, 70.1 per cent of the non-whites were employed as factory operatives, service workers, and laborers, while 36.1 per cent of the whites were so employed. Among employed females, 55.2

per cent of the non-whites were in domestic or service employment, compared to 19.7 per cent of the whites. This distribution is disheartening, considering that there have been two or three decades of Negro advancement in occupational opportunities within the state.

Employment trends for non-whites indicate a continuation of the decline in the proportion of jobs held by non-white males in the laborer and service worker category; a concurrent decline in the proportion of non-white females in private household jobs as a result of their increased employment in clerical and service work is expected to continue. It is expected that the proportion of professional and technical jobs among non-whites will continue to increase, with females showing a greater increase than males.

Several factors should improve the prospects for Negro employment in Michigan in general, and Detroit in particular, over the next decade. First, the Negro will no doubt profit from the recognition of his right to equal opportunity for employment. Second, the growing needs for skilled persons will emphasize the recruitment of workers on the basis of capacity and ability rather than race. Third, given the short supply of certain occupational specialists, Negro professionals and technicians who have the training will have unprecedented opportunities for employment.

There are, however, strong impediments to a full utilization of the Negro labor force. The most serious of these is the differential in education between whites and Negroes. Even with more opportunities available for Negroes it is possible that *there will be no substantial increase in Negro employment because too few Negroes possess the education and training required.* Negroes as a group missed boarding the educational escalator to those new jobs in the mid- and late 1950's.

The Negro also faces difficulty in gaining admission to the apprenticeship programs of craft unions. Without progress here, little hope can be seen for increased Negro participation in the skilled jobs associated with construction and maintenance.

Finally, there is the question of motivation. Unless there are increasing numbers of examples of success in the Negro community, it will be difficult to get young Negroes to stay in school or to go into training for skilled jobs. Past history indicates that some assurance of employment must exist if efforts to improve the education or training of underprivileged persons are to succeed.

Education, training, and retraining of workers

The number of persons entering the Michigan labor force in the next decade and the rising level of the skills needed for employment emphasize the urgency of a comprehensive educational and vocational training program in Michigan. Such a program must prepare and train youths for jobs, provide compensatory education and job training for disadvantaged workers, provide programs of training in skill categories that are in short supply, and offer training to unemployed workers to permit them to adjust to changes in job requirements. Although these goals may overlap, the Michigan labor market of the 1970's will require that all of them be recognized and that an effective program be implemented to achieve them.

The future of vocational education in Michigan is dependent upon the reimbursement practices of the federal and state government and the willingness and ability of local communities to diversify their investment in education. The present structure of vocational education in Michigan is not geared to the needs of the labor market at present or to the evolving world of work in the 1970's. Unless there is a marked change from current trends in federal and state reimbursement practices and local community investment in education, there is little hope that Michigan will have a viable vocational education program commensurate with the needs of the years ahead.

The data in Table VII-14 indicate that over half the enrollees in the state's vocational education program were concentrated in homemaking and agricultural courses. These concentrations reflect the force of tradition as well as the influence of the reimbursement programs of the federal and state governments, which favor these areas. Table VII-15 indicates that, unfortunately, the greatest reduction in reimbursement for courses has been in the occupational categories most in demand—trade and industrial, distributive and office. The differential rates of reimbursement have contributed to the schools' failure to expand training in these crucial areas and to reduce training in occupations and skills that are becoming obsolete.

Although changes in reimbursement patterns are urgently required, the major factor in the development of a strong vocational education system is the willingness and capacity of local communities to establish and pay for such education. Because of ever-increasing demands being placed on local school systems by the large numbers of students entering the elementary and high schools, there is little hope that local systems will be able to develop the required vocational programs. Even if they were able to do so, there are inherent defects in local programs. These include the tendency to provide training for skills needed locally, without regard for the state's labor market as a whole, and a great variation in the number and quality of programs offered by communities with varied resources.

The limitations of the local community are most evident in Detroit. Nowhere in Michigan are the needs for a comprehensive system of vocational education more pressing, and nowhere in Michigan do the prospects appear so bleak. As the city's needs for education have been increasing at a rapid rate, its tax base has been eroding.

In summary, current practices in Michigan regarding reimbursement and responsibility for vocational education in Michigan do not give grounds for optimism that a comprehensive program of vocational education will be developed in the near future, although recent federal legislation will help reduce the burden falling on state and local governments. The retraining of unemployed workers will continue under the emergency programs set up by the Area Redevelopment Authority and the Manpower Development and Training Act. The nature of these programs indicates that they will be able to train only a limited number of unemployed persons. Finally, the training and retraining concept has become a recognized part of a broad-gauged manpower utilization plan. There is danger that the complex problems of the decade ahead may be reduced to a need for more retraining. Recognition must be given to the fact that retraining is only meaningful when there is an active demand for workers who have acquired new skills or upgraded old ones.

II

THE NATIONAL ECONOMY

Sidney Sonenblum

Following the initial shock of discovery in the postwar period that the U. S. economy was not entering a depression or even a period of slow growth, a number of economists became deeply involved with considerations of the pace at which the economy could be expected to grow under conditions of reasonably full employment. These considerations have lead to the construction of a number of new and sophisticated model formulations of economic development, chiefly with reference to so-called aggregate production function analysis; but they have also led to a number of empirical exercises concerned with quantifying the likely economic environment in the United States for five to twenty-five years into the future.

Those making and using the statistical projections included primarily business economists, concerned with long-range marketing and investment decisions of their firms, and government economists interested in questions of fiscal policy and labor demand-and-supply balances.

The public became an acutely interested observer of the nation's economic growth in the late 1950's, when the high unemployment affected an increasing number of communities and households, and incomes failed to increase as rapidly as expected. The extent of the public involvement is evidenced less by legislation than by the "growth debate" of the 1960 presidential campaign and the attention given to economic questions at congressional hearings and in the press. Perhaps the most striking aspect of this public soul-searching concerning what economic achievements are feasible, what can be done about improving the national economic performance, and what role the government should play in this process was the rather high degree of sophistication expressed in the various arguments—a sophistication in no small measure attributable to the educational efforts of the Joint Economic Committee of Congress and the Council of Economic Advisers.

As we review the economic growth debate of the 1950's it is convenient to distinguish between those who took the position that a "slow" rate of noninflationary GNP growth (something around 3 per cent) was the most useful for planning purposes and those recommending that a "rapid" rate of noninflationary growth (something around 4 per cent) was the most useful. The "slow"-growth proponents seem to be saying that if we look at the record of the past and speculate about the future there is no evidence that economic factors will change sufficiently for the nation to depart from its average long-run growth of 3 per cent since 1929. The "fast"-growth proponents, however, seem to be saying that given the recent environmental changes in the economy the pace of future growth *could* be much faster than the long-term growth of the past and, even allowing for some slippage from the potential, the pace of future growth *would* be faster; further if the future GNP growth turns out to be no faster than the long-run growth the "GNP gap" would inevitably mean serious pressures from unemployment, budget deficits, lagging international trade and payments, and attempts to get a reduced work week.

Looking back at some of the major economic changes since the war, we can find evidence that would support either position: a decade of rapid postwar growth in output up to the mid-1950's, characterized by substantial increases in business investment, government expenditures, and consumer purchases; a poor economic performance relative to our potential in the past five years, characterized by high unemployment and low levels of business investment but showing a faster growth in output than that usually associated with high unemployment; many changes in technology and business management which have not only improved productivity, often at a faster pace than in the past, but also resulted in the creation of some new job opportunities at a faster pace than these jobs could be filled with available skills; the elimination of a large number of old jobs whose disappearance has caused substantial pockets of distress in certain occupations, industries, age and ethnic groups, and geographic areas of the economy.

What are the major areas of information which would throw light on whether the national economy can expect to grow at a relatively rapid or slow pace?

First, we must identify the quantitative impact on economic growth which improvements in knowledge and technology and the growth in the supply of labor and capital have had in the past. These are the considerations included in aggregate production function analysis.

Next, we must ask whether there are "institutional" rigidities which might prevent these factors from having their full effect in the future. Specifically, we must judge whether there is a conflict between expansionary policies on the one hand, and international payments equilibrium, the federal budget position, domestic price stability, and investment fund requirements, on the other hand; whether the fruits of rapid improvement in productivity are dissipated by persistent unemployment, manpower bottlenecks, and a reduced work week; and whether government economic policy will be legislated in time and in such a way as to encourage expansionary responses from the private sector.

We must, in addition, specify the form which economic growth will take: Is consumer demand sufficient to support economic growth, and what kinds of goods and services will households be purchasing? Which public goods and services will be growing and which declining? What kinds and levels of investment goods will be required?

The Decision and Judgment Models

To aid in the interpretation of such information Gerhard Colm has developed, and the National Planning Association Center for Economic Projection has implemented, a framework of analysis for making economic projections which distinguishes among possible alternative policies. This framework takes account of the realization that economic projections are used specifically for the kind of planning in which risks and benefits must be weighed against each other. The users of economic projections in evaluating their own cost-benefit calculus will often find reasons for preferring projections based on one rather than another set of policy assumptions. This is particularly so with the broad group of government planners on the one hand and the broad group of business planners on the other, although there is considerable room for difference among individual decision makers within each of these groups.

Briefly, this framework incorporates three kinds of projections. The *present policy* projection forecasts economic developments on the assumption that there will be no future change from the current policies of government and attitudes of consumers, business, and labor. Such a projection, of course, does not mean that things stay as they are, since account must be taken of foreseeable developments in population and productivity under present policy assumptions as well as of government commitments which have already been made about the future.

The *target projection* describes economic targets which are believed attainable if it is possible to bring about the changes in government policy and in the attitudes of business, labor, and consumers which are needed to achieve these targets. The *target projection* not only evaluates the consistency of economic relationships but also recognizes that some policies are not generally acceptable in our society, even if they result in more rapid economic development or greater price stability. That is, the target projection does not simply postulate a target in terms of a desirable rate of economic growth and then seek out the policies needed to achieve that target; rather, it finds out what a reasonable target is by testing the consistency between targets and possible policies. Taken together, the present policy projection, the target projection, and the packages of policies considered necessary to move from the current situation to the target can be called the Decision Model. Since the Decision Model throws light on the kinds of future economic programs needed to sustain a given rate of growth or achieve a higher one, it is of particular value to government officials and those who want to evaluate government policies.

Distinguished from the Decision Model is the Judgment

Model, which includes a *judgment projection* reflecting a probable, rather than feasible, course of economic developments. It is based, as are the present policy and target projections, on consideration of objective economic relationships, but it also depends on judgments about changes in policies and attitudes which appear likely under foreseeable circumstances. Since such judgments are often uncertain it is useful to supplement the judgment projection with alternative projections based on differing assumptions about defense expenditures and other such factors.

The projections in the Decision and Judgment Models are independent. However, in the developing of these projections there is a constant analytical feedback to determine for the *target projection* a reasonable target that can be attained with policies that are compatible with existing economic and social institutions.

The major advantages of such an approach are that it permits the user of projections to judge for himself how his plans may be affected by the differing policies which might be adopted and enables him therefore to decide which set of projections (modified as necessary) are most useful to him.

Decision and Judgment Model projections

Table II-1 compares the three types of projections with each other as well as with the relatively fast economic growth of 1948-57 and the relatively slow growth of 1957-62; this comparison throws some light on the forces affecting over-all economic growth.

As Table II-1 shows, the growth rate in real GNP slowed down by 25 per cent from the 1948-57 interval to the 1957-62 interval; accompanying this we find a 20 per cent slowdown in labor productivity (as measured by GNP per man-hour). In the present policy projection we find about the same growth in GNP and productivity as in the 1957-62 slow growth interval. The judgment projection shows a 15 per cent faster growth in output than during the 1948-57 interval. However, this is almost wholly attributable to the unemployment and underemployment of plant and people in 1962; for if we measured the growth rate from a

Table II-1

DECISION MODEL PROJECTIONS TO 1973

A. Projections

	1948	1957	1962	1973		
				Present Policy	Target	Judgment
Population (millions)	146	171	187	225	227	227
Labor participation (percentage of total population in labor force)	42.9	41.3	40.0	38.9	40.2	39.8
Total labor force (millions)	62.9	70.7	74.7	87.5	91.3	90.1
Civilian labor force (millions)	61.4	67.9	71.9	85.1	88.9	87.7
Total employment (millions)	60.6	67.8	70.6	82.0	87.9	86.6
Civilian employment (millions)	59.1	65.0	67.8	79.6	85.5	84.2
Unemployment rate (percentage of civilian labor force)	3.8	4.3	5.6	6.5	3.8	4.0
Unemployment number (millions)	2.3	2.9	3.9	5.5	3.4	3.5
Average weekly hours (total economy)	41.6	39.5	38.7	34.9	36.1	35.9
Total man-hours in economy (billions)	131	139	142	149	165	162
Value of stock of private plant and equipment* (billions of dollars)	465	630	659†	850	1,015	965
Gross national product* (billions of dollars)	342	480	554	775	950	905
GNP per capita*	$2,335	$2,804	$2,968	$3,440	$4,185	$3,993
Personal consumption per capita*	$1,521	$1,772	$1,912	$2,170	$2,510	$2,394
Federal Reserve Board Index of Production (1957/59=100)	68.4	100.7	118.2	175.0	225.0	212.1
Percentage distribution of GNP:						
Household consumption	69	64	65	63	60	60
Residential construction	4	4	4	4	4	4
Business investment	14	12	10	10	13	12
Federal goods and services	7	11	11	11	10	11
State and local goods and services	6	8	10	12	13	13

*Based on 1962 dollars.
†Estimated for the year 1961.

B. Average Annual Percentage Growth

	1948 -57	1957 -62	1962–73 Projected From				
			Potential 1962 level*			Actual 1962 level	
			Target	Judgment	Present Policy	Target	Judgment
GNP	3.9	2.9	4.5	4.1	3.1	5.0	4.6
GNP per man-hour	3.1	2.5	3.3	3.1	2.6	3.6	3.3
GNP per capita	1.8	1.1	2.7	2.2	1.3	3.2	2.7
Personal consumption per capita	1.6	1.5	2.1	1.6	1.1	2.5	2.1

*The potential 1962 GNP, given full employment, is estimated at about $585 billion.

potential full employment level in 1962, thus measuring the long-run full employment growth, the projected growth rate of output and productivity would be the same as in the earlier interval. The target projection, even measured from a 1962 full employment base, shows a growth rate faster than we have generally experienced over long, full employment intervals in the past.

To examine the sources of output growth more closely we will use an expository device developed by Denison.[1] In this device, the GNP growth rate is shown as the sum of the percentage point contributions to growth of the separate components of labor and capital inputs plus the combined productivity of these inputs.[2]

When we compare the relatively slow growth interval (1957-62) with the relatively fast growth interval (1948-57) in the past fifteen years we note that, in both cases, combined factor productivity contributes substantially more to output growth than do increases in the supply of factor inputs.[3] However, it should also be noted that the slowdown in output growth was accompanied by virtually no change in the percentage point contribution

[1] Edward F. Denison, *The Sources of Economic Growth in the United States and the Alternatives before Us*. Supplementary Paper No. 13 (New York: Committee on Economic Development, 1962).

[2] These data are derived by taking the annual growth rates of the separate factor inputs shown in Table II-1 and weighting the labor inputs by 80 per cent and the capital inputs by 20 per cent—their approximate contribution to the national income. Technically, this procedure implies that the national income shares are equal to the output elasticities of labor and capital. The results are highly sensitive to this assumption. If, for example, the factor elasticities are obtained by regression estimation the relative importance of factor productivity would be much reduced. (Richard R. Nelson, *Aggregate Production Functions and Medium Growth Projections*, Memorandum RM-3912-PR [New York: Rand Corp., December, 1963].) When the weighted inputs are summed the residual from the GNP growth rate represents combined factor productivity—analagous to the concept used by John Kendrick. (J. W. Kendrick, *Productivity Trends in the United States* [Princeton, N. J.: National Bureau of Economic Research, 1961].)

[3] This observation also depends on the particular model form implicit in the analysis (see preceding footnote). If, for example, the growth in capital was measured to include the "embodied" improvements in the quality of the capital, as is done by Solow (Robert M. Solow, "Technical

of productivity, so that almost the entire slowdown in growth could be arithmetically ascribed to a reduction in the increase of the labor and capital inputs. Thus we have the somewhat paradoxical situation that while productivity improvement is the major source of output growth its relative importance declines as the rate of output growth speeds up.

If there were no interaction between improvements in productivity and increases in the supply of factor inputs, in the coming decade we could expect productivity to improve at least at the same pace as in the past, and probably faster, as the effects of expanded research and development are felt through the economy; we could expect man-hours of labor input to grow at a faster pace than in the past because of the large additions to the labor force assured us by demographic forces; we could expect an increase in the plant and equipment input (the faster the rate of increase in output, the larger this input becomes) to be modified by a long-term decline in plant and equipment needs as capital efficiency improves.

However, there are interactions among the factor inputs and productivity which are of critical importance. One such interaction develops when a "slow" increase in expenditures by consumers and government holds back labor and capital employment and thus creates resistance by labor to efficiency improvements, reduces labor's mobility, and promotes the expectation among businessmen of low market potentials, with the final result of holding back productivity improvements that were otherwise likely to develop. This seems to have occurred in the 1957-62 interval, as measured both by the combined factor productivity of Table II-2, and more strikingly by the man-hour productivity shown in Table II-1.

Another possibility of interaction is that productivity might improve at such a rapid pace that the required types of labor

Progress, Capital Formation, and Economic Growth," *American Economic Review*, LII [May, 1962]), or if the growth in labor was measured to include improvements in the quality of labor because of increased education as is done by Denison, then the relative contribution to output growth of combined factor productivity would be smaller, while the contribution of the factor inputs would be larger.

Table II-2

SOURCES OF OUTPUT GROWTH

	1948 –57	1957 –62	1962–73 Present Policy	Target	Judgment
Percentage point contribution to growth:					
Total man-hours of labor input	0.6	0.3	0.4	1.1	1.0
+ Plant and equipment input	0.7	0.2	0.4	0.8	0.6
= Total factor input	1.3	0.5	0.8	1.9	1.6
+ Combined factor productivity	2.6	2.4	2.3	3.1	3.0
= Gross national product	3.9	2.9	3.1	5.0	4.6
Percentage of GNP growth rate:					
Total man-hours of labor input	15	10	13	22	22
Plant and equipment	18	7	13	16	13
Total factor input	33	17	26	38	35
Combined factor productivity	67	82	74	62	65
Gross national product	100	100	100	100	100

cannot be made available, a condition which, by holding back employment growth and consumer income, would also hold back growth in total demand. A third possibility of interaction is that productivity could improve so rapidly that even if labor skills were adequate the demands of consumers and government could not increase sufficiently to absorb both the productivity improvement and a growth in labor inputs consistent with full employment.

Our judgment estimate of the future (for reasons discussed in the section "Judgment Projections") is that neither a scarcity of labor skills nor of consumer and government demand is likely to hold back growth in productivity and total output—provided that some current policies and attitudes are changed. Rather we conclude that, within the limits of a 3 per cent to 5 per cent GNP growth rate, a faster productivity improvement will mean a still faster growth in labor and capital inputs, providing a reinforced or dual impact on the pace of GNP growth.

Considering the possible consequences of such interactions

we have projected the present policy growth in output (Table II-1) to be at about the same pace as in the 1957-62 interval because a slow growth in demand holds back the growth in both productivity and factor inputs; we project the judgment growth to be at a faster pace than in the 1948-57 interval because productivity increases its contribution, and labor and capital both resume their long-term growth pattern as they recover from their current underutilization; we project the target growth at the fastest pace of all because full employment of labor does not constrain the introduction of productivity improvements, and more women and older persons stay in the labor force when job opportunities are plentiful.

The contribution of the man-hours input to economic growth is critical and is examined in some further detail in Table II-3.

Table II-3

PERCENTAGE POINT CONTRIBUTION TO ANNUAL GNP GROWTH

			1962–73		
	1948 –57	1957 –62	Present Policy	Target	Judgment
Population	1.4	1.4	1.4	1.4	1.4
+ Labor participation rate	-0.3	-0.5	-0.2	0.0	0.0
= Total labor force	1.1	0.9	1.2	1.4	1.4
+ Employment rate	-0.1	-0.2	-0.1	0.2	0.1
= Total employment	1.0	0.7	1.1	1.6	1.5
+ Average weekly hours	-0.4	-0.3	-0.7	-0.5	-0.5
= Total man-hours of labor	0.6	0.3	0.4	1.1	1.0

Although we have assumed that the relatively low level of economic prosperity in the present policy projection will hold back population increases somewhat, this would have relatively little effect on the contribution which a growing population will make to output growth in the coming decade. We expect population to increase at about the same rate in each projection, that is, at about the same rate as that since 1948.[4] As the propor-

[4]For a more detailed examination of this assumption, see pp. 55-58.

tion of total population in the younger and older age brackets increases there is a tendency for a decline in the over-all labor participation rate, a tendency which therefore acts as a negative influence in GNP growth. This participation rate decline was particularly sharp during the 1957-62 interval when the lack of job opportunities forced some persons out of the labor force and discouraged others from entering. In the projections we note that a continuation of present policy would have a continued negative effect on the participation rate, whereas recovery to full employment in the target and judgment projections implies no subtraction from growth because of participation rate changes. Taken together, the projected population and participation rate changes show the labor force's contribution to growth in the target and judgment projections to be above its contribution in the past. Reductions in the unemployment rate from 1962 to the target and judgment projections act as a positive contribution to growth, whereas the increased unemployment in the present policy projection continues to act as a negative factor. Finally, the average number of hours worked per week is expected to continue its long-term decline in each projection, although the decline is most rapid in the present policy projection because high unemployment leads to work-sharing arrangements.

We have examined the supply factors contributing to growth and found that the absolute and relative importance of these factors can be expected to change with time even when economic policy does not change; however, still further changes in the importance of the supply factors can be expected with policy shifts. The same can be said for the distribution of total output among the various demand sectors in the economy. As shown in Table II-1, there is a long-term increase in the share of state and local government expenditures as public goods become increasingly important, and there is a decline in the share of household expenditures. We expect these shifts to continue in each of the projections. Also, we have not projected a relative increase for federal expenditures, since defense is assumed to increase far less rapidly than total output. Because of improvements in capital efficiency as time passes, business investment is expected to furnish a declining share of total output for equal growth rates; the share of business investment in total output is expected to go up, however, with faster increases in output during the same interval of time. This is reflected in our projections, which show the present policy share at the same level as in 1962, while the target projection goes above the share experienced in 1957, which was a high investment year.

Policy Considerations

Economic projections can never be wholly accurate in predicting the economic environment of the future. Our tools for economic analysis are not precise enough, even with the most complicated models, to relieve us from introducing considerable dosages of judgment about interrelations among economic variables and the probable consequences of a given set of actions. This fact, however, does not invalidate the potential utility of such projections, since the precise figures presented are meant to illustrate only general orders of magnitude of trends which appear probable under reasonable assumptions. Yet the changes implied by such calculations are often so large that it is prudent to consider their magnitudes in evaluating current and prospective business plans and public policies.

Our experience with such projections in the past indicates that they are sufficiently reliable for this purpose. In fact, the major reason why economic projections go "wrong" appears to lie less in poor assumptions about changing economic interrelationships than in incorrect assumptions about the introduction of new legislation and the adaptation of the private sector to public policy.

There seem to be political and economic mechanisms in a democracy which induce the transition from things which "should" happen to things which "do" happen. This transition from the ideal to the real appears to be most effectively accomplished when the gap between the two is most keenly felt. Thus we often find ourselves in a situation where we must expect things to get worse before current policies will be modi- to make them better. This does not invalidate the longer-term projection. For example, increases in the number of persons and areas which are by-passed by economic prosperity are themselves a critical force in changing the direction of future developments.

However, it is not suggested that we should be sanguine about the adoption of policy changes necessary for realizing economic developments that will bring us closer to our economic potential than has been the case in recent years. At the very least we should be always interested in reducing the time gap between the recognition of need for new policies and their adoption. And, as the prolonged debate over tax reduction and reform indicated, we cannot be certain that our institutions will always work effectively in this direction.

The Decision Model permits us to identify those soft spots in the economy which require attention as well as to judge the feasibility of achieving specified targets. As we look at the data of the Decision Model (and the further detail of the judgment projections shown in the section "Judgment Projections") it appears that the magnitude of the changes required for achieving reasonably full employment of resources at high levels of productivity is not so large that these changes cannot be brought about.

However, for feasibility to become actuality it is necessary to stimulate the growth in consumer demand, probably through appropriate tax policy. Also, there are a number of important international and domestic programs in which government expenditures play a critical role; some of these programs need to be expanded during the coming decade. Although the primary purpose of such programs is to meet emerging needs in our society, they will also improve aggregate demand and generate manpower requirements both directly and indirectly when the program's effects are felt in the private sector. The growing demand for professionals must be met, probably by improving educational programs. Workers need to be retrained to meet the increasing demand for craftsmen and technicians and to offset the relative decline in demand for operatives. Our young people should be trained in those clerical, sales, and craftsman skills which will be needed in the future. We should recognize that the economic circumstances of the non-whites in our society require special attention if their position in relation to whites is not to deteriorate still further.

These are some of the areas in which current economic policy is inadequate to achieve full employment growth. However, the question remains as to whether policy changes are likely to overcome those "rigidities" in our society which, as some people argue, can be expected to impede a pick-up in the pace of economic growth by holding back productivity improvements, increasing unemployment, and reducing the work week and labor participation.

1. It is argued that productivity advances are changing the requirements for manpower so rapidly that labor force skills cannot adapt sufficiently, the consequence being a substantial number of unemployables in the economy. These difficulties are compounded by the large number of young people entering the labor force, the large number of school drop-outs, and the large number of persons without sufficient education to adapt to new opportunities. Our judgment projection examines the relation between labor supply and demand by skill categories and leads us to conclude that productivity is not likely to increase so much more rapidly than in the past that it will create a basic conflict. This assumes, however, that job training programs will increase. The most important programs for learning new skills involve the formal and informal on-the-job training which is motivated by management's desire to improve productivity and by the individual's desire for advancement.[5] Substantial results from these programs are likely to continue and even to increase to a modest extent, particularly in the light of management's recognition that training is required in periods of surplus as well as scarce labor supply. In addition, however, there will be a need for substantial increases in public training programs–particularly for the unemployed, who

[5]A recent survey by the Federal Reserve Bank of Boston showed that seven out of ten New England manufacturing firms have industrial training programs which cost, in the aggregate, over $70 million per year and involve, in any year, training for one-fifth of New England's manufacturing labor force. This training is not concentrated in special areas but spread throughout the occupational and industrial structure.

have no opportunity for on-the-job training. Since such programs are not currently very large, even substantial increases in expenditures will not involve excessive sums from public funds. In spite of the success we assume from such programs, we can also expect part of the labor force in some areas to lack the needed skills, and we also find it likely that there will be some scarcities of key personnel—all of which will restrain economic growth from its full potential.

2. It is argued that consumer demand in an affluent society cannot grow sufficiently to support both full employment and rapid productivity improvement. This argument is based either on a suggestion of satiety on the part of consumers, or, more realistically, on the idea that the shape of the income distribution is such that it cannot support full employment consumption. The latter may mean that the income distribution is shifting in favor of the upper income, high-saving groups and thus reducing the share of aggregate income being spent. Or it may mean that, although no such shift in the income distribution is occurring, a shift is needed in favor of the low-income groups if full employment consumption is to be maintained. On this question the judgment projections suggest that neither consumer satiety nor income distribution effects will significantly restrain economic growth.

3. The argument that household consumption will be inadequate leads some to conclude that a major shift from "conventional" to "unconventional" purchases, i.e., from private to public goods and services, is required if full employment is to be maintained. Our judgment projections suggest that although a proportionate shift to productive government expenditures is to be expected (with or without a rising defense budget), this shift is not out of line with past trends. Some argue further that the needed shift to public goods, if full employment is to be maintained, will mean domestic inflation and aggravated balance of payments difficulties, situations which the nation cannot afford. Our judgment projection implies

the opposite conclusion: that increased government expenditures are compatible with cuts in tax rates. Tax cuts would, in turn, relieve the effects of the current high tax rate structure which absorbs rising income and profits into the Treasury and thus tends to blunt the forces of expansion.

4. It is argued that a shortage of investment funds limits the growth in plant and equipment, thereby holding back economic growth. Because of mutual interactions, it cannot be directly ascertained from the historical data whether a lack of investment funds or lack of expected growth in market opportunities has held back investment. It does not seem likely, however, that at this point in time there are serious shortages of investment funds; and as we look into the future, it appears that if such a shortage does develop it will be a consequence rather than a cause of slow aggregate economic growth.[6]

5. Finally, and of utmost importance, it is argued that in order to reduce the pressure on our balance of payments we must necessarily adopt domestic policies which will restrain expansion. However, it is becoming increasingly recognized that a slow rate of economic growth tends to aggravate rather that solve the balance of payments problem. For, although rapid expansion in the short run does tend to expand imports faster than exports, a more important consideration is that in the long run slow growth and continuing high unemployment will increase labor's resistance to productivity improvements and agitation for reduced work weeks in the labor force. These cost-raising factors will make us less, not more, competitive in world markets.

Judgment Projections

This section shows further detail regarding the judgment projection of population and labor force, allocation of national

[6]A detailed examination of the capital markets of the future appears in Chapter III.

output, industry production, and employment characteristics. The detail shows only highlights of some of the trends which are described more comprehensively in various reports of the National Planning Association Center for Economic Projections. It is hoped that the magnitudes which are presented will permit the reader to evaluate their probability in the light of past developments and to group the implications of these developments in respect to future changes. But it is also hoped that through this analysis of the change between projected and current magnitudes the reader can evaluate the probable effectiveness of public policy in ameliorating the stresses imposed by the interactions of potentially conflicting forces. The analysis bears particularly on the relations between productivity change and full employment growth, affluence and consumer demands, public and private goods, and finally the need for and availability of investment funds.

Labor supply

Population (Table II-4). The U. S. population has increased from 4 million persons in 1790 to 180 million in 1960. Before 1900, both because of immigration and net natural increase, the population grew about 30 per cent per decade; since 1900 immigration has been relatively low, and hence reproduction accounts for most of the population increase of over 15 per cent per decade. Beginning with World War II, the pace of increase in population growth was stepped up to such an extent that the population increased by almost 50 million persons between 1940 and 1960. The growth rate of the last decade, however, has been almost 30 per cent higher than the rate between 1940 and 1950.

Long-term projections of population growth are always hazardous; but they are particularly so at this time, when recently published data on population show some marked shifts from past behavior. Since 1960 there has been a substantial slowdown in the rate of population increase. This fact can be attributed to a leveling off in the decline of the average marriage age and an "unfavorable" shift in the age distribution of the population away from women of childbearing age. Taking account of these phenomena and considering the changes in the age distribution of the population which will develop in the coming decade, the Census Bureau has revised downward an earlier projection of the 1975

Table II-4

POPULATION—1957, 1962, AND 1973
(Distribution by Sex and Age)

	Millions of Persons			Percentage of Totals		
	1957	1962	1973	1957	1962	1973
Total	171.1	186.6	226.6	100.0	100.0	100.0
Under 14	49.2	54.6	68.4	28.8	29.3	30.2
14-19	14.8	18.5	23.9	8.6	9.9	10.5
20-24	10.7	11.9	18.3	6.3	6.4	8.0
25-54	66.7	68.2	74.8	39.0	36.5	33.0
55+	29.7	33.4	41.3	17.3	17.9	18.3
Males—total	84.8	92.1	111.7	49.6	49.4	49.3
Under 14	25.1	27.8	34.9	29.6	30.2	31.2
14-19	7.5	9.4	12.1	8.8	10.2	10.8
20-24	5.4	5.9	9.2	6.4	6.4	8.2
25-54	32.8	33.5	36.9	38.6	36.3	33.1
55+	14.0	15.5	18.7	16.5	16.9	16.7
Females—total	86.3	94.5	114.9	50.4	50.6	50.7
Under 14	24.1	26.9	33.5	27.9	28.5	29.1
14-19	7.3	9.2	11.8	8.5	9.7	10.3
20-24	5.3	5.9	9.1	6.1	6.2	7.9
25-54	33.9	34.6	37.9	39.3	36.6	33.0
55+	15.7	17.9	22.6	18.2	19.0	19.7

population, which showed a 1.8 per cent annual growth; the most recent projection shows a 1.5 per cent annual growth. This projection is consistent with anticipation surveys showing the number of children the family is expected to include when it is completed.

However, in our judgment, insufficient weight is given in these calculations to the positive effect of economic prosperity on family size. Since the nation experienced relatively slow economic growth in the past five years, whereas our judgment projection shows a relatively fast growth, we have also projected a relatively high fertility rate--approximating that of the past decade—which would result in a population of 227 million by 1973. We project the age groups between 25 and 65 to decline as a percentage of the population, while the groups below 25 and over 65 can be expected to increase in relative importance.

Although our population estimate will not affect the labor force projection, it does influence our projection of total demand for goods and services and would significantly influence the projections for separate regions in the country. This influence can be demonstrated by comparing David Goldberg's estimate of population in Michigan for 1975, as shown in Chapter IV, with an estimate that we have made. Goldberg, using a much more detailed analysis, assumes a decline in the national fertility rate, a continuation of the higher than national rate for Michigan women, and no net migration from Michigan, and he arrives at a 1975 population of 9.5 million. Our projection, which assumes a high fertility, arrives at a population estimate of 10 million for 1975 in spite of our estimate of 400,000 out-migrants from Michigan between 1960 and 1975.

Labor force (Tables II-5, II-6). The relentless pressure of population growth assures a rising labor force for the nation. The labor force has increased from 23 million persons in 1890 to current levels of about 75 million and is expected to reach 90 million by 1973. The increase in the labor force has been at about the same pace as the growth in population--the relation between labor force and population showing relatively little variation since 1890 (varying from 36.9 per cent to 42.6 per cent for decade years).

As we look to the future we expect that the growing-up of the postwar baby crop will add substantially more persons to the labor force during the coming decade than were added during the preceding decade. That is, there will be some 6 million *net* additions in the coming five years and 15 million between 1962 and 1973. These are not additions to the labor force in the sense that they represent the number by which new entrants into the labor force exceed deaths and retirements. Since about 2 per cent of the men and 5 per cent of the women leave the labor force for various reasons each year, we can expect about 20 million persons to be separated from the labor force between 1962 and 1973. With 15 million net additions, therefore, we would expect 35 million "new faces" (new entrants and reentrants) looking for jobs between 1962 and 1973. Put in another way, about one-third of the projected 1973 labor is not currently in the labor force.

Table II-5

TOTAL LABOR FORCE—1957, 1962, AND 1973
(Distribution by Age and Sex)

	Millions of Persons			Percentage of Totals		
	1957	1962	1973	1957	1962	1973
Total	70.7	74.7	90.1	100.0	100.0	100.0
14-19	5.9	6.6	8.9	8.3	8.9	9.9
20-24	7.3	8.1	12.1	10.3	10.8	13.4
25-54	45.5	47.0	52.8	64.3	62.9	58.7
55+	12.1	13.0	16.2	17.1	17.4	18.0
Males—total	48.6	50.2	59.2	68.7	67.2	65.7
14-19	3.7	4.0	5.4	7.6	8.0	9.1
20-24	4.8	5.3	7.9	9.9	10.5	13.4
25-54	31.5	32.0	35.3	64.8	63.9	59.7
55+	8.7	8.8	10.5	17.9	17.6	17.8
Females—total	22.1	24.5	30.9	31.2	32.8	34.3
14-19	2.2	2.6	3.5	10.0	10.7	11.4
20-24	2.5	2.8	4.2	11.3	11.5	13.6
25-54	14.0	15.0	17.4	63.4	61.1	56.5
55+	3.4	4.1	5.8	15.4	16.7	18.5

The aggregate growth projection fails to reveal some significant aspects of the age, sex, and color composition of the labor force. Because of the aging process we can expect the age brackets up to 24 to make up about half the total increase to 1967; after 1967 the age groups over 25 begin to dominate the total labor force growth. If jobs are not quickly found for those in these younger groups they will fail to gain the experience needed for their later years when they are usually at the most productive stage in their lives and have the greatest responsibilities.

Since 1947 women have dominated the labor force growth: 60 per cent of the labor force increase between 1947 and 1957, and again between 1957 and 1962, was accounted for by women. Almost half the increase could be found among married women, between the ages of 25 and 54. Although our projections show a continued growth in the number of women in the labor force, women will account for less than 40 per cent of the increase in

Table II-6

CIVILIAN LABOR FORCE—1957, 1962, AND 1973
(Distribution by Color, Sex, and Age)

	Millions of Persons			Percentage of Totals		
	1957	1962	1973	1957	1962	1973
Total	67.9	71.9	87.7	100.0	100.0	100.0
White	60.6	64.0	77.8	89.2	89.0	88.7
Males	41.4	42.7	50.8	60.9	59.4	58.0
Females	19.2	21.3	27.0	28.3	29.6	30.7
Non-white	7.3	7.9	9.9	10.8	11.0	11.3
Males	4.5	4.7	5.8	6.6	6.5	6.6
Females	2.9	3.2	4.1	4.3	4.5	4.6
Total Males	45.9	47.4	56.6	67.5	65.9	64.6
Total Females	22.1	24.5	31.1	32.5	34.1	35.3
White—Ages	60.6	64.0	77.8	89.2	89.2	88.7
14-19	4.8	5.6	7.6	7.1	7.8	8.7
20-24	5.3	6.2	9.9	7.8	8.6	11.1
25-54	39.5	40.6	45.7	58.1	56.5	52.3
55+	11.0	11.7	14.6	16.2	16.3	16.6
Non-white—Ages	7.3	7.9	9.9	10.8	10.8	11.3
14-19	0.6	0.7	1.0	0.9	1.0	1.0
20-24	0.9	0.9	1.2	1.3	1.3	1.4
25-54	4.8	5.1	6.2	7.1	7.1	7.0
55+	1.0	1.1	1.5	1.5	1.5	1.6

the coming decade. With a projected increase of over 8 million in the male labor force, as compared with a 3.5 million increase in the preceding decade, the task of finding new job opportunities for household heads is much larger than in the past.

Non-whites represent about 11 per cent of the civilian labor force and are projected to account for a slightly larger share. Although non-whites represent one-tenth of the labor force, they currently account for over two-tenths of the unemployed. This implies a serious adjustment problem for the future, particularly since half the growth of the non-white labor force in the coming five years (as compared with a quarter of the white labor force growth) is projected to be in the 25-54 bracket--containing those age groups which are potentially most productive and which have the greatest family responsibilities.

Labor participation rates (Table II-7). The size of the labor force depends not only on the age and sex composition of the population but also on the share of the population in each age-sex bracket which is willing and able to work. These labor participation rates depend in turn on such factors as the level of economic prosperity, the racial composition of the labor force, the extent of urbanization, the availability of pensions, and educational achievement.

In the past these various factors have interacted in such a way that the labor force share of the population over 14 has changed very little over long periods, ranging between 55 per cent and 58 per cent in decade years between 1890 and 1960. However, the participation rate for males has been declining, whereas females have increased their participation. We have projected a slight decline in the participation rates of males between 25 and 65, with sharper declines in the rates for males below 25, a reflection of a rising demand for higher education; a sharp increase in the participation rates for females over 25, particularly in the 45-and-over age group, significantly influenced by part-time employment opportunities and trends toward a shorter work week; and a slight decline in the rate for females below 25.

Table II-7

LABOR PARTICIPATION RATES—1957, 1962, AND 1973
(Percentage Employed by Age and Sex)

	Males and Females			Males			Females		
	1957	1962	1973	1957	1962	1973	1957	1962	1973
All ages	41.3	40.0	39.8	57.3	54.5	52.9	25.6	25.9	26.9
14-19	39.9	35.7	37.3	49.7	42.6	44.6	30.6	28.3	29.8
20-24	68.2	68.1	66.4	89.8	89.8	85.9	46.0	47.5	46.5
25-34	65.0	65.8	67.0	97.3	96.4	96.2	35.6	36.3	37.8
35-44	69.0	69.4	71.7	97.9	95.8	96.7	43.3	44.0	47.5
45-54	70.6	71.7	74.5	96.4	94.2	94.8	46.5	50.0	55.4
55-64	59.1	60.9	62.6	87.5	84.6	85.0	34.5	38.6	42.3
65+	23.3	18.5	17.1	37.5	38.6	25.8	10.5	9.4	10.5
14 and over	58.0	56.6	57.0	82.7	78.1	77.0	35.9	36.2	38.0
25-54	68.2	68.9	70.6	96.0	95.5	95.7	41.3	43.4	45.9
55+	40.7	38.9	39.2	62.1	56.8	56.1	21.7	22.9	25.7

The changing labor participation rates are particularly critical in the non-white labor force. Non-white women have traditionally participated at a higher rate than white women, but the difference is becoming smaller; we expect this closing-up trend to continue. Non-white males, however, who participated in the labor force at a higher rate than white males in the late 1940's, have fallen increasingly below the white rates during the 1950's. This appears related to the lack of job opportunities (aggravated by the decline in agriculture, where non-whites are rather heavily concentrated) particularly for the younger and older age brackets.

Since 1961 neither men nor women, white or non-white, have entered the labor force at the rate which would be suggested by their past trends. According to Otto Eckstein there was a shortfall of about one-half million persons in 1962 alone, heavily concentrated among women over 45 and men over 55.[7] We attribute this shortfall to the lack of job opportunities in recent years. In the judgment projections, however, we have assumed that job opportunities would not be so scarce that those who wish to seek jobs would be discouraged from entering the labor force. If this judgment proves wrong and something more like the current policy projection evolves over the coming decade, we can expect labor participation to be reduced from its expected trend in the younger as well as older age brackets. If our young people who do not go on to a higher education are also discouraged from entering the job market, then there is not only an immediate loss of income to themselves and society but also a personal and social loss, which can never be regained, of opportunity for future development of productive abilities.

Average work week (Table II-1). The American economy has taken a share of its improved productivity in the form of leisure time, which has been increasing at a rate of about 2 hours per decade and by 1962 reached a level just below 39 hours per week for the total economy. In the judgment projection we have continued this trend to a 36-hour week by 1973. If high levels of un-

[7]U. S. Senate, Committee on Labor and Public Welfare, *Hearings before the Subcommittee on Employment and Manpower, Nation's Manpower Revolution,* Part 5, Otto Eckstein, "Unemployment and Economic Growth," 88th Cong., 1st sess., 1963-64.

employment are to continue, however, it is probable that labor pressures will force a faster decline in the work week, with unfortunate consequences for productivity and our balance of payments.

Taken together, the projected growth in employment and the decline in the work week imply an increase of 20 billion man-hours that will reach a level of 160 billion man-hours of labor input in the 1973 economy.

Distribution of national output

The nation's total output and income, in any given year, are distributed among households, government, and domestic and foreign investment. The most convenient way of summarizing the developments in each of these sectors and their interrelationships is in the form of a national economic budget which shows the expected expenditures for goods and service by each sector, their revenues, and their resultant saving or dissaving, as shown in Table II-8.

The most striking aspect of this table is the expected substantial increase in expenditures and revenues by each sector as a concomitant of aggregate growth. The relatively slight projected change from recent patterns in the distribution of expenditures and revenues is consistent with developments in the past half-century. These distributional changes are not large, but they are critical to the process of economic development. Although consumers are projected to purchase a smaller share of national output, and government an increasing share, these shifts are not so large as to be out of line with past trends or likely to result in inflationary pressures.

Households (Table II-9). Households, defined in the national accounts to include nonprofit institutions as well as families and individuals, are projected to purchase 60 per cent of the national output and earn 65 per cent of the national revenues by 1973. In addition, households benefit directly and indirectly from the many services provided by government.

Currently, households are purchasing three times the quantity of goods and services they purchased in 1930; this represents an average annual increase of 3 per cent for the entire period and 3.5 per cent since the war. Per capita expenditures

Table II-8

NATION'S ECONOMIC BUDGETS—1957, 1962, AND 1973

	Disposable Receipts		Purchase of Goods and Services		Excess of Receipts	
	Amount*	Percentage of GNP	Amount*	Percentage of GNP	Amount*	Percentage of Disposable Receipts
1957						
Households	308.8	69.7	285.2	64.4	23.6	7.6
Domestic investment	45.6	10.3	66.1	14.9	-20.5	...
Net international	1.5	0.3	4.9	1.1	- 3.5	...
Government	87.5	19.8	86.5	19.5	1.0	1.1
Statistical discrepancy	- 0.6	- 0.1	...	...	- 0.6	...
GNP (in 1957 prices)	442.8	100.0	442.8	100.0	...	...
GNP (in 1962 prices)	480.1	...	480.1	...	...	...
1962						
Households	382.9	69.1	356.7	64.4	26.2	6.8
Domestic investment	58.1	10.5	76.6	13.8	-18.2	...
Net international	1.7	0.3	3.3	0.6	- 1.5	...
Government	114.9	20.7	117.3	21.2	- 2.4	-2.1
Statistical discrepancy	- 3.8	- 0.7	...	...	- 3.8	...
GNP (in 1962 prices)	553.9	100.0	553.9	100.0	...	...
1973						
Households	591.0	65.3	542.5	60.0	48.5	8.2
Domestic investment	103.0	11.4	140.0	15.5	-37.0	...
Net international	0.8	0.1	4.5	0.5	- 3.7	...
Government	210.1	23.2	217.9	24.1	- 7.8	-3.7
GNP (in 1962 prices)	904.9	100.0	904.9	100.0	...	...

*In billions of dollars.

have almost doubled since 1930, a fact which implies an annual increase of over 1.5 per cent before and after the war. The judgment projection shows a faster rate of increase than in the past five years for total, per capita, and per household personal expenditures.

Why do we expect this pick-up in the pace of personal expenditures? It is our conviction that the slow growth of household purchases in recent years is a direct result of the slow growth in consumer income. Provided that incomes increase adequately, the relative slack in purchases of consumer durables during the last five years is likely to give rise to a period of high expenditures as the deferred demands of recent years become realized, and as the rising income of families at the lower end of the income scale enables them to afford the volume and diversity of purchases now enjoyed by families in the middle income brackets. Nondurables and services, as well, are likely to increase (although services at a somewhat reduced pace from the rapid rise of recent years) as rising income levels open up whole new styles of life for many families.

Consumers are not expected to become so affluent that further increases in income will hold back consumer purchases sufficiently to restrain the growth in GNP. We expect disposable income to increase at a rate of 4 per cent per year and to reach a per capita level of $2,600 by 1973. We project almost twice as many consumer units in the $7,500 to $15,000 pre-tax income bracket as there were in 1962, and this group is expected to earn over 40 per cent of the total income. Consumer units earning over $15,000 are expected to more than double in number and to earn about 35 per cent of total income. Consumer units earning less than $7,500 are expected to be below the 1962 number, and this group will earn about 20 per cent of total income.

As more families move into higher income brackets we can feel fairly confident that their expenditures will at least equal those of families in similar income brackets today and probably be greater as the demonstration effect of still higher incomes spills downward. Of the 50 per cent increase in total personal expenditures over current levels that is expected by 1973, we expect two-thirds to be accounted for by an increase in the num-

Table II-9

PERSONAL INCOME AND EXPENDITURES—1957, 1962, AND 1973

A. Household Income and Expenditures

	At 1962 Price Level			Percentage of Average Annual Growth			Percentage of Total Personal Expenditures		
	1957	1962	1973	1948 -57	1957 -62	1962 -73	1957	1962	1973
Personal consumption expenditures									
Per capita (dollars)	1,772	1,912	2,394	1.6	1.5	2.1			
Per household (dollars)	6,133	6,532	8,359	1.2	1.3	2.3			
Total (billions of dollars)	303.6	356.7	542.5	3.5	3.3	3.9	100.0	100.0	100.0
Durables	40.6	47.5	80.3	5.1	3.3	4.9	13.4	13.3	14.8
Nondurables	144.6	162.0	231.1	2.6	2.3	3.3	47.6	45.4	42.6
Services	118.4	147.1	231.1	4.1	4.5	4.2	39.0	41.2	42.6
Personal disposable income									
Per capita (dollars)	1,919	2,052	2,608	2.0	1.3	2.2			
Per household (dollars)	6,640	7,012	9,100	1.4	1.1	2.4			
Total (billions of dollars)	328.7	382.9	591.0	3.8	3.1	4.1			

B. Income Distribution of Consumer Units

Income Brackets: 1957 at 1961 Price Level 1962 and 1973 at 1962 Price Level	Percentage of Consumer Units in Each Income Bracket			Percentage of Consumer Unit Income in Each Income Bracket		
	1957	1962	1973	1957	1962	1973
Below $2,000	13	12	8	2	2	1
2,000 - 3,999	20	19	12	9	8	4
4,000 - 5,999	23	21	15	18	14	8
6,000 - 7,499	14	13	12	15	12	9
7,500 - 9,999	14	16	19	18	20	17
10,000 - 14,999	9	12	20	17	20	25
15,000 - 19,999	3		7	7		11
20,000 - 24,999	1	7	3	4	24	7
25,000 and above	2		4	10		18
Total consumer unit income (billion dollars)	354	419	643			
Number of consumer units (millions)	53.6	58.6	69.2			
Average income per consumer unit (dollars)	6,610	7,140	9,285			

ber of households and upgrading in income levels. Accounting for the other third will be reduced saving rates in each income bracket, a reflection of the desire of families at given income levels to improve their living standards by purchasing new goods and services as well as increasing their purchases of existing goods and services.

The distribution of personal expenditures is also likely to change, not only because of changing consumer preferences and the introduction of new goods and services but also because of the changes in the number of consumer units in each income class which accompany the growth in economic prosperity. We expect a continuation of the historical increase in the proportions of durable goods expenditures, and a continuation of the decline in the share of spending on nondurables—the decline being concentrated in food expenditures. Services are likely to receive a still higher portion of the consumer's dollar in 1973 than currently, although the rate of increase in services expenditures is likely to slow down from its recent pace.

To a large extent the rather high per capita incomes in Michigan are related to the state's capacity to produce consumer durables. This is not an unmixed blessing, however, because erratic swings in demand for these goods have a magnified effect on the stability of the Michigan economy and also because a long-term relative shift away from these goods would require a basic structural adjustment for the state.

We have noted our expectations that consumer durable expenditures will not only rise but even increase as a share of household expenditures. Much of this expected increase is attributable to the influence of the projected increase in the number of families which by today's standards would be considered to have high incomes. These families will not only increase the share of their expenditures which they devote to services but also will buy larger quantities and a better quality of consumer goods and will constitute a particularly strong market for new products. We expect the increase in the proportion of household expenditures for durables to be shared about equally between expenditures for automobiles, on the one hand, and for furniture and other household equipment, on the other.

The consequences of these changes for the growth in Michigan's income are more difficult to trace than on the national level. What we expect is that, although Michigan's average household income will continue to grow, its excess over the national average will decline.

Business investment (Table II-10). The combined total of plant and equipment outlays, residential construction, and net inventory accumulation constitutes gross private domestic investment in the national accounts. Its general decline in relation to GNP (from 20 per cent in 1929 to 14 per cent in 1962) is in large part accounted for by the slow growth in business spending for plant.

Business Plant and Equipment Investment

The mutual interdependence of plant and equipment investment and aggregate output means that a speed-up in the GNP growth cannot proceed without a significant increase in the volume and rate of investment. This is not the same, however, as saying that "to raise output all that is needed is to raise investment," a prescription for growth which operates only within the limits permitted by other factors such as growth in manpower and productivity. In our projections we have stipulated a restoration of the fairly persistent long-run relation of investment to output—modified somewhat by likely changes in future trends.

Since 1957 the nation's capital stock has advanced at an average rate not only below the relatively high rate of the 1948-57 interval but also below the rate deemed consistent with current growth potentials of output and labor force. The slow growth of capital stock has shown up in the currently low share of plant and equipment investment expenditures in the GNP.

The projections show a growth rate in capital stock that will be faster than in the past five years and slower than in the postwar decade. The growth in investment expenditures, however, is substantially faster than even that of the postwar decade as investment in replacement and modernization, particularly in the first part of the coming decade, adds substantially to expansion requirements.

The projected expansion in plant and equipment is consistent with past trends in improvements of capital efficiency (declining

Table II-10

INVESTMENT, FOREIGN TRADE, AND AVERAGE ANNUAL PERCENTAGES OF GROWTH

A. Business Investment and Foreign Trade

	Billions of Dollars at 1962 Price Level			Percentage of GNP		
	1957	1962	1973	1957	1962	1973
Gross private domestic investment	70.2	76.6	140.0	14.6	13.8	15.5
Plant and equipment expenditures	49.9	49.5	90.5	10.4	9.1	10.0
Plant	20.0	20.6	30.8	4.2	3.9	3.4
Equipment	29.9	28.9	59.7	6.2	5.2	6.6
Residential construction*	18.8	23.9	40.5	3.9	4.3	4.5
Net inventory change	1.5	3.2	9.0	0.3	0.6	1.0
Exports of goods and services	26.4	28.4	45.2	5.5	5.1	5.0
Imports of goods and services	20.1	25.2	40.7	4.2	4.5	4.5

*Private nonfarm housing starts numbered 990,000 in 1957; 1,430,000 in 1962; and are projected at 2,100,000 in 1973.

B. Average Annual Percentage Growth (In Terms of Plant, Equipment, and Man-Hours)

	1929 –49	1949 –57	1957 –62	1962 –73
Value of stock:				
Of private plant	-0.3	1.5	2.1	2.1
Of private equipment	2.3	6.0	0.0	4.4
Of private plant and equipment	0.5	3.5	1.1	3.2
Per worker	-0.4	2.3	0.5	1.6
Per $1 of output	-1.7	-0.8	-1.0	-0.8
Plant and equipment investment expenditures	1.4	3.6	-0.1	5.6
GNP per man-hour	2.1	3.1	2.5	3.3
GNP	2.6	3.8	2.9	4.6

capital stock to output ratio), increases in the capital to labor ratio, and shifts in the product mix of output. However, the projected level of annual investment is so high that it raises the question of whether business will undertake the investments called for by the potential growth in output. Here some actions taken in the past few years are likely to strengthen businessmen's readiness to invest. The 1962 investment tax credit and depreciation revisions, along with the corporate income tax reduction in the 1964 tax bill, have increased the business cash flow and the after-tax rate of return on investment. Corporate profits have increased in 1963, and corporate liquidity appears ample to finance the substantial capital expansion in the judgment projection, provided, of course, that a favorable outlook for sustained market expansion is maintained.

Residential Construction

Compared to 1.4 million housing starts and total housing expenditures of $24 billion in 1962, we have projected 2.1 million starts and expenditures of $40 billion for 1973. For both years housing outlays represent about 4.5 per cent of GNP.

The housing market of the coming decade appears likely to be governed by a combination of factors different from that of the 1950's. One of the key factors will be the reduced importance of household formation as a determinant of new construction. During the decade of the 1950's about 80 per cent of the housing starts were attributable to the creation of new households; the projected figure is 60 per cent. The factors likely to accompany this change include public programs for urban renewal and other projects which speed up obsolescence by providing direct and indirect stimulus to residential construction. Also, rising personal incomes, particularly at the lower end of the income scale, and the drive for better housing for Negroes will permit existing substandard and inadequate housing to be dropped from the housing supply. Apartment construction is likely to keep growing in relative importance, largely as a result of the increasing proportion of young and old households in the population. The booming trend in expenditures for additions and alterations, and for nonhousekeeping units, is likely to continue. Finally, the average expenditure per housing start is likely to increase as it has done in the past.

Government (Table II-11). Through its fiscal operations the government exerts a major impact on the level and type of output by private industries, the distribution of income, the level of employment, and the rate of economic growth. Economic growth not only requires government programs of expenditure to support growth but leads in turn to a rising tax base and makes the financing of some of these programs possible without preventing improvements in other areas and without necessarily requiring higher taxes.

Within the coming decade we find no drastic changes in the traditional division of responsibilities between the government and the private sectors of the economy. Nor do we assume a major change in the traditional division of responsibility among the different jurisdictional levels of government, although state and local spending for goods and services is likely to jump ahead of federal outlays, largely as a result of the relatively slow rise of federal defense purchases.

Substantial increases in government expenditures have been projected, amounting to $283 billion of all government—federal, state, and local—expenditures in 1973 as compared with $160 billion in 1962. In the perspective of a growing economy, these expenditures will represent 31 per cent of the GNP, a somewhat higher ratio than currently. (Government expenditures on goods and services only are projected at 24 per cent of GNP.)

The rising relative importance of government outlays in the past has been primarily the result of war and postwar defense requirements. In the decade ahead requirements for national security will continue to pre-empt a sizable part of government expenditures. Regardless of the level of defense needs, however, continued economic growth will require substantial government expenditures for such programs as urban renewal, water resource development, air pollution control, transport facilities, and research.

National security expenditures, including funds spent on research and space, are projected to reach $80 billion by 1973—a growth of $2.5 billion per year. In spite of this increase,

Table II-11

GOVERNMENT EXPENDITURES AND REVENUES--1957, 1962, AND 1973

	Billions of Dollars at 1962 Price Level			Percentage of GNP		
	1957	1962	1973	1957	1962	1973
Total government expenditures	129.4	160.6	282.8	26.0	29.0	31.2
Goods and services	98.4	117.4	217.9	19.5	21.2	24.1
Transfers, interest, subsidies	31.0	43.2	64.9	6.5	7.8	7.1
Total federal expenditures	88.0	109.5	179.1	18.0	19.8	19.8
Goods and services	55.5	62.4	101.2	11.2	11.3	11.2
Defense	49.6	53.4	80.5	10.0	9.6	8.9
Other	5.9	9.7	20.7	1.2	1.8	2.3
Transfers, interest, subsidies, grants	32.5	47.1	77.9	6.8	8.5	8.6
Total state and local expenditures	45.9	58.8	122.7	8.9	10.6	13.6
Goods and services	42.9	55.0	116.7	8.3	9.9	12.9
Education	15.6	22.0	47.1	3.0	4.0	5.2
Highways	8.5	9.9	14.5	1.6	1.8	1.6
Housing and community development	0.2	0.4	9.0	0.1	0.1	1.0
Public health and sanitation	5.4	6.6	16.5	1.0	1.2	1.8
Other programs	13.2	16.1	29.6	2.6	2.9	3.3
Transfers, interest, subsidies	3.0	3.8	6.0	0.6	0.7	0.7
Total government revenues	126.0	158.1	275.0	26.3	28.6	30.4
Personal tax and nontax	46.2	57.6	96.2	9.6	10.4	10.6
Corporate tax	22.6	25.0	40.0	4.7	4.5	4.4
Indirect business tax and nontax	41.5	51.6	92.3	8.6	9.3	10.2
Social insurance contribution	15.7	23.9	46.5	3.3	4.3	5.1

defense expenditures are expected to decline as a share of GNP and of government outlays. They will decline still more if the Administration's recent efforts to hold back increases in the defense budget prove successful in the long run.

Over half the projected federal expenditures are not directly associated with defense. These include outlays for Old Age and Survivors' Insurance, veterans, interest, grants-in-aid to states and localities, subsidies, and unemployment insurance. All but the last of these are projected to increase. Also projected to increase, somewhat in line with population growth, are outlays for such federal nondefense goods and services as water development, air transportation facilities, research and development, and hospital construction.

State and local expenditures are projected to grow at a faster pace than federal outlays. Expenditures on education are expected to continue as the most important component (one-third) of state and local expenditures. Highway expenditures are expected to increase at their past pace, and a substantial increase is projected for public health and sanitation, recreation, water resource development, and welfare programs. Housing and community development, however, for which the current level of expenditure is very low, is projected to grow at the fastest pace of all programs, approaching 8 per cent of total state and local expenditures by 1973.

The total of government revenues is projected to increase somewhat more slowly than government expenditures, the result being an excess of government expenditures over receipts (in the Income and Product Account) mostly accounted for by increased indebtedness of state and local governments. Implied in these projections is a cut in both personal and corporate effective tax rates. Personal and indirect business taxes are each expected to constitute about one-third of total revenues, whereas corporate taxes and social insurance contributions each constitute about one-sixth of the total--about the same shares as in recent years.

Employment

Although we have shown the projected trends in the labor supply, we have yet to indicate the prospective trends in labor demand. To judge whether a future balance between the supply of and requirements for labor is feasible, an analysis of both these trends is necessary. The prospective changes in manpower requirements are related to prospective developments in production levels, technological improvements, population growth, increases in capital, consumption behavior, and developments in the international environment. Some of these changes have been discussed in the preceding sections. However, for purposes of estimating employment needs it is appropriate to translate these changes into projections of net output by industry and of improvements in productivity by industry, as shown in Tables II-12 and II-13.

Both output and productivity are expected to increase more rapidly than in the past. The industries where output is projected to grow most rapidly, however, are durables manufacturing, finance and insurance, communications, public utilities, and services; the industries where relatively rapid productivity improvements can be expected are agriculture, mining, manufacturing, transportation, communication, and public utilities.

Given these changes, the demand for employees is projected to increase by 16.5 million from 1962 to 1973 in an economy where total output will increase by $350 billion in the same interval. Such an increase in employment, twice the growth of the last eleven years, would not only create jobs for most of the new labor force entrants but also reduce the unemployment rate to 4 per cent--the "interim objective" of the Council of Economic Advisers.

Employment by age, sex, and color (Table II-14). We can expect women and non-whites to account for slightly increasing shares of the total employed. We can also expect a major part of the employment increase to be found in the 25-54 age bracket, even though this group's share of total employment will decline and young people (below 24) are expected to increase their share.

Industry employment (Table II-15, II-16). The growth in total output does not mean that the demand for employment in each industry will grow at the same rate. First, there are long-run shifts in consumer purchasing habits which favor growth in trade, services, and construction employment. Second, the current level and composition of demand is such that unemployment

Table II-12

INDUSTRY NET OUTPUT AND GNP—1957, 1962, AND 1973
(By Originating Sector)

	Billions of Dollars at 1962 Price Level			Percentage of Total		
	1957	1962	1973	1957	1962	1973
GNP	480.1	553.9	904.9	100.0	100.0	100.0
Agriculture, forestry, fisheries	24.0	23.2	30.0	5.0	4.2	3.3
Mining	12.7	11.4	16.1	2.7	2.1	1.8
Construction	22.1	25.5	39.3	4.6	4.6	4.3
Manufacturing	139.4	156.7	262.4	29.0	28.3	29.0
Durables	78.7	93.9	163.7	16.4	17.0	18.1
Nondurables	60.6	62.8	98.7	12.6	11.3	10.9
Trade	85.5	96.8	145.3	17.8	17.5	16.1
Finance, insurance, real estate	56.7	67.3	112.6	11.8	12.1	12.4
Finance, insurance	16.3	19.8	35.7	3.4	3.6	3.9
Real estate	40.4	47.5	76.9	8.3	8.6	8.5
Transportation	24.0	23.3	31.6	5.0	4.2	3.5
Communication, public utilities	22.5	26.0	57.0	4.7	4.7	6.3
Communication	9.7	11.6	22.7	2.0	2.1	2.5
Public utilities	12.8	14.4	34.3	2.7	2.6	3.8
Services	30.2	39.1	64.1	6.3	7.1	7.1
Households and institutions	16.3	21.6	31.5	3.4	3.9	3.5
Government	44.2	60.4	109.0	9.2	10.9	12.0
General government	38.9	54.4	98.5	8.1	9.8	10.9
Government enterprises	5.3	6.0	10.5	1.1	1.1	1.2
Rest of world (net product originating from abroad)	2.4	3.2	6.0	0.5	0.6	0.7

Table II-13

TRENDS IN OUTPUT AND OUTPUT PER WORKER

	Average Annual Percentage Growth					
	Output			Output Per Worker		
	1948 -57	1957 -62	1962 -73	1948 -57	1957 -62	1962 -73
Total GNP	3.9	2.9	4.6	2.5	2.1	2.7
Agriculture, forestry, fisheries	0.8	1.5	2.4	3.6	5.2	3.9
Mining	2.5	0.0	3.2	4.7	-0.3	4.0
Construction	4.1	0.4	4.0	1.3	-0.4	1.2
Manufacturing	3.5	3.2	4.8	2.8	3.4	3.3
Durables	4.2	3.5	5.2	2.6	4.0	3.3
Nondurables	2.8	2.8	4.2	3.0	2.6	3.1
Trade	3.2	2.6	3.8	1.6	1.7	1.6
Finance, insurance	4.6	3.9	5.5	1.0	1.2	1.3
Transportation	2.2	0.9	2.8	2.7	3.1	2.9
Communication, public utilities	8.5	5.7	7.4	6.5	6.8	6.5
Communication	6.7	5.2	6.3	4.5	7.2	6.1
Public utilities	10.3	6.1	8.2	8.3	5.9	6.5
Services	2.2	4.3	4.6	-0.1	1.4	1.0

is particularly high in manufacturing, mining, construction, and trade. With the changes in the composition of demand brought about by increased employment, we would expect employment in these industries to improve quite rapidly. For example, we would expect that a rapid increase in investment and expenditures for consumer durables would increase the demand for employees in manufacturing at a rather rapid pace. Finally, there are differential changes in technology which affect productivity and therefore the manpower needs in each industry; the industries with rapid productivity improvements such as agriculture, mining, and manufacturing therefore tend toward a relative reduction in employment.

Table II-14

CIVILIAN EMPLOYED PERSONS BY AGE, SEX, COLOR—1957, 1962, AND 1973

	Number of Employed (In Millions)			Percentage of Civilian Employment		
	1957	1962	1973	1957	1962	1973
Total	65.0	67.8	84.2	100.0	100.0	100.0
14–19	4.8	5.4	7.9	7.4	8.0	9.4
20–24	5.6	6.5	10.9	8.6	9.6	12.9
25–54	42.9	43.6	50.2	66.0	64.3	59.6
55+	11.7	12.2	15.2	18.0	18.0	18.1
Males	44.0	44.8	54.5	67.7	66.0	64.7
14–19	2.8	3.1	4.6	4.3	4.6	5.5
20–24	3.3	3.9	6.9	5.1	5.7	8.1
25–54	29.5	29.5	33.3	45.4	43.5	39.5
55+	8.4	8.3	9.7	12.9	12.2	11.6
Females	21.0	23.0	29.7	32.3	33.9	35.3
14–19	2.0	2.3	3.3	3.1	3.4	3.9
20–24	2.3	2.6	4.0	3.5	3.8	4.8
25–54	13.4	14.1	16.9	20.6	20.8	20.1
55+	3.3	3.9	5.5	5.1	5.8	6.5
White	58.3	60.7	75.1	89.7	89.5	89.2
Males	39.9	40.7	49.2	61.4	60.0	58.3
Females	18.4	20.1	25.9	28.3	29.6	30.8
Non-white	6.7	7.1	9.1	10.3	10.5	10.8
Males	4.1	4.2	5.3	6.3	6.2	6.3
Females	2.6	2.8	3.8	4.0	4.1	4.5

The net effect of these competing forces is that the demand for employment in agriculture, mining, manufacturing, private households, and transportation-communication-utilities is projected to decline as a share of total employment demand; while in construction, finance-insurance, real estate, trade, services, and government, the relative demand is projected to increase. In absolute numbers, however, employment in each industry (except agriculture and mining) is expected to grow between 1962 and 1973.

Table II-15

CIVILIAN EMPLOYED PERSONS BY INDUSTRY—1957, 1962, AND 1973

	Number of Employed (In Millions)			Percentage of Total		
	1957	1962	1973	1957	1962	1973
Total civilian employment	65.0	67.8	84.2	100.0	100.0	100.0
Agriculture, forestry, fisheries	6.3	5.2	4.4	9.7	7.7	5.3
Private households	2.4	2.7	3.0	3.7	4.0	3.6
Mining	0.7	0.6	0.5	1.1	0.9	0.6
Contract construction	3.6	3.7	5.1	5.6	5.5	6.0
Manufacturing	17.6	17.4	20.5	26.9	25.6	24.3
Durables	9.9	9.7	11.8	15.3	14.3	14.1
Nondurables	7.6	7.7	8.6	11.7	11.3	10.3
Transportation, communication, utilities	4.5	4.1	4.3	6.9	6.0	5.0
Transportation	2.9	2.5	2.6	4.4	3.7	3.0
Communication	0.9	0.8	0.9	1.4	1.2	1.0
Public utilities	0.7	0.7	0.8	1.1	1.0	1.0
Trade	12.4	13.0	16.3	19.1	19.1	19.3
Finance, insurance, real estate	2.6	3.0	4.4	4.0	4.4	5.2
Finance and insurance	2.0	2.2	3.5	3.0	3.3	4.2
Real estate	0.6	0.7	0.9	1.0	1.1	1.1
Services	7.8	9.5	13.9	12.0	14.0	16.5
Government	7.2	8.7	11.8	11.1	12.9	14.0
Government enterprises	0.9	1.0	1.4	1.4	1.5	1.7

Over the next decade the employment increase in services and government is projected at about the same rate as between 1957 and 1962; for manufacturing, construction, and trade the projected increase is substantially above the rate of increase in the past five years. Manufacturing, trade, services, and government are each projected to increase employment by over 3 million persons during the next decade, and together they account for over 80 per cent of the total projected increase in demand for manpower.

In Table II-16 we present 1976 employment projections for detailed industry groupings. (The tabulation shows 106 industries or industry groupings at three different levels of disaggregation.) These projections for 1976 are based on generally the same assumptions as the 1973 projections. However, since they were completed before the 1973 projections, there will occasionally appear to be relatively minor differences in trend.

The detailed industry projections support the feasibility of further rapid output growth in mining, manufacturing, utilities, and other sectors of the economy. We expect a continuation of output expansion in each two-digit Standard Industrial Classification industry, although employment in metal mining, coal mining, tobacco, textiles, petroleum refining, and leather and lumber industries is expected to decline, primarily as a result of increases in labor productivity. When we look at the three-digit industry groupings we again expect to find output increases for each industry, although accompanied in a number of cases by decreasing employment.

Two particularly fast-growing industries in nondurables manufacturing are paper products and chemicals; relatively slow-growing nondurables are textiles and food products. Among the durables industries, electric machinery is projected to grow relatively rapidly, while primary metals and transportation equipment fall somewhat below the growth of all durables industries combined.

The national demand for durables is projected to increase at so rapid a pace as to compensate for the substantial improvements in productivity and to result in employment increases for almost all specific durables industries. However, as Tables II-17 and II-18 indicate, the same cannot be said for durables employment in Michigan.

The projected stability in Michigan durables employment is particularly critical for the state, which depends heavily not only on direct employment in the industry but also on the indirect employment generated in other industries to support the purchases

Table II-16

TOTAL EMPLOYED PERSONS BY INDUSTRIES—1947, 1957, AND 1976
(Industries at Various Levels of Aggregation)*

S.I.C.[†] Industry Group			Description	Number of Employees (In Thousands)		
Major Division	2-Digit	3-Digit		1947	1957	1976
			Total economy	59,402	67,808	92,400
01-9			Agriculture, forestry, fisheries	8,340	6,300	4,600
10-14			Mining	889	698	680
	10		Metal mining	96	94	80
		101	Iron ore mining	32	33	30
		102	Copper ore mining	26	27	23
		103-9	Misc. metal mining	38	34	27
	11,12		Coal mining	471	218	150
	13		Oil and gas mining	231	289	330
	14		Misc. mining	91	97	120
15-17			Construction	2,850	3,617	5,980
19-39			Manufacturing	16,408	17,610	21,720
	19		Ordnance	29	144	200
	20		Food and kindred products	1,899	1,851	1,800
		201	Meat products	290	341	400
		202	Dairy products	346	335	270
		203	Canning	269	246	250
		204	Grain mill products	144	134	120
		205	Bakery products	296	311	330
		208	Beverages	238	224	200
		206-7, 209	Misc. food products	316	260	230
	21		Tobacco	125	99	80
	22		Textiles	1,371	1,006	800
		225	Knitting mills	255	220	210
		221-24, 226-29	Misc. textiles	1,116	786	590
	23		Apparel	1,218	1,241	1,400
	24		Lumber	892	672	600
	25		Furniture	355	383	500
		251	Household furniture	257	274	345
		252-59	Misc. furniture	98	109	155
	26		Paper	491	586	800
		261-63	Pulp and paper	267	291	370
		264-65	Paper containers	224	295	430

*These data differ from the major division data shown in Table II-15, in that they include (1) the military in government and total employment, (2) government enterprise employment in the private sectors of transportation, communication, utilities, and services, and (3) private household employment with services.

† Standard Industrial Classification.

Table II-16 *(Continued)*

S.I.C.† Industry Group			Description	Number of Employees (In Thousands)		
Major Division	2-Digit	3-Digit		1947	1957	1976
	27		Printing and publishing	761	892	1,300
		271	Newspapers	263	323	500
		275	Commercial printing	247	290	400
		272–74 276–79	Misc. printing	251	279	400
	28		Chemicals	685	831	1,200
		281	Industrial chemicals	247	296	400
		282	Synthetics	118	156	230
		283	Drugs	91	103	150
		284	Soap	71	87	130
		285	Paints	53	66	100
		286–89	Misc. chemicals	105	123	190
	29		Petroleum	233	238	200
	30		Rubber and plastics	341	381	500
	31		Leather and leather products	434	383	360
	32		Stone, clay, and glass	567	610	700
		321–23	Glass products	152	157	180
		324	Cement products	40	45	50
		325–26	Clay products	142	134	100
		327	Concrete products	120	148	220
		328–29	Stone products	113	126	150
	33		Primary metals	1,350	1,389	1,400
		331	Steel mills	693	738	700
		332	Steel foundries	271	240	210
		333	Nonferrous primary metals	54	70	90
		334–36 392–99	Misc. primary metals	285	289	340
		391	Steel forgings	47	52	60
	34		Fabricated metals	1,042	1,195	1,400
		344	Structural fabricated metals	231	369	560
		341–43 345–49	Misc. fabricated metals	811	826	840
	35		Nonelectrical machinery	1,451	1,626	2,200
	36		Electrical machinery	1,092	1,378	2,750
		361	Distribution equipment	119	180	370
		362	Industrial apparatus	180	186	230
		363	Household appliances	194	165	200
		364	Lighting and mining equipment	110	134	210
		365	Radio and TV sets	72	108	190
		366	Communications equipment	222	315	820
		367	Electronics	84	178	600

†Standard Industrial Classification.

Table II-16 *(Continued)*

S.I.C.[†] Industry Group			Description	Number of Employees (In Thousands)		
Major Division	2-Digit	3-Digit		1947	1957	1976
		369	Misc. electrical mach.	111	112	130
	37		Transportation equipment	1,346	1,957	2,500
		371	Motor vehicles	810	788	1,000
		372	Aircraft	252	919	1,200
		373	Shipbuilding	168	157	180
		374-79	Misc. transport equipment	116	93	120
	38		Instruments	282	351	600
		381	Scientific instruments	29	73	190
		382	Measuring instruments	56	96	200
		383-87	Misc. instruments	197	182	210
	39		Misc. manufacturing	444	397	430
40-47			Transportation, communication, utilities	4,666	4,724	5,730
	40-47		Transportation	3,174	2,932	3,230
	40		Railroad transportation	1,557	1,121	600
	42		Motor freight transport	609	863	1,300
	45		Air transportation	95	163	400
	41,43 44,46		Misc. transport	913	785	930
	48		Communication	804	920	1,230
	49		Utilities	688	872	1,270
		491,part 493	Electric utilities	396	492	700
		492,part 493	Gas utilities	178	209	300
		494-99	Misc. utilities	114	171	270
50-59			Trade	10,672	12,416	18,520
	50		Wholesale trade	2,813	3,300	4,520
	52-59		Retail trade	7,859	9,116	14,000
60-67			Finance, insurance, real estate	1,860	2,593	4,300
70-89			Services	7,717	10,737	19,270
	72		Personal services	1,262	1,396	1,800
	73		Business services	429	811	3,000
	80		Health services	1,044	1,803	3,800
	81		Legal services	218	278	470
	82		Educational services	377	617	1,700
	86		Nonprofit organizations	584	845	1,700
	88		Private households	1,843	2,582	3,500
	70,71 74-9 83-5 87,89		Misc. services	1,960	2,405	3,300
91-93			Government	6,000	9,113	11,600
	91		Federal	3,006	4,497	4,200
			Civilian	1,416	1,697	1,900
			Military	1,590	2,800	2,300
	92,93		State and local	2,994	4,615	7,400

[†]Standard Industrial Classification.

made by the durables industry and its employees. The significance of durables production to the Michigan economy can be seen from the data showing that the proportion of durables in total Michigan employment is twice the national ratio, although this difference is narrowing.

Part of the comparatively poor prospects for durables employment in Michigan relates to this state's relatively low current activity in rapidly growing industries. Thus, for example, the electric machinery industry shows the best prospects for employment growth on a national basis. However, although Michigan's current proportion of total employment in durables is twice the national average, for the electric machinery industry the Michigan proportion to total employment is below the national average. Although our projections do not show a change in this relationship, opportunities appear present in Michigan for a greater increase in electric machinery employment than we have shown.

A more important aspect of Michigan's relatively poor prospects for durables employment is its inability to maintain its shares of national employment in transportation equipment, nonelectric machinery, and fabricated metals at their historically high rates. Thus employment in transportation equipment and fabricated metals is projected to decline in Michigan (while increasing nationally), and employment in nonelectric machinery, although projected to increase, does so at a slower rate than in the nation as a whole. There is some doubt that Michigan can compete effectively against the geographic redistribution trend in these industries.

Employment by occupation (Table II-19). With the development of new technologies, growth in output, and changes in the mix of industry, there are also changes in manpower requirements, as defined by occupational characteristics. Variations in the demand for employees in each occupational category can be traced to the changing importance of each occupation in a given industry as technology affects the manpower needs of that industry; such changes can also be related to shifts in the relative importance of each industry in total national employment as shifts in demand affect the composition of the national output.

As in the past, the most significant growth is projected to

Table II-17

EMPLOYMENT IN SELECTED DURABLES INDUSTRIES—1947, 1957, AND 1976
(United States and Michigan)

S.I.C.*	Description	Employment in Michigan (In Thousands)			Industry Employment as Percentage of Total Employment					
					United States			Michigan		
		1947	1957	1976	1947	1957	1976	1947	1957	1976
24	Lumber	20	13	10	1.5	1.0	.6	.8	.5	.3
25	Furniture	22	22	17	.6	.6	.5	.9	.8	.5
32	Stone, clay, glass	16	18	19	1.0	.9	.8	.6	.6	.5
33	Primary metals	82	92	77	2.3	2.1	1.5	3.3	3.2	2.1
19,34	Ordnance, fabricated metals	106	122	112	1.9	2.0	1.7	4.3	4.2	3.1
35	Nonelectric machinery	140	148	187	2.4	2.4	2.4	5.6	5.1	5.1
36	Electrical machinery	41	40	52	1.8	2.0	3.0	1.7	1.4	1.4
37	Transportation equipment	463	411	312	2.3	2.9	2.7	18.7	14.3	8.5
38	Instruments	6	9	24	.5	.5	.6	.2	.3	.7
39	Miscellaneous	14	14	11	.8	.6	.5	.6	.5	.3
	Total durables	910	889	821	15.1	15.0	14.3	36.7	30.9	22.4

*Standard Industrial Classification.

Table II-18

TOTAL EMPLOYMENT IN DURABLES INDUSTRIES
(United States and Michigan)

	1947	1957	1960	1976
Durables employment (millions):				
United States	8.9	10.1	9.6	13.3
Michigan	0.9	0.9	0.7	0.8
Percentage of total employment in durables:				
United States	15.1	15.0	14.5	14.3
Michigan	36.7	30.9	25.5	22.4

occur among white-collar workers, notably the professional-technical and clerical workers. We expect each sector, particularly manufacturing, services, and government, to show a rising share of its total employment engaged in professional-technical work; hence by 1973 we find 16 per cent of the national employment in this occupational category, as compared with the current 12 per cent. The projected increase of 5.5 million professional-technical workers suggests the strong possibility that manpower bottlenecks might develop in this area.

Growth in clerical personnel is expected, in spite of the continuing increase in the use of computer and highly automatic office equipment, because of the still larger increase in the need for such services by business. Clerical employment, particularly in trade, services, and the category comprising finance, insurance, and real estate, is expected to show a large increase. The projected increase in sales workers derives largely from the over-all growth in trade employment and from the increasing proportion of sales workers found in manufacturing establishments.

We project an increase of over 2 million in the demand for blue-collar workers between 1962 and 1973, in spite of the decline in their number since 1957. Although craftsmen-foremen are projected to have about the same share of manufacturing employment as they hold currently, an increase in their number is

Table II-19

CIVILIAN EMPLOYMENT BY OCCUPATION AND COLOR—1957, 1962, AND 1973

	Number of Employees (In Millions)			Percentage of Civilian Employment		
	1957	1962	1973	1957	1962	1973
Total	65.0	67.8	84.2	100.0	100.0	100.0
White-collar workers	26.5	29.8	42.3	40.6	44.1	50.2
Professional, technical	6.5	8.0	13.5	9.9	11.9	16.0
Managerial, proprietors	6.7	7.4	9.4	10.3	10.9	11.2
Clerical	9.2	10.1	13.6	14.1	14.9	16.1
Sales	4.1	4.3	5.8	6.3	6.4	6.9
Blue-collar workers	24.9	24.3	26.8	38.3	35.7	31.9
Craftsmen, foremen	8.7	8.7	10.4	13.3	12.8	12.4
Operatives	12.5	12.0	12.9	19.3	17.7	15.3
Laborers	3.7	3.6	3.5	5.7	5.2	4.2
Service workers	7.6	8.8	11.1	11.7	13.0	13.2
Private household	2.1	2.3	2.5	3.2	3.5	3.0
Other service	5.5	6.5	8.6	8.5	9.5	10.2
Farmers	6.1	4.9	4.0	9.3	7.2	4.7
White total	58.3	60.7	75.1	100.0	100.0	100.0
White-collar workers	25.5	28.6	40.1	43.9	47.2	53.5
Professional, technical	6.2	7.6	12.8	10.7	12.6	17.0
Managerial, proprietors	6.5	7.2	9.1	11.2	11.9	12.1
Clerical	8.8	9.6	12.6	15.1	15.8	16.9
Sales	4.0	4.2	5.6	6.9	6.9	7.5
Blue-collar workers	22.1	21.5	23.5	37.9	35.3	31.3
Craftsmen, foremen	8.3	8.3	9.7	14.3	13.6	12.9
Operatives	11.1	10.6	11.1	19.0	17.4	14.8
Laborers	2.7	2.6	2.7	4.6	4.3	3.6
Service workers	5.4	6.5	8.2	9.3	10.7	11.0
Private household	1.1	1.3	1.4	1.9	2.1	1.9
Other service	4.3	5.2	6.8	7.4	8.6	9.1
Farmers	5.2	4.1	3.3	8.9	6.8	4.1
Non-white total	6.7	7.1	9.1	100.0	100.0	100.0
White-collar workers	1.0	1.2	2.2	13.3	16.7	24.2
Professional, technical	0.3	0.4	0.7	4.0	5.3	7.7
Managerial, proprietors	0.2	0.2	0.3	2.4	2.6	3.3
Clerical	0.4	0.5	1.0	5.5	7.2	11.0
Sales	0.1	0.1	0.2	1.4	1.6	2.2
Blue-collar workers	2.8	2.8	3.3	41.1	39.5	36.3
Craftsmen, foremen	0.4	0.4	0.7	5.4	6.0	7.7
Operatives	1.4	1.4	1.8	20.5	19.9	19.8
Laborers	1.0	1.0	0.8	15.2	13.6	8.8
Service workers	2.1	2.3	2.9	32.1	32.8	31.9
Private household	1.0	1.0	1.1	14.8	14.7	12.1
Other service	1.1	1.3	1.8	17.3	18.1	19.8
Farmers	0.9	0.8	0.7	13.5	11.0	7.7

expected because of the over-all increase in manufacturing employment; the growing construction industry also provides a major reason for the craftsmen's increase despite the declining share of craftsmen in construction employment. The growth in construction and manufacturing is also expected to stabilize the decline in the demand for industrial laborers.

The need for operatives is expected to decline and thus reduce their share of employment in each industry (except construction). Despite this, the growth in over-all employment, particularly in trade, construction, and manufacturing, is expected to raise the future demand for operatives by almost a million persons.

Service worker employment during the decade ahead is projected to increase by about the same number as in the preceding decade, primarily because of its growth in the trade and service industries.

It should be emphasized that these changes in demand for manpower by occupation imply a minimum of education, training, and retraining required to develop the new talents and skills to fill the new job opportunities. For, since our estimates are for broad occupational groupings, we have ignored the extensive job mobility which occurs *within* each broad group. Also, we have ignored the fact that whenever deaths and retirements cause separation from the work force the skills of the separated workers must be replaced. If we estimate an inventory of available skills in 1962 (including both employed and unemployed) and subtract from this inventory the estimated number of separations from the work force between 1962 and 1973, we are left with about 50 million persons who are currently in the work force and will still be there in 1973. Since the manpower demand in 1973 is projected at 84 million, there are conservatively 30 million persons (ignoring re-entrants) for whom education, training, and retraining must be provided in the coming decade if these people are to have the talents and skills needed to fill the new job opportunities.

It is possible to estimate crudely how these 30 million would be categorized by broad occupational grouping. In spite of deaths and retirements we find no need to "train" more laborers and farmers than we have currently. However, we do need to train roughly 2 million persons in each of the following occupational groups: sales personnel, craftsmen-foremen, and operatives. In addition we need to train about 4 million service workers and the same number in the manager-proprietor groups. Finally, we require about 7 million more persons trained in each of the professional-technical and clerical groups.

The non-white distribution of employment is quite different from that of whites. White-collar employment among non-whites accounts for less than 20 per cent of total employment, as compared with almost 50 per cent for whites. Although the percentage of blue-collar workers is about the same for non-whites as for whites, the non-white workers in this category are heavily concentrated among industrial laborers. Similarly, the non-white service workers are concentrated in the low-wage service occupations, such as private household work.

The occupations in which the non-whites are concentrated are not only the low-income occupations; they are also those which tend to have the highest unemployment rates and unemployment duration. In these projections, non-whites continue to be concentrated in the group comprising operatives, laborers, and service workers, even though some improvement is expected, both absolutely and in relation to whites, in their employment as white-collar workers and craftsmen. Given the projected occupational distribution, we can expect the income and employment opportunities for non-whites to improve. Our projections imply little if any improvement, however, in the opportunities for non-whites compared to those for whites. It is to be hoped that the drive for equal rights will help in changing this trend. But since the mid-1950's, contrary to earlier postwar developments, the educational attainment of non-whites, particularly at the high school level, has not improved in relation to that for whites. Reductions in job discrimination must clearly be supported by education and training programs. The need for improvement in the relative economic position of the non-white group demands vigorous public policy.

Regional employment (Table II-20). The changing mix of industry growth will affect the regional distribution of economic activity, since some areas are favorably endowed with rapidly growing industries while others are not. In addition, business

Table II-20

REGIONAL DISTRIBUTION OF POPULATION AND CIVILIAN EMPLOYMENT—1957, 1962, AND 1973*

	Population						Civilian Employment					
	Number of Persons (In Millions)			Percentage of Total			Number of Persons (In Millions)			Percentage of Total		
	1957	1962	1973	1957	1962	1973	1957	1962	1973	1957	1962	1973
Continental United States	170.3	184.9	224.5	100.0	100.0	100.0	65.0	67.7	84.1	100.0	100.0	100.0
New England	9.9	10.6	13.9	5.8	5.7	5.7	4.2	4.3	5.1	6.5	6.4	6.2
Middle Atlantic	36.8	39.5	53.2	21.6	21.4	21.1	15.7	16.3	19.9	24.1	24.0	23.7
Great Lakes	34.7	37.0	47.1	20.4	20.0	19.6	14.2	14.5	17.7	21.8	21.4	21.0
Southeast	37.2	40.1	42.2	21.8	21.7	21.3	12.2	12.7	15.8	18.8	18.8	18.8
Plains	15.1	15.7	18.2	8.9	8.5	8.1	5.7	5.8	6.8	8.8	8.6	8.1
Southwest	13.4	15.1	16.8	7.9	8.2	8.6	4.5	4.8	6.3	6.9	7.1	7.5
Mountains	4.2	4.7	4.9	2.5	2.5	2.4	1.4	1.5	1.9	2.2	2.2	2.2
Far West	19.0	22.2	28.1	11.2	12.0	13.2	7.1	7.8	10.6	10.9	11.5	12.5

*The regional grouping of states conforms to that developed by the U.S. Department of Commerce.

will relocate its new capacity to areas where it can reduce costs and get closer to population centers which have become more important as people have migrated to them.

We project population to increase in each of the multi-state regions shown in Table II-20. The increases during the 1962-73 interval will be slightly above the population increases of the preceding decade. We also expect a slow redistribution of the population toward the Southwest and Far Western states and away from the Middle Atlantic, Great Lakes, Plains, and Southeastern states, as people seek out their best job opportunities and the amenities of life. Accompanying the interregional migration we can expect a continuation of the move towards urban areas, with 80 per cent of the national population being urbanized by the mid-1970's.

The redistribution of employment is expected to be the same as that for population, namely, towards the Far West and Southwest. The dominant characteristic of industry employment trends in this century has been the decline in agriculture and mining employment and the growth in manufacturing and noncommodity activity, such as services and government. Increasing noncommodity employment opportunities have provided the major source of new jobs in all regions and states. During the projected interval, total civilian employment is expected to increase not only in each multi-state region, but in each state as well. The projected growth in noncommodity employment is expected to offset the absolute decline in resource employment and the relative decline in manufacturing employment in most states.

Although regions and states are tending to become more similar in the industrial composition of their employment, significant interstate differences are likely to remain. In the New England, Middle Atlantic, and Great Lakes states, manufacturing employment is expected to continue to be relatively important; in the Southeast, Plains, Southwest, and Mountain states the natural resources sector (agriculture and mining) is likely to be relatively important, as it is currently; in the Middle Atlantic, Southwest, Mountain, and Far West states, the noncommodity sector is expected to be relatively important, just as it is currently.

Accompanying the employment growth and productivity advances, we expect increases in the personal income and per capita income of each state. Paralleling the population growth, the largest increase in the states' shares of the nation's personal income is expected to be in the Far West and Southwestern regions. However, because of varying state population growths, differing trends toward urbanization and industrialization, shifts in the industrial and occupational mix of employment, and differential changes in wage rates, the per capita income expectations of the states tell a different story from that of state trends in total personal income. The states which currently have relatively low per capita income levels (tending to be those in the Southeast, Plains, and Southwest) are those states where per capita income is expected to increase most rapidly. Both the richer and poorer states are expected to show increases in per capita income. The increase will be somewhat faster in the poorer states, but we do not expect the differential to be overcome; the New England, Middle Atlantic, Great Lakes, and Far West states will continue to have per capita income levels substantially above those of the other states. Indeed, measured in number of dollars, the differences among state per capita incomes are projected to be larger than the current differences.

III

THE SUPPLY OF CAPITAL IN THE UNITED STATES

James J. O'Leary

The purpose of this chapter is to shed some light on the prospects for long-term capital financing in the next decade. To present these prospects in perspective, the first part reviews the behavior of the market for loanable funds during the period 1948-63. The general economic characteristics of the period are outlined, trends in the sources and uses of capital funds are analyzed, and the behavior of long-term interest rates is traced. The experience of the past will provide a valuable basis for looking ahead. The second part discusses the prospects for the national economy as a whole in the next decade. The final part considers the outlook for long-term capital financing in the decade ahead.

Behavior of the Market for Loanable Funds, 1948–63

General economic characteristics of the period

1948–59. In this review of the general economic characteristics of the period 1948-63, it is useful to distinguish between the period 1948-59 and the years since 1959. We had, of course, during 1948-59 an outstanding period of expansion in the American economy. In current dollar terms, the gross national product rose from $234.3 billion in 1947 to $482.7 billion in 1959, or by about 106 per cent. Corrected for changes in the price level (that is, in terms of 1962 prices), GNP rose in real terms from $327.9 billion in 1947 to $502.6 billion in 1959, or about 53 per cent.

What forces powered the expansion of 1948-59? Through much of the period the huge pent-up demands of the wartime years, and in some degree of the Great Depression, provided a tremendously favorable climate for expansion. These accumulated demands were supported by a large supply of liquid savings, built up by the American people during the war as well as by a great expansion of consumer and home mortgage credit. Nowhere was the pent-up demand more evident than in housing. With the burst of new family formations after the war—reaching an annual average of 1,525,000 in 1947-50—and with the availability of easier and easier home mortgage financing through VA and FHA, we had an unparalleled level of home construction. Under the circumstances, it was inevitable that there would be a corresponding burst of state and local government spending for schools, roads, and public improvements of all types. Similarly, the large current demand for all kinds of goods, plus the huge backlog of demands, encouraged a high level of capital spending by business and industry. Overexpansion of plant and equipment seemed hardly a problem in a national economy so characterized by strong current and accumulated demand. Like housing, the durable consumer goods—automobiles, washing machines, refrigerators, and all the rest—received a great stimulus from the backlog of demands. In addition to the huge deferred demands and easy credit, the persistence of heavy deficit financing by the federal government in many of these years facilitated the rise of general economic activity.

But along with the expansion of national output, the period 1948-59 was also characterized by an upward push of the general price level. From 1947 to 1959 the Consumer Price Index rose from 77.8 to 101.5 (1957-59=100), or by more than 30 per cent. More than two-thirds of the price rise occurred in three of the years—1948, 1951, (Korean War), and 1957. In other years, however, the price level moved up gradually, giving rise to the focus on the "cost-price push" pattern of inflation. Regardless of the fact that in many of the years during 1948-59 there was little actual general price rise, in the late 1950's the general public became extremely concerned about inflation. A public expectation of inflation was rampant. Nowhere was this more evident than in the great "bull" market in stocks from 1949 through 1959, in fact through late 1961. Capital gains, in turn, provided a most favorable climate for general economic expansion.

One of the very significant developments of 1948-59 was the changing position of the United States in regard to international balance of payments. In the first several years after the war the prostrate economies of western Europe and Japan needed large inflows of goods and services from the United States for reconstruction. In those days the problem of such countries was the "dollar problem"—how to acquire enough dollars to pay for needed imports from the United States. However, as a result of the Marshall Plan and other U. S. loans and grants, by the middle of the 1950's the reconstruction of western Europe and Japan was largely accomplished, and the economies in these areas had the advantages of modern, efficient plants and equipment. Moreover, labor costs in these countries were far below those in the United States, where the cost-price push was taking its toll. The result was that increasing foreign competition cut down our ability to generate an export surplus, and we began to find that our continuing foreign loans and grants, as well as military expenditures abroad, were producing a deficit in our international balance of payments. In 1958 the deficit suddenly jumped to $3.5 billion, and in 1959 it increased to $3.7 billion. In a country which had never had to worry about the balance of payments, we suddenly became aware that steps must be taken to correct the deficit if we were to preserve our gold reserves. Great pressure was placed on the government to halt the rise in the price level which handicapped our ability to sell goods and services abroad.

1960–63. In many ways the period 1960-63 has been a rather different one so far as the national economy is concerned. After a modest recession in 1960, the national economy has expanded steadily since early 1961. GNP has risen from a seasonally adjusted annual rate of about $500 billion in the first quarter of 1961 to $600 billion in the fourth quarter of 1963, or 20 per cent. A very important force behind this rise has been government policy measures—easy money and deficit financing. In spite of the favorable record of expansion, however, the Administration has been frustrated in its objectives of encouraging full employment of both our labor force and our productive capacity and bringing about an acceleration in the rate of economic growth. Although total civilian employment has risen markedly, the rate of unemployment still remains high—about 5.5 per cent in December, 1963, compared with 6.9 per cent in February, 1961.

Why has the expansion failed to be stronger in the face of the efforts the Administration has exerted? Several possible reasons may be advanced. First, by the end of the 1950's the largest part of the accumulated demand for consumer goods and housing had been satisfied. The extra push which this backlog had imparted to economic expansion had become exhausted. The seemingly insatiable demand for housing gave way to increasing concern about vacant housing units and unsold houses. Similarly, the sellers' market for automobiles and other consumer goods yielded to more selective buying by consumers. One very important effect was decreased willingness on the part of the manufacturing industry to expand productive capacity.

Secondly, in the early 1960's the rate of family formation has been comparatively low--about 1,130,000 units as compared with 1,525,000 in the years 1947-50. Thirdly, there is evidence that as costs pushed up there has been a "squeeze" on the rate of corporate profits, which has served to dampen enthusiasm for capital expenditures by business and industry. This squeeze has been alleviated by the improvement in profit margins as the economy has expanded, but it is still a factor in many industries. Contributing to the profits squeeze has been a burdensome federal corporate tax system. Finally, concern about the large deficit in our international balance of payments has undoubtedly exerted some restraint upon federal monetary and fiscal policies directed toward expansion.

Developments with regard to the balance of payments have been of particular interest and importance since 1959. After the deficits of $3.5 billion in 1958 and $3.7 billion in 1959, the deficit rose to a peak of $3.9 billion in 1960. During the first two years of the Kennedy administration the problem of a large deficit appeared to be approaching a solution, with the deficit declining to $2.4 billion in 1961 and $2.2 billion in 1962. This improvement was more apparent than real, however, since the lower figures were attributable in large part to special measures such as advance repayment of debt by foreign countries. In any event, in the first half of 1963 the payments deficit increased to the very high annual rate of $4.2 billion. This increase was due primarily to a sharp rise in both short- and long-term net capital outflows, which were running at an annual rate of $5 billion in the second quarter. However, the capital outflow has been reduced, partly by a rise in the Federal Reserve rediscount rate in July, 1963—and a consequent rise in other short-term interest rates—and partly by the Administration's introducing the Interest Equalization Tax Bill in July. Although not yet enacted, this bill has checked the outflow of long-term capital. The deficit for the year 1963 as a whole will probably amount to about $2.6 billion. During the past six years the United States has lost about $7 billion of gold reserves, and our monetary gold stock has been reduced to $15.9 billion. Moreover, in addition to withdrawing gold, foreigners (excluding international institutions) have built up their holdings of liquid assets in the country to about $21.5 billion. Of our gold reserves, about $12.3 billion is needed under statute as reserves against Federal Reserve notes and deposit liabilities, so that our "free gold reserves" have shrunk to $3.6 billion, as compared with foreign liquid asset holdings of $21.5 billion.

Why are these developments so important? The primary reason is that they have contributed to a situation where it is imperative to keep the general price level in the United States stable to prevent any further decline in the salability of American goods abroad. The United States cannot push expansionary fiscal and monetary policies at home without facing the risk of a new round of inflation which would very likely provoke a pronounced outflow of gold and a crisis in our international position.

Sources and uses of loanable funds, 1948–63

As a further aid to making an intelligent appraisal of the prospects for long-term capital financing in the decade ahead, it will be helpful to study Table III-1, which presents a picture of sources and uses of loanable funds since 1948.

Before trends in the sources and uses of loanable funds are analyzed, some general comment on the nature of the data may be useful. Under uses of funds for 1962 the figure of $5.0 billion for corporate bonds is shown. This is the amount by which total outstanding corporate bonds increased in 1962. All other figures under "uses" represent the *net increase* in outstanding debt or equity instruments. Similarly, in the upper portion of the table, in 1962 the life insurance company figure is $5.7 billion. This figure represents the *net increase* in available funds for investment by life insurance companies. Similarly, the other figures for sources of funds indicate the net increase in available funds. One other point about the table is essential. In 1959, for example, the total uses of funds amounted to $57.3 billion. These were the uses that were satisfied, as is indicated by the fact that total sources also amounted to $57.3 billion. The table does not show those potential uses of funds which were not satisfied because available sources were not great enough. Certainly in 1959, a year of heavy demand for loanable funds, there were many demands which went unsatisfied.

Uses of funds. If we turn first to trends in the uses of loanable funds, we note that the figures for net increase in corporate bonds exhibit two main characteristics. First, the data show some cyclical fluctuation—in 1957 and 1958, for example, as a result of pronounced corporate expansion, there were peaks in the increase in outstandings. More importantly, however, when the entire period is viewed, there appears to be no evidence of a trend in the annual figures. Rather, they show a high degree of stability in the range of $4-$5.5 billion. This may seem surprising at first glance in view of the great growth in corporate business in the postwar period, but corporations have increasingly resorted to financing themselves internally through retained earnings and the use of depreciation allowances.

Generally speaking, there has also been quite a bit of stability in the net increase in outstanding corporate stocks. The generally prevailing range has been from $2.0 to $2.5 billion. In looking at these figures, one is impressed by the comparatively modest extent to which corporations finance themselves by means of equity issues. The reasons are probably two: (1) the desire to avoid dilution of ownership and control of a corporation; and (2) the natural preference of corporations for debt financing because interest is a deductible item for income tax purposes. In any event large amounts of equity capital are provided through retained earnings. Under conditions in which the net additions to supply have been comparatively small, and in which investors' interest in common stocks has been rising, it is easy to understand the upward pressures in the common stock market.

In contrast with the corporate financing picture, the net increase in state and local government securities outstanding has shown an upward trend. Here again the figures have been subject to some cyclical fluctuation. Generally speaking, in periods of tight money the increase in outstandings has been reduced, but for the period as a whole the trend in the increase in outstandings each year has been upward. This has reflected, of course, the pronounced rise in state and local government spending since the war to meet the need for highways, schools, bridges, sewerage systems, and many other public improvements.

The figures in the period for the net increase or decrease (-) each year in the U. S. government debt are, of course, a reflection of the position of the federal budget. As is readily apparent, in some of the years, e.g., 1952-53 and 1958-59, the net increase in federal debt was an especially important, and perhaps decisive, factor in placing pressures on the money and capital markets. The figures reflect also the fact that federal deficits have been used to combat cyclical downturns in the economy.

The next item in Table III-1 shows the net increase in federal agency debt. This includes the increase in outstanding debt of such agencies as the Federal National Mortgage Association (FNMA), the Federal Land Banks, and the Federal Home Loan Banks. Here again there is evidence of a cyclical pattern in that such agencies normally step up their own borrowing in periods of recession. Inspection makes it apparent, however,

Ta

SOURCES AND USES OF FUNDS
(In Billi

	1948	1949	1950	1951	195
Sources of funds:					
Life insurance companies	3.4	3.6	3.7	3.7	4.
Savings and loan associations	1.2	1.3	2.1	2.0	3.
Mutual savings banks	1.0	1.0	1.0	0.8	1.
Corporate pension funds	0.7	0.7	0.9	1.3	1.
Commercial banks	- 1.7	6.1	6.6	6.0	9.
Federal Reserve Banks	0.8	- 4.4	1.9	3.0	0.
State and local funds	1.0	1.0	1.5	1.5	2.
U.S. investment accounts	3.0	2.0	- 0.1	3.1	3.
Federal loan agencies	0.1	0.4	0.4	0.9	0.
Corporations	3.6	3.0	8.1	3.0	2.
Fire and casualty companies	1.0	1.1	0.8	0.7	1.
Foreigners	- 0.1	0.1	1.5	...†	1.
Individuals and others	4.3	3.1	1.8	1.7	4.
Total sources ‡	18.1	18.9	30.0	27.8	36.
Uses of funds:					
Corporate bonds	4.7	3.3	2.0	3.6	4.
Corporate stocks	1.1	1.3	1.5	2.3	2.
State and local government issues	2.2	2.3	3.1	2.4	3.
U. S. government issues	- 4.1	4.3	- 0.4	2.7	8.
Federal agency issues	0.3	- 0.1	0.4	0.2	..
Mortgages: 1-4 family	5.1	4.3	7.6	6.5	6.
Other	2.2	2.1	2.6	2.9	2.
Business credit	2.3	- 2.5	8.1	5.2	2.
Consumer credit	2.8	2.9	4.1	1.2	4.
All other credit	1.7	1.0	1.1	0.7	1.
Total uses ‡	18.1	18.9	30.0	27.8	36.

* Estimated.
† $50 million or less.
‡ Because of rounding, components may not add to totals shown.

I-1

HE U.S. CAPITAL MARKET, 1948–63
f Dollars)

1953	1954	1955	1956	1957	1958	1959	1960	1961	1962	1963 *
4.7	5.0	5.3	5.0	4.7	4.9	4.9	5.1	5.2	5.7	5.9
3.7	4.2	5.7	4.9	4.9	6.3	8.3	7.1	9.3	10.2	13.1
1.8	2.0	2.1	2.0	1.7	2.4	1.5	1.5	2.2	3.3	3.5
1.7	1.9	1.9	2.1	2.6	2.6	3.0	3.2	3.2	3.3	3.6
4.1	10.2	4.8	4.4	5.1	15.2	4.2	9.2	16.1	18.9	18.6
1.2	- 1.0	- 0.1	0.1	- 0.7	2.1	0.3	0.7	1.5	1.9	2.8
2.5	2.9	2.1	2.3	2.1	1.8	3.3	2.7	2.7	3.1	3.0
2.4	1.3	2.1	2.3	1.2	- 0.9	- 0.7	1.4	- 0.6	1.0	2.5
0.2	- 0.1	0.6	0.9	1.6	0.6	2.5	1.5	1.0	0.9	- 0.6
2.4	0.5	11.7	- 1.2	1.8	3.7	10.9	1.2	3.7	6.4	7.6
1.3	1.1	0.9	0.5	0.7	0.8	1.5	1.1	1.3	1.2	1.2
0.6	0.6	1.3	0.5	...†	...†	4.5	1.0	1.1	2.1	1.2
5.1	1.5	7.7	8.2	7.6	2.6	12.9	2.8	3.3	4.9	5.5
31.9	30.0	46.1	32.1	33.4	42.2	57.3	38.6	49.8	63.0	68.2
4.8	3.8	4.2	4.7	7.1	5.9	4.1	5.0	5.1	5.0	5.6
1.9	1.8	1.9	2.5	2.7	2.1	2.4	1.6	2.6	0.5	- 0.3
3.5	4.2	3.5	3.3	4.8	5.7	5.0	4.0	5.3	5.7	6.4
7.8	3.5	2.0	- 4.1	- 1.7	8.0	7.9	- 0.6	6.1	7.5	6.1
...†	...†	1.5	0.6	2.1	- 0.5	2.2	0.1	0.7	1.6	1.5
7.6	9.6	12.6	10.8	8.6	10.1	13.2	10.4	11.8	13.4	15.9
2.3	2.8	3.6	3.8	3.5	5.2	5.9	5.8	7.7	11.9	13.8
- 1.8	1.4	9.5	7.4	3.1	2.9	8.4	5.5	5.6	8.3	10.2
3.9	1.1	6.4	3.5	2.6	0.2	6.2	4.5	1.6	5.5	6.6
1.9	1.9	0.9	- 0.4	0.5	2.7	2.1	2.2	3.3	3.6	2.4
31.9	30.0	46.1	32.1	33.4	42.2	57.3	38.6	49.8	63.0	68.2

that the level of net increase in this debt has tended to move upward.

We now come to a use of loanable funds which has shown a dramatic rise—mortgages on 1-4 family properties. Here again the figures reflect cyclical fluctuations. For example, the net increase in 1-4 family mortgage debt rose in 1953-55 and then declined in 1956-57. With an easy credit policy by the Federal Reserve in 1953-54, the institutional funds poured into 1-4 family mortgages in the years 1953-55, particularly into government-insured and guaranteed mortgages, because of inflexible regulated rates in this area. With a more restrictive credit policy in 1955-57, the availability of home mortgage financing declined, particularly for FHA and VA mortgages, again because interest rates on these mortgages are government regulated. In spite of cyclical fluctuations, the strongly rising trend is clear, from a net increase of $5.1 billion in outstandings in 1948 to $15.9 billion in 1963. By 1963 the net increase in 1-4 family debt was three times the net increase in corporate debt.

The trend in net increase in "other mortgages" is equally dramatic. These have risen from a $2 billion level in 1948 to $13.8 billion in 1963. Included are mortgage loans on farms, apartment buildings, hotels, motels, shopping centers, bowling alleys, warehouses, department stores, office buildings, and a host of other commercial and industrial facilities. Here again, the recent figures have far outstripped corporate financing.

The next item, business credit, is a form of shorter-term credit, but it is so related to other forms of credit that it needs to be recorded if we are to understand the total financial picture. Business credit takes two main forms: (1) commercial bank credit to business, and (2) trade credit, i.e., the credit extended by one business concern to another. As can be seen in the table, the figures are highly cyclical and are closely related to business inventory cycles.

The net increase in consumer credit is also, as would be expected, cyclical in its behavior. It is related to cyclical fluctuations in consumer expenditures for automobiles and durable consumer goods. The general level of net increase has tended to rise as the economy has grown.

Finally, "all other credit" includes such heterogeneous uses of credit as loans to finance purchases of securities, policy loans of life insurance companies, and so forth.

Adding all of the uses together, it is not surprising to see that the totals have fluctuated more or less in accord with the general cyclical fluctuations in business. But it is also clear that the general level of the aggregate uses has risen markedly from about $18 billion in 1948 to $68.2 billion in 1963. The explanation is clear. The rising figures are in part the product of the real growth of the American economy. They are also the product of the rising general price level in the period through 1959. As the prices of capital goods have risen, it has been inevitable that total uses of loanable funds have also increased.

Sources of funds. If we turn now to the upper portion of the table, what were the trends in various sources of funds to meet the rising volume of uses? The first item shows the gradual rise in net available funds coming into the capital markets from life insurance companies—from $3.4 billion in 1948 to $5.9 billion in 1963. Although the funds available from life companies are very large, it will be noted that the annual amount showed little growth in the years 1954-61. The explanation is not simple, but it is clear that the concern about inflation which infected the American public in this period favored equity types of investment and tended to militate against saving in fixed-dollar terms through life insurance. Since 1961, with the lessening of the public's fear of inflation, life insurance saving appears to be on the rise again. This is important from the viewpoint of availability of corporate financing. During the period 1948-62 the life insurance companies increased their holdings of corporate bonds by $34 billion, or 50 per cent of the aggregate increase of $68 billion in corporate debt in the period.

As is apparent from the table, there has been a phenomenal growth in the net available investment funds of savings and loan associations—from $1.2 billion in 1948 to $13.1 billion in 1963. The big questions today are whether the future growth of home mortgage credit will be sufficient to satisfy the appetite of the savings and loan industry, and whether these institutions will succeed in obtaining broader investment powers, e.g., to buy municipal bonds, make consumer loans, and acquire a larger proportion of nonresidential mortgage loans. Strong efforts are already being made to accomplish these objectives. The picture is one of structural imbalance in our capital markets: institutions designed for local home mortgage lending are garnering a proportion of the nation's savings which threatens to exceed the needs for home mortgage credit.

The mutual savings banks showed only a moderate growth prior to the past two years. Net available funds rose markedly in 1962 and 1963, the result of an expanding economy as well as a shifting of the public's savings away from equities into institutions paying an attractive return on deposits. Here again, as the savings banks have seen their savings volume rise, there has been a need for wider investment powers, a fact which explains the mutual savings banks' drive for federal charters with broader investment authority.

The table also shows the steady and marked growth, from $0.7 billion in 1948 to $3.6 billion in 1963, in net available funds from corporate pension funds. These are, of course, uninsured pension funds administered by banks and corporate trustees. Barring renewed inflation it may be expected that a rising proportion of the pension funds business will be in insured plans, particularly since newly enacted "separate accounts" legislation has given life companies unrestricted power to invest in equities. The expansion of corporate pension funds has been favorable for corporate financing because most of the pension fund money has gone into this area.

The next item in sources of funds is the commercial banks. As is apparent, the availability of funds from the commercial banks has shown a cyclical pattern because it is affected by the willingness of the Federal Reserve authorities to supply reserves to the banking system. The great increase in 1958, for example, was the product of monetary easing, and the sharp decline in 1959 was the result of monetary restriction. The figures for 1961-63 deserve special attention. Net available funds from the banks increased by $16.1 billion in 1961, by $18.9 billion in 1962, and by $18.6 billion in 1963, and much of this tremendous expansion came into the long-term capital market. During the easy credit policy that the authorities have followed since early 1960, great amounts of reserves have been made available to the banks. As a result the banks have expanded their total loans and investments by $60 billion since early 1960. Normally, with a rise in loans and investments of this magnitude there would have been a correspondingly sharp rise in the "money supply"—cash and demand deposits. Actually, there has been only a comparatively modest increase in the money supply so defined. Since early 1960, particularly since early 1962, when the commercial banks were permitted to pay 4 per cent on time and savings deposits, a great shifting of deposits from the demand to the time category has been occurring. Because the banks have had to pay 4 per cent on these funds, there has been a natural pressure to acquire higher-yielding, long-term investments—mortgages, term loans, municipal bonds, etc. Thus, with the combined effect of easy credit policy and the 4 per cent rate on time deposits (necessary to compete with the savings and loan and mutual savings banks), the commercial banks have become a major factor in the bond and mortgage markets.

The item Federal Reserve Banks in the table simply represents the net purchases of government securities each year by the authorities in their open market purchases. The amounts vary cyclically, therefore, depending upon whether the authorities desired to ease credit by purchasing government securities or to tighten it by selling government securities.

Another fast-growing source of funds has been state and local funds, that is, pension funds for teachers, policemen and other state and municipal employees, and so forth. As is evident, the net amounts available from these funds have increased steadily from $1.0 billion in 1948 to $3.0 billion in 1963. In the early years of this period most of the money went into municipal bonds and U. S. government bonds, but in recent years the state and local funds have gone aggressively into corporate bonds and to a modest extent into mortgages.

"U. S. investment accounts" in the table are such sources of funds as the Old Age and Survivors' Disability and Insurance Fund and the Railroad Retirement Fund. These funds are largely invested in U. S. government bonds.

Federal loan agencies are such agencies as the Federal Land Banks and the Federal National Mortgage Association (FNMA). The figures for this item show a distinct cyclical pattern. The reason is that FNMA buys home mortgages in periods of general credit tightness and sells them when money is easy.

As is apparent, corporations provide a very important source of loanable funds. The corporations provide trade credit to other corporations and acquire short-term government securities, certificates of deposit, and other investments. Loanable funds available from corporations show cyclical fluctuations. For example, these funds reached peaks in 1950, 1955, 1959, 1962, and 1963. It is not surprising that in each of these years inventory expansion was taking place and so trade credit increased.

The funds available from fire and casualty companies have been comparatively small. They have tended to go into securities with a high degree of marketability—common and preferred stocks, municipal bonds, and so forth. The figures for "foreigners" represent the net purchase of securities by foreigners in the U. S. capital market. In recent years, as the deficit in the U. S. international balance of payments has reached large amounts, foreigners have added significantly to their holdings of short- and longer-term securities in the United States.

Finally, "individuals and others" have been an important source of loanable funds. These figures do not merely represent the increase in holdings of securities and mortgages by individuals. This item is a statistical "residual." It includes funds made available by unincorporated business concerns, investment companies, finance companies, and other investors.

One final word about sources of loanable funds: As the national economy has expanded, total sources of funds have risen from $18 billion in 1948 to $68.2 billion in 1963. In other words, as total uses for funds have grown, total sources have also grown. As we indicated earlier, in this table sources and uses of funds must be equal because the table shows those uses which were satisfied.

General Economic Prospects in the Decade Ahead

Against this background of the behavior of the national economy and the market for loanable funds in the United States during the period 1948-63, what can be said about the general economic prospects in the decade ahead, and then the prospects for long-term capital financing? The question of what lies ahead for financial markets cannot be answered unless we first reach some conclusions about prospects for the national economy as a whole. If the next decade should bring an acceleration in the economic growth of the country under full employment conditions, as set forth in the Judgment Model in Chapter II, Table II-1, it is clear that our economy would generate high and rising demands for capital funds and that monetary policy would have to lean much of the time toward restraint of credit in the interest of preserving reasonable general price stability. The big question is, therefore, whether full employment and an accelerated rate of sustained economic growth can be achieved in the years ahead.

One thing is certain. Whether a Democratic or Republican administration is in office, the prime economic objectives of the government will be full employment and faster growth as far as these are consistent with the maintenance of general price stability. These objectives have certainly been the focus of policies of the present Administration. The efforts of the Administration to bring about the tax reduction recently enacted by Congress are clear evidence of the aim to push the economy to full employment and faster growth.

Just as has been true in the past several years, the position of the U. S. balance of payments with the rest of the world will be extremely important in the picture. Some progress has been made toward solving our balance of payments problem; but it has been slow, and the problem is likely to remain with us in the foreseeable future. It is quite unlikely that any dollar crisis will arise, because the free world depends heavily on the dollar as the cornerstone of its currency system. This dependence explains the extraordinary degree of co-operation which has been developed among countries of the western world to control speculation in gold and foreign currencies and to conserve the gold position of deficit countries such as the United States. However, it is vital that we avoid a rise in the general price level at home, because our hope for eliminating the payments deficit depends on increasing our export surplus and because this can be done only if our products are available at competitive prices. If we can hold the line on the U. S. price level, the rise in costs and prices in many foreign countries which have surpluses in their balance of payments will help improve the competitive position of our products and services. Thus, our very difficult problem is to encourage a stronger expansion of our economy, full employment, and faster economic growth, and to do these things without provoking a new round of inflation at home and hence a deterioration in our international balance of payments position.

The fiscal policy measures which are now emerging offer considerable promise of generating sustained expansion and full employment. The tax cut will bring about a total reduction in individual income taxation, phased over two years, of an estimated $8.8 billion. The cut will also mean a reduction of about $2.3 billion in corporate income taxes, in addition to the reduction of about $2.2 billion that occurred in 1962 as a result of the investment credit and the liberalized depreciation guidelines. The tax program is designed to release more of the energies of the private sectors of the economy by stimulating consumer and investment spending. One can question whether the tax cut will give us the proper balance between stimulating mass consumption and investment spending on the one hand and personal incentives on the other. But the important thing is that it seeks to release the energies of the private economy. As Congressman Mills pledged in the debate in the House on the bill, the government cannot travel both roads—tax reduction and rising federal spending. If federal spending is controlled, the tax reduction route gives great promise of encouraging a sustained secular expansion.

Most economists now believe that the economic expansion which began in February, 1961, will continue through 1964. With the national economy expanding as the result of a strong use of fiscal policy, it seems quite likely that monetary policy will be more freely used to protect against the resurgence of inflationary forces at home and against any threat to the dollar abroad. This is all the more likely because the Federal Reserve authorities have pursued an easy credit policy for three years, and there is evidence that credit excesses are occurring.

Beyond 1964, there is little reason to doubt the potential of the American economy to operate at a full employment level and to maintain a satisfactory growth rate. We are now taking only the first steps toward reducing the burden of high tax rates. Additional tax steps can be taken to keep the economy moving strongly *if we can control federal spending*. We are living in the midst of a technological revolution and in the early stages of the space age. The rate of capital spending should be high. The rate of new family formation is due to increase markedly in the years ahead, producing an enlarged demand for housing, community facilities, and durable consumer goods.

One cannot, however, rule out the business cycle. The path toward expansion will not, of course, be a smooth one—there will be ups and downs. However, the postwar experience indicates that the amplitude of business fluctuations has moderated considerably. Through better understanding of our economy and hence wiser public and private policy, and through "built-in stabilizers" like unemployment insurance, and so forth, there is a good chance that major business swings are a thing of the past. It seems reasonable to anticipate, therefore, that on the average in the next decade the American economy will perform at a high level. If world tensions should ease, and if the need for military spending should be reduced, further reduction in the burden of federal taxation would be possible.

The picture painted here may turn out to be much too optimistic. The great danger, of course, is that in pursuing policies to promote full employment and faster economic growth the government may provoke a renewed upward push on the general price level. The consequences could well be a boom-bust pattern in the next couple of years and very serious difficulties in the balance of payments. However, this does not need to happen if firm control on federal spending is exerted, and if monetary and debt management policies are efficiently employed to temper inflationary forces.

Accordingly, the Judgment Model in Chapter II, which suggests an average annual growth in GNP of 4.6 per cent during the next decade, with GNP rising to $905 billion in 1973, seems a useful projection for considering possible sources and uses of capital funds in 1973.

Prospects for Long-Term Capital Financing

If the pattern of general business activity is as suggested above, that is, strong economic growth in the decade ahead at a full employment level, interrupted only by comparatively moderate cyclical fluctuations, then it seems clear that the total uses of credit will increase steadily with the growth of the economy just as they did during the period 1948-63, as shown in Table III-1. The "mix" of these uses may change significantly, just as it did during 1948-63, but the totals will certainly swell. Total uses in 1973, for example, might run in the order of $110 billion. This prospect in itself, however, does not suggest that there would be serious shortages of available funds to finance desired uses. The experience of 1948-63 makes it clear that the American economy has developed a very efficient system for providing financing of all types. Again, Table III-1 demonstrates how the sources of funds have grown along with the expansion of the economy. There does not appear to be any convincing reason why the aggregate sources of funds in the years ahead will not keep pace with the uses.

Table III-2 presents a projection of sources and uses of funds in the U. S. money and capital markets in 1973. This projection is based on the Judgment Model for the economy as a whole as set forth in Chapter II. The figures in the projection made here are at best a rough indication of what the funds in these categories may possibly amount to ten years from now. Total sources and uses of funds in 1973 are projected at $110.7 billion, compared with $68.2 billion in 1963, as shown in Table III-1.

A brief explanation of how the individual items in Table III-2 were determined will be helpful. The net available funds from life insurance companies are directly related to total personal disposable income. In the years before 1956 life insurance funds tended to amount to about 2 per cent of per-

Table III-2

PROJECTED SOURCES AND USES OF FUNDS IN
U.S. MONEY AND CAPITAL MARKETS, 1973
(In Billions of Dollars)

Sources:		*Uses:*	
Life insurance companies	11.8	Corporate bonds	14.0
Savings and loan associations	14.8	Corporate stocks	6.3
Mutual savings banks	5.3	State and local government issues	11.7
Corporate pension funds	4.1	U.S. government issues	2.0
Commercial banks	30.9	Federal agency issues	2.5
Federal Reserve Banks	5.0	Mortgages	
State and local funds	4.1	1-4 family	24.3
U.S. investment accounts	2.5	Other	15.4
Federal loan agencies	3.0	Business credit	16.3
Corporations	14.3	Consumer credit	10.8
Fire and casualty companies	1.8	All other credit	7.4
Foreigners	2.0		
Individuals and others	11.1		
Total sources	110.7	Total uses	110.7

sonal disposable income. This percentage declined steadily to 1.4 per cent in 1961 but rose in 1962 and 1963 to 1.5 per cent. The projected figure of $11.8 billion in 1973 assumes that by 1973 the net available funds from life companies will have returned to the level of 2 per cent of personal disposable income, which in the Judgment Model in Chapter II (Table II-9) is placed at $591 billion. The belief that life insurance funds will rise to their historic level is based on several indications: (1) a good chance that the general price level will be quite stable in the period 1964-73, making life insurance more attractive; (2) the improved ability of life companies to compete for pension fund business with the aid of "separate fund" legislation (which permits life companies to invest in equities on an unrestricted basis for such separate funds) and with more equal tax treatment; and (3) increased emphasis by the companies on the sale of permanent insurance which produces savings.

In Table III-2 the funds available from savings and loan associations in 1973 are projected at $14.8 billion. Here again these funds are directly related to total personal disposable income. In 1963 the funds available from savings and loans amounted to 3.2 per cent of personal disposable income, a figure considerably higher than in earlier years. In the projection of $14.8 billion it is assumed that the relationship will be 2.5 per cent of the $591 billion disposable income. It is further assumed here that in the next ten years savings and loans will not continue the accelerated rate of growth of the past decade. The projected figure of $5.3 billion for mutual savings banks is based on the fact that in 1962 and 1963 the net available funds from this source amounted to .9 per cent of personal disposable income, which was close to the relation existing in 1953–58. This percentage declined in the period 1959–61, but in recent years the savings banks have shown a capacity for more vigorous growth. The $5.3 billion figure in Table III-2 is .9 per cent of the $591 billion personal disposable income projected for 1973.

The projected figure of $4.1 billion for corporate pension funds in 1973 is based on the assumption that such funds will be .7 per cent of the personal disposable income of $591 billion. This is a lower percentage than the prevailing one in the past decade, which has moved upward from .7 per cent to .9 per cent in 1960-63. The lower figure assumed in 1973 is based on the belief that with the rise in the percentage of the population 65 years old and over the growth of pension fund savings will level out and that in coming years a higher proportion of the pension fund business will be placed with life insurance companies.

The projected figure of $30.9 billion for commercial banks in 1973 is based on the assumption that funds available from commercial banks will expand in line with the growth in GNP. Since GNP, measured in 1962 prices, rose from $554 billion in 1962 to $905 billion in 1973 in the Judgment Model in Chapter II, or 63.4 per cent, the figure of $18.9 billion from the commercial banks in 1962 has been increased by the same percentage to obtain the projected figure of $30.9 billion for 1973. The figure of $5 billion for the Federal Reserve Banks in 1973 is pretty much a guess about the net increase in holdings of government securities by these banks.

The projected figure of $4.1 billion for state and local government funds is based on the fact that historically the net increase in money from such institutions has ranged around .7 per cent of personal disposable income. The .7 per cent figure takes account of the aging of the population and the effect this may have on pension savings. There is little basis for projecting funds from the U. S. investment accounts. The figure of $2.5 billion for 1973 assumes that the level will remain the same as in 1963. This seems realistic in view of the fact that OASDI is on a pay-as-you-go basis. The figure of $3 billion projected for federal loan agencies assumes, as does the Judgment Model, that the federal government will become more active in such areas as urban renewal and slum clearance.

The figure of $14.3 billion projected for corporations is based on the assumption that funds available from corporations are related to the volume of GNP. As may be seen in Table III-1, the years 1955, 1959, 1962, and 1963 were the years in which available funds were at high points. The average of $9.1 billion for these four years was expanded by 57 per cent (the growth of GNP from 1963 to 1973) to produce the projection of $14.3 billion for corporate funds in 1973. The projected figure of $1.8 billion for fire and casualty insurance companies in 1973 was based on the fact that historically the funds available from such institutions have been about .3 per cent of personal disposable income, and so this ratio was applied to the $591 billion personal disposable income projected in the Judgment Model. It is impossible to anticipate the net available funds from foreigners; the $2 billion figure in Table III-2 is hence merely a guess that seems reasonable in the light of the data in Table III-1. Finally, the projected figure of $11.8 billion for "individuals and others" in 1973 is based on the assumption that available funds from this source will be 2 per cent of personal disposable income of $591 billion. This is a difficult item to project because it includes funds from unincorporated business and other sources, as well as from individuals. For this reason, the relation to personal disposable income has not been stable in the past. The 2 per cent figure seems to be a reasonable one, however.

With respect to the uses of capital funds as shown in the projections for 1973 in Table III-2, the projected figure for the net increase in corporate bonds is $14 billion. Historically, it appears that the net increase in corporate bonds has amounted to about 14.5 per cent of total plant and equipment expenditures. In arriving at the figure of $14 billion for 1973, we have assumed that net corporate bond issues would amount to 15.5 per cent of the $90.5 billion total of plant and equipment expenditures for 1973 projected in the Judgment Model. The higher ratio for 1973 is based on the assumption in the Judgment Model that the communications and public utilities industries will have a proportionately larger place in the economy in the next decade, and corporations in these fields characteristically draw on the capital markets to a greater degree than other industries. Also, it seems likely that commercial banks will be obliged to raise substantial funds in the capital markets during the next decade. The figure of $6.3 billion projected for the net increase in corporate stocks in 1973 is taken as 7 per cent of the $90.5 billion of plant and equipment expenditures projected for that year. Historically, the 7 per cent relationship has been quite constant.

The net increase in state and local government debt is a function of state and local government expenditures. The projected figure of $11.7 billion in 1973 assumes that the net increase in such debt will amount to 9.5 per cent of the total of $122.7 billion for state and local government expenditures projected for 1973 in the Judgment Model. This percentage is in line with the ratio which has existed in the past decade.

There is no satisfactory way to project the net increase in U. S. government issues. Assuming that 1973 is a full employment, high-growth year, the federal budget should be close to being in balance. Accordingly, the net increase of $2 billion in federal debt in 1973 is a figure consistent with an economy such as we assume. At a GNP of $905 billion, the $2 billion increase in federal debt represents virtually a balanced budget. There is also no satisfactory method for projecting the net increase in federal agency issues. The $2.5 billion figure seems reasonable in view of the Judgment Model projection that the federal government will play a greater role than in the past in housing, education, and other areas.

Historically, the net increase in 1-4 family mortgage debt has amounted to 55-65 per cent of the national expenditures for residential construction. The projected net increase in 1-4 family mortgage debt of $24.3 billion for 1973 assumes that the ratio will be 60 per cent of the residential construction expenditures, which amount to $40.5 billion as projected in the Judgment Model. The projection of net increase in "other" mortgage debt is more difficult to determine. The projected figure of $15.4 billion for 1973 is based on the assumption that the net increase in other mortgages will be 50 per cent of the expenditures for "other construction," i.e., other than residential construction, which in the Judgment Model for 1973 are placed at $30.8 billion. The 50 per cent ratio seems appropriate in view of the relation between the net increase in "other mortgages" and "other construction" expenditures during 1959–63.

The figure of $16.3 billion projected for business credit in 1973 assumes that the total of business credit is a function of the size of GNP. From the average of the years 1955, 1956, 1959, 1962, and 1963, when the net increase in business credit was comparatively high, it appears that the net increase in such credit in years of high-level business activity tends to be about 1.8 per cent of GNP. When this percentage is applied to a projected GNP in 1973 of $905 billion, the net increase in business credit is $16.3 billion.

Similarly, the projected figure of $10.8 billion for the net increase in consumer credit in 1973 is taken as 2 per cent of the $542.5 billion of consumer expenditures projected for 1973 in the Judgment Model. The 2 per cent ratio is consistent with the ratio in other years during 1953-63 in which the increase in consumer credit was high. The figure for "all other credit" is a residual.

One thing does seem clear—there are likely to be significant changes in the years ahead in the institutional structure of the money and capital markets. As noted earlier, the growth in funds flowing into institutions which specialize in home mortgage loans has proceeded so strongly that such institutions are now having difficulty in finding an adequate supply of mortgages at yields they consider necessary. This is particularly true of the savings and loan associations. The hearings which were held in September, 1963, before the House Banking and Currency Committee certainly illustrate the problem of institutional restrictions. The savings and loan associations, with the support of the chairman of the Home Loan Bank Board, are actively seeking much broader investment powers. Similarly, the mutual savings banks are also seeking broader investment powers through the vehicle of federal charters. It is important to the public interest to ask whether such institutions should have broader investment powers in the absence of additional regulatory measures. But discussion of this matter would go beyond the scope of this chapter. Experience of the period 1948–63 suggests that the flows of funds will be adjusted and that institutional rigidities will not be a serious problem.

A crucial question again in financial markets is how succesful we will be in maintaining general price stability. If, in pursuing the objectives of full employment and faster economic growth, the government and private policy-makers take steps which produce a renewed upward pressure on the general price level, the implications for financial markets would be similar to those of the 1950's. For one thing, a rising price level would undoubtedly inflate the amount of short- and long-term credit requirements of the economy. At the same time, because of the desire to hedge against inflation, investors would tend to shift away from interest-bearing obligations, and from institutions which invest in debt instruments, and would move more strongly into equities. Moreover, under such conditions the monetary authorities would be obliged to pursue a very restrictive credit policy. Obviously, the effect of these forces would be rising interest rates.

Even if wise public and private policy succeeds in avoiding renewed upward pressures on the price level in coming years, it seems likely that sustained high employment and strong growth will keep long-term interest rates as high as they are at present. The best possibility is that long-term interest rates will move within the levels of the high of early 1960 and the low of mid-1960. In an economy characterized by full employment and strong growth, the monetary and debt management authorities will be required to guard against the possible renewal of inflationary forces. Moreover, even though over the next few years the deficit in the U. S. balance of payments should be whittled down, it seems likely that interest rates in this country must stay in line with rates abroad because of the large liquid asset holdings which foreigners have built up here in the past fifteen years. The fact that interest rates abroad will probably remain high will tend to place some floor under rates in the United States.[1]

Looking ahead for the next decade, therefore, it seems likely that, barring a renewal of inflationary forces, there should be ample funds to finance a strong growth of the country.

[1]A more extensive analysis of the capital market would have to give consideration to the behavior of interest rates in the recent past and to the expected behavior of these rates in the future. It has been assumed in the projections that the levels of interest rates in the 1970's will be between those of early 1960 and mid-1960.

IV

A DEMOGRAPHIC ANALYSIS OF MICHIGAN 1960–80

David Goldberg

The link between economic progress and population change has always been a source of considerable concern and speculation. Several writers have gone so far as to attribute the economic stagnation of the 1930's to declining growth rates, and similarly they have found their economic optimism of the 1960's associated with the expected rapid growth of population. Although this orientation is unusually extreme, most writers would agree that population size and characteristics affect labor force, division of labor, labor mobility, consumption, savings, and the growing stock of knowledge, all of which ultimately determine per capita product or some other measure of economic prosperity.

Modern economic growth is generally characterized by rapid structural changes—shifts in the relative importance of various industries as well as in their location. This condition requires great mobility of the population in order to sustain economic growth. Insufficient labor supply in areas of expanding economic opportunity or excess labor supply in places of deteriorating opportunity, both conditions of labor immobility, would present major obstacles to economic expansion. The redistribution of population is necessary for achieving a balance between opportunities and labor supply. If migration is viewed as the means through which the balance of opportunities is continuously restored, then it must certainly be considered an important symptom or index of economic conditions for a local area. Therefore, we begin the assessment of Michigan's economic past and future by examining its migration pattern.

Analysis of Michigan's Population Growth

The state has had a long history of rapid population growth. During the past hundred years Michigan has grown more rapidly than the nation, with the exception of the period 1890-1910. By 1960, Michigan's share of the national population had reached 4.38 per cent as compared to 3.06 per cent in 1910 (Table IV-1).

Table IV-1

POPULATION GROWTH AND SOURCE OF GROWTH IN MICHIGAN, 1870-1960*

Date	Percentage of U.S. Population in Michigan	Total Population	Increase during Preceding Decade	Natural Increase	Net Migration	Net Migration as Percentage of Total Increase
1960	4.38	7,823	1,451	1,292	159	11.0
1950	4.23	6,372	1,116	787	329	29.5
1940	3.98	5,256	414	387	27	6.5
1930	3.94	4,842	1,174	463	711	60.6
1920	3.47	3,668	858	355	503	58.6
1910	3.06	2,810	389	249	140	36.0
1900	3.19	2,421	327	253	74	22.6
1890	3.33	2,094	457	251	206	45.1
1880	3.26	1,637	453	260	193	42.6
1870	3.07	1,184	435	...	...	...

*All population data in this table are reported in thousands.

The fact that Michigan's growth rate has been faster than the national rate reflects primarily the net balance of migration into Michigan from other states. In each decade since 1870 there have been more migrants coming into the state than leaving the state for other areas. Between 1870 and 1910 about 38 per cent of the total growth in the state population could be attributed to net migration. The establishment of the automobile industry in Michigan is undoubtedly responsible for the exceptional migration to the state between 1910 and 1930, a period during which three out of five persons added to the population were migrants. If, today, we think of a place like California as representing an attractive, booming state loaded with growth industry, then the Michigan of 1910-30 must be viewed in similar terms. The growth experienced by the two places, at two different points in time, was very similar. During the past decade, 60 per cent of the California growth resulted from net in-migration, just as happened in Michigan thirty to fifty years ago.

In the post-depression period, Michigan was still experiencing a heavy in-migration. Its total of 329,000 net in-migrants between 1940 and 1950 was exceeded only by California, Florida, and Washington. And in the most recent decade, Michigan still ranked tenth among the states in net in-migration. Although migration in relation to population growth has declined considerably since the peak years of 1910-30, the fact that there was always been a net balance of in-migrants to the state, when viewed at ten-year intervals, would at least suggest that opportunities were more prevalent in Michigan than in the nation as a whole.

When the 1950-60 decade is broken down into yearly intervals, a totally different picture of the economic climate of the state is obtained in relation to the demographic pattern for individual years.

Estimates of the state population for each year from 1950 to 1962 were prepared by using a composite estimation technique.[1] This method yields fairly reliable estimates of the state population for intercensal years. With annual data on natural increase (births minus deaths) available from the Michigan Department of Health, it is possible to obtain annual estimates of net migration to Michigan using the simple relationship: total population increase = natural increase + net migration. In each year from 1950 to 1956 there was a net balance of in-migrants to Michigan from other states (Table IV-2). About 400,000

[1]Composite estimates of population may be the most accurate means of estimating population in intercensal years for large population units such as states. The details of this technique as applied to Michigan are given in: David Goldberg, Allen Feldt, and J. William Smit, *Estimates of Population Change in Michigan, 1950-1960* (Ann Arbor: Dept. of Sociology, Institute of Public Administration, Univ. of Michigan, 1960).

Table IV-2

POPULATION, AGE DISTRIBUTION, AND COMPONENTS OF GROWTH IN MICHIGAN, 1950–62*

Age	1950	1951	1952	1953	1954	1955	1956	1957	1958	1959	1960	1961	1962
0–19	2,176	2,261	2,348	2,458	2,576	2,696	2,815	2,915	3,005	3,076	3,156	3,226	3,275
20–44	2,432	2,500	2,523	2,562	2,613	2,652	2,709	2,681	2,637	2,560	2,524	2,492	2,456
45–64	1,302	1,325	1,350	1,384	1,409	1,457	1,444	1,484	1,464	1,492	1,505	1,510	1,535
65+	462	485	486	518	536	547	565	570	580	600	638	654	673
Total	6,372	6,571	6,707	6,922	7,134	7,352	7,533	7,650	7,686	7,728	7,823	7,882	7,939

	1950–51	1951–52	1952–53	1953–54	1954–55	1955–56	1956–57	1957–58	1958–59	1959–60	1960–61	1961–62
Population increase	199	136	215	212	218	181	117	36	42	95	59	57
Natural increase	138	118	122	128	134	139	144	141	136	92	168	121
Net migration	61	18	93	84	84	42	- 27	-105	- 94	3	-109	- 64
	(49)†									(-24)†	(-82)†	
Migration rate	.0076	.0027	.0139	.0121	.0118	.0057	-.0036	-.0137	-.0122	-.0031	-.0105	-.0081

*All population data in this table are reported in thousands.

†July through June estimates, comparable to the estimates for the period 1951–59.

more persons came to Michigan than left the area. Korean war production and fairly low unemployment levels (except for 1954) may have been largely responsible for the massive movement to the state during this period. By 1956-57 the economic circumstances of the state had been altered to the point where it could be characterized as an area with an overabundant labor supply for the diminishing opportunities available. Beginning with 1956, Michigan experienced an out-migration of population. This out-migration continued in every year through 1962, the last year for which data are available. The net movement away from the state amounted to about 400,000 persons, approximately equal in magnitude to the net number entering Michigan during the first six-year interval examined.

Out-migration from 1956-62 cannot have solved Michigan's economic problems, but in its absence the difficulties would have been magnified considerably. We cannot expect the redistribution of population to match perfectly the continuous economic changes. Frictional factors, including the accuracy of communication about existing opportunities in an area as well as familial and social ties to an area, prevent a perfect fit of migration to changing opportunity. In Michigan, the previously expanding job market may have closed up well before 1956, the last year of in-migration. The total labor force of the state was about the same size in 1953 as it was in 1960, and the number employed in the former year may have been greater. In-migration between 1954 and 1956 was essentially a lag or carry-over from the peak war production year of 1953 and its unusually low unemployment level of 2.1 per cent.

The balance between shifting economic conditions and migration is not fully described by reference to numbers of migrants. Characteristics of in- and out-migrants from the state would be most useful in attempting to evaluate the effect of migration on economic conditions. Unfortunately, only a limited amount of such data is actually available, although there has been considerable speculation in many quarters about the backflow of unskilled labor to the South during the past several years.

If the decade is divided at 1955 (the only date that can be used with respect to available data) we find that whites accounted for about three out of five net in-migrants during the

Table IV-3

NET MIGRATION TO MICHIGAN BY RACE
1950-55 and 1955-60

	1950-55	1955-60	1950-60
White	+210,000	-183,000	+ 27,000
Non-white	+127,000	+ 5,000	+132,000
Total	+337,000	-178,000	+159,000

first five-year period (Table IV-3). In contrast to this, the recession period was characterized by a heavy out-migration of whites and a small in-migration of non-whites.

For the decade as a whole, 83 per cent of the net in-migration was non-white, compared to about 65 per cent in the 1940-50 decade. Poor conditions in this state clearly do not result in a return migration to the South for non-whites, but such conditions do have the effect of cutting down the size of the stream of southern migration headed for Michigan. Between 1955 and 1960 Michigan gained non-white migrants from the South and lost white migrants to all other regions of the country. Apparently the recession conditions of Michigan still represented a more attractive set of opportunities than those available to non-whites in the South.

In the net outward movement of more than 180,000 whites from Michigan between 1955 and 1960, more than half the migrants were headed for the western states, the secondary target being the South. On the surface it would appear that there was a substantial backflow movement to the South. However, more than two-thirds of the net movement to the South was to the state of Florida.[2] Migration to Florida should probably be

[2]All data on migration to and from Michigan between 1955 and 1960 were estimated from: U. S. Bureau of the Census, *Census of Population: 1960*, Subject Reports *Mobility for States and State Economic Areas* and *Lifetime and Recent Migration* (Washington: Government Printing Office, 1963).

interpreted in the same way that one would interpret migration to the West—a movement of people to places of greater opportunity. Whether the search is for economic advantages or opportunities for leisure or retirement is irrelevant. These data at least suggest that impressions of a substantial return migration of so-called "hillbilly" labor are false.

When the migration data are reported in net figures, the potential importance of migration for a local labor force is grossly understated. For example, the 180,000 net loss of whites from Michigan in 1955-60 represents a movement of more than 500,000 from the state and more than 300,000 to the state. Coupled with differential interchange of migrants between regions, even a small net movement could have a substantial effect on the skill level of a local population.

Although there are no data available on the occupational skills of in- and out-migrants from Michigan, a special report of the U.S. Bureau of the Census does contain data on the educational level of interregional migrants for the period 1955-60.[3] The experience of the East North Central division (Michigan, Illinois, Indiana, Ohio, and Wisconsin) is probably representative of the Michigan experience.[4] In order to avoid confounding the educational data because of age and race differentials in migration, one group was selected for analysis—white, male interdivisional migrants, aged 25-29.

Table IV-4 contains data on the median educational level of migrants leaving and entering the East North Central division in 1955-60. Only in-migrants born outside of the East North Central Division and out-migrants born outside of the division that is their destination are included in this table. By this means the problem of backflow migration is minimized, and for the most part only those born in the division in which they were residing in 1955 are counted in the population. In the exchange of migrants between the East North Central division and the

[3] *Ibid.*

[4] The pattern of migration for each of the five states in the East North Central division was very similar for the years 1950-55 and 1955-60. All but Wisconsin experienced a heavy in-migration during the first five years and all states experienced an out-migration of lesser magnitude during the second five years.

Table IV-4

MEDIAN SCHOOL YEARS COMPLETED BY MIGRANTS TO OR FROM THE EAST NORTH CENTRAL DIVISION, 1955-60
(White Males, Aged 25-29)

Origin or Destination	Median Education of In-Migrants to E.N.C. States	Median Education of Out-Migrants from E.N.C. States
Northeast	16+	16+
Middle Atlantic	14.8	16+
West North Central	13.0	13.9
South Atlantic	12.3	12.8
East South Central	10.4	12.9
West South Central	12.7	12.9
Mountain	12.9	12.9
Pacific	12.8	12.9

remaining eight divisions, it can be seen that in any interchange between the East North Central division and any other division the educational level of migrants lost by the East North Central was as high or higher than that of migrants gained from any particular division. For example, migrants originating in the East North Central states who went to the Middle Atlantic states had a median education of more than 16 years, whereas those who came to this area from the Middle Atlantic division had a median education of 14.8 years. The loss of education talent by the E.N.C. division in this exchange was fairly typical of the eight interdivisional exchanges involving the East North Central states. In fact, this division lost in six of the exchanges and "traded" migrants of equal educational levels in two exchanges (Northeast and Mountain). There were no exchanges in which this area obtained migrants of higher education than those being given up.

A full matrix of the median education of interdivisional migrants is given in Table IV-5A. Each row of the table indicates the educational level of in-migrants to a division, with each column showing the education of out-migrants from that

Table IV-5

MEDIAN EDUCATION OF INTERDIVISIONAL MIGRANTS; 1955–60

A. Median School Years Completed for White, Male, Interdivisional Migrants, Aged 25–29

Destination of Migrants (1960 Residence)	Origin of Migrants (1955 Residence)								
	North-east	Middle Atlantic	East North Central	West North Central	South Atlantic	East South Central	West South Central	Mountain	Pacific
Northeast	...	15.7	16+	14.9	12.9	12.8	13.6	12.9	12.9
Middle Atlantic	16+	...	16+	16+	13.4	13.1	15.3	14.4	15.2
East North Central	16+	14.8	...	13.0	12.3	10.4	12.7	12.9	12.8
West North Central	15.4	15.6	13.9	...	12.9	12.9	12.9	13.0	12.8
South Atlantic	14.3	13.6	12.8	12.9	...	12.6	12.9	12.8	12.6
East South Central	13.0	14.3	12.9	13.3	12.9	...	13.0	12.9	12.7
West South Central	13.2	13.9	12.9	13.0	12.8	12.8	...	12.8	12.7
Mountain	12.9	13.7	12.9	12.8	12.8	12.7	12.7	...	12.7
Pacific	13.0	13.2	12.9	12.8	12.7	12.5	12.5	12.7	...

B. Educational Level of Interdivisional Streams of Migrants

	In-Migrants Have Higher Education	In- and Out-Migrants Have Same Education	Out-Migrants Have Higher Education
Northeast	1	2	5
Middle Atlantic	6	0	2
East North Central	0	2	6
West North Central	3	2	3
South Atlantic	5	2	1
East South Central	8	0	0
West South Central	3	0	5
Mountain	0	4	4
Pacific	3	2	3

division. The first-row entry for the Northeast division is 15.7 for the Middle Atlantic states, meaning that in-migrants to the Northeast whose origin was the Middle Atlantic had a median education of 15.7 years. Similarly, the first column entry for Northeast is 16+ for Middle Atlantic. In other words, migrants originating in the Northeast (1955) and settling in the Middle Atlantic division (1960) had a median education of more than sixteen years. In this case the exchange migration between Northeast and Middle Atlantic resulted in an educational loss to the Northeast. Focusing on the appropriate row and column will give the exchanges of any pair of divisions for the period 1955-60.

The experience of each division in their eight inter-divisional exchanges of migrants is summarized in Table IV-5B. It can be seen that no division did as poorly, i.e., lost as much educational talent, as the East North Central states. The region was clearly losing those people in whom it had the greatest investment.

These data are summarized in another form in Table IV-6. Here we see that 50 per cent of the white, male out-migrants from the East North Central division states had completed at least one year of college, whereas 41 per cent of the in-migrants had as much education. At the other extreme, 8 per cent of the out-migrants had no more than a grade school education, while 20 per cent of the in-migrants had not been educated beyond grade school.

The excess of poorly educated persons, resulting from exchange migration with other regions, can only intensify the already existing problems of unemployment, partial employment, and retraining. But these are problems that, to some extent, can be handled with money. It is the loss through exchange of the highly educated population that may be more disturbing in the long run to the economy of the region and the state. The innovations of this group are largely responsible for the development of new manufacturing and service industries. If their potential contributions are leaving the area because of out-migration, the effect will eventually be felt–even in good automobile years.

The net movement of population in and out of Michigan has not been evenly distributed throughout the state. The net in-

Table IV-6

EDUCATIONAL DISTRIBUTION OF IN- AND OUT-MIGRANTS, EAST NORTH CENTRAL DIVISION, 1955–60
(White Males, Aged 25-29)

Years in School	In-Migrants to E.N.C. Division (Per Cent)	Out-Migrants from E.N.C. Division (Per Cent)
Grade School:		
Under 8	10	3
8	10	5
High School:		
1-3	15	15
4	24	27
College:		
1-3	12	15
4+	29	35
Total	100	100

migration to the state as a whole over the past two decades has been almost entirely a function of the ability of the state's ten standard metropolitan areas to attract migrants.[5] This condition is not an unusual one. The continuing concentration of population and economic functions in metropolitan areas can be interpreted as evidence bearing on the emergence of a metropolitan economy, an economy in which the future of regions or states is almost completely tied to the growth of its metropolitan centers.

[5]Standard metropolitan areas consist of a central city of 50,000 or over and the county containing that central city. When adjacent counties appear to be economically integrated with the central city county, they may be included in the metropolitan area. The central cities of Michigan's ten standard metropolitan areas are: Ann Arbor, Bay City, Detroit (three counties), Flint, Grand Rapids, Jackson, Kalamazoo, Lansing (three counties), Muskegon, and Saginaw.

Between 1940 and 1955, as shown in Tables IV-7A and IV-7B, which should be combined, the metropolitan areas of the state experienced a net in-migration of about two-thirds of a million persons. In addition more than 100,000 net migrants were added to the populations of the highly urban nonmetropolitan counties of the southern part of the Lower Peninsula. In contrast to the southern portion of the state, the northern section of the Lower Peninsula and the Upper Peninsula had a continuous net out-migration. For the period 1955-60 all sections of the state lost migrants to other areas, although approximately 85 per cent of the net out-migration had as its source the Detroit metropolitan area. The similarity in migration patterns for Detroit, other metropolitan areas, and the remainder of the southern part of the Lower Peninsula is not coincidental. The economies of most of these areas are strongly tied to the automobile industry. Only Ann Arbor, Grand Rapids, Kalamazoo, and Muskegon do not have the largest part of their employed labor force engaged in the manufacture of motor vehicles and related equipment.

Given the industrial profile of most of the metropolitan areas in the state and in particular that of Detroit, which makes up nearly half of the state population, the probability that the state will approach the growth rates achieved in the 1940's or even the 1950's appears to be very slight. During the past decade the rates of net migration to metropolitan areas in Michigan (3.6/100 population) lagged behind the rates for metropolitan areas in the East North Central states (5.1) and were much less than the national rates for metropolitan areas (9.2). It was the nonmetropolitan areas of the state which appeared to be relatively healthy with respect to net migration, having lost only .4 migrants per 100 population in contrast to the national rate of -8.7 for nonmetropolitan areas. However, the future growth pattern of Michigan will not be determined by its nonmetropolitan areas.

The Future Population of Michigan

Projections of the future population of an area must involve assumptions about (1) mortality, (2) fertility, and (3) migration.

Table IV-7

NET MIGRATION FOR SELECTED AREAS, 1940–60

A. Net migration—1940–50 and 1950–60

	1940–50		1950–60	
	Net Migrants	Rate*	Net Migrants	Rate*
All metropolitan areas	339,000	9.4	166,000	3.6
Detroit	258,000	10.9	92,000	3.1
Other	81,000	6.5	74,000	4.8
Nonmetropolitan areas	- 10,000	- 0.6	- 7,000	- 0.4
Southern part of Lower Peninsula	56,000	5.7	44,000	3.8
Northern part of Lower Peninsula	- 12,000	- 3.6	- 19,000	- 5.3
Upper Peninsula	- 54,000	-16.8	- 32,000	-10.6
Total	329,000	6.3	159,000	2.5

*Decade rates of net migration represent the net number of migrants per 100 persons living in the area at the beginning of the decade.

B. Estimated Net Migration—1950–55 and 1955–60

Area	1950–55	1955–60
All metropolitan areas	323,000	-157,000
Detroit	242,000	-150,000
Other	81,000	- 7,000
Nonmetropolitan areas	14,000	- 21,000
Southern part of Lower Peninsula	48,000	- 4,000
Northern part of Lower Peninsula	- 14,000	- 5,000
Upper Peninsula	- 20,000	- 12,000
State total	337,000	-178,000

These components are not equally important in projections for local or national units. For all types of units, however, mortality projections are relatively unimportant with respect to the future size of population, provided current mortality is at the level experienced in most western countries. Mortality is now so low that immortality would have a smaller effect on eventual population size than a 10 or 15 per cent rise in completed family size. For local areas, then, fertility and migration assumptions are the crucial determinants of future population size. In countries where immigration is restricted and predictable, the accuracy of projections about future size are almost a function of the accuracy of projections of fertility. The assumptions about each of the components of the projection for Michigan are discussed below.

Mortality

Life tables were constructed on the basis of the mortality figures in Michigan for the years 1959-61. The probability of surviving from age 5 to age 25 for the total population of the state is .986. In other words, fewer than 1.5 per cent of the five-year-olds in Michigan will die before they reach age 25, if their mortality experience is comparable to that of 1959-61. Similarly, fewer than 3.9 per cent of the population aged 25 are expected to die before they reach age 45. The twenty-year intervals are illustrated because they are equivalent to our projection interval, 1960-80. Obviously, even if there are major improvements in health, projections of the number of survivors of the 1960 population cannot be in error by a great amount. For this reason, 1959-61 life tables, specific for sex and race, without any adjustment for future mortality trends, were used in projecting the survivors of the current population. To illustrate the force of mortality, the 7,823,000 persons residing in the state in 1960 are expected to be represented by 7,500,000 survivors in 1965.

Fertility

Fertility is a much more complex phenomenon to predict because the population exerts much more direct control over timing of births than deaths. As a result there have been great changes in fertility from period to period, making it exceptionally difficult to imagine what is "normal" at any given point in time. For example, in 1960 married women aged 20-24 had an average of 1.46 births, whereas married women aged 25-29 in 1960 had 1.30 births when they were 20-24 years old. This does not necessarily mean that women aged 20-24 will eventually have more children than women aged 25-29. In fact recent studies of the expected number of children married women will have by the time they complete their families indicate that the younger group will have fewer children. In other words, the timing patterns of these two groups of women are different, the younger group having a greater proportion of their children earlier in life.

Since 1955 several studies of "expected" fertility have been conducted in the United States. In addition many reinterview studies have been carried out over intervals of one to seven years to discover if women who say they will have *x* children over a given interval do in fact have *x* children. In general these studies show that the aggregate expectations of women are accurate predictors of their future fertility behavior.[6] These studies provide the basis for the fertility projections used here.

The fertility assumptions used in the projections may be summarized in the following tabulation of total fertility rates.[7]

[6]Several of these studies have been summarized by Ronald Freedman, David Goldberg, and Doris Slesinger, "Current Fertility Expectations of Married Couples in the United States," *Population Index,* XXIX (Oct., 1963), 366-91.

[7]The total fertility rate is the sum of the period age specific birth rates. Hypothetically, a cohort of women subject to the age specific with rates of a given period would eventually have the number of children shown in the total fertility rate. At any given period the total fertility rate may be much higher or lower than the number of children the actual cohorts will eventually have. Therefore, the projections of population are

Year	White	Non-white
1960	3.81	4.11
1965	2.95	3.75
1970	2.95	3.50
1975	2.95	3.25
1980	2.95	3.25

The implications of these assumptions may be described in several ways. First, they imply that the crude birth rate will decline from an annual average of 26.1 births per 1,000 persons in Michigan during the period 1955-60 to averages of 22.4, 20.6, 22.4, and 23.8 for the periods 1960-65, 1965-70, 1970-75, and 1975-80 respectively. The rise in the crude rates between 1970 and 1980 is simply due to the presence of more women at child-bearing ages at that time, not to an expected rise in family size. Second, the net effect that the operation of the assumed total fertility rates will have on the eventual number of children born per woman in Michigan is as follows: white women aged 15-44 in 1960 will average 3.1 children per woman by the time they complete their families at various times in the future. White women aged 15-44 in 1980 will average 3.0 children when they complete their families. For non-white women the more gradual decline in total fertility rates will result eventually in an average of 3.4 children per woman for the group who are 15-44 years old in 1980, a drop from 3.5 children for the comparable group in 1970. These figures correspond fairly well with the number of children expected by married women, according to national sample surveys conducted in 1960 and 1962.[8]

an attempt to focus on the number of children women will actually have, according to their statements of expectation, rather than some particular period measure of fertility.

[8]The data shown above were taken from Freedman, Goldberg, and Slesinger, pp. 366-91.

Age at Year of Interview	Expected Number of Children 1960 Sample	Expected Number of Children 1962 Sample
18–24	3.1	3.1
25–29	3.4	3.3
30–34	3.3	3.3
35–39	3.0	3.1

With adjustments for the fact that the fertility of Michigan women is from 3 to 7 per cent higher than the national level, depending on the fertility measure used, and that about 95 per cent of all American women eventually marry, the assumptions employed in the projections fit the most up-to-date information available from the national population. If these assumptions are met, there will be approximately 1.8 million births in Michigan in the 1960 decade and 2.2 million births between 1970 and 1980.

Migration

Since the experience of the past decade or two usually provides a reasonable prediction of the future, we could expect a continuation of net in-migration. However, the abrupt change in the migration pattern for Michigan, beginning about 1956, leaves much to be desired with respect to an extrapolation of a smooth trend in the past. From this vantage point, it appears likely that the 1950's marked the end of a distinct phase in Michigan population growth, a period during which the state was able to attract large numbers of migrants because of the presence of growth industries. It is not even totally unreasonable to argue that the end of this growth period came long ago and that rapid growth was sustained only because of the "unnatural events" of World War II and the Korean War.

The characteristics which appear to attract migrants today include: the presence of extensive tertiary industry, high standards of public education, high proportions of workers in white-collar occupations, and the presence of modern growth industries (machinery, electronic, chemical, communications). In an affluent society such as this one, noneconomic factors like climate and opportunities for recreational and cultural activity also play an important role in the redistribution of population. Clearly, if we were to array the states according to their potential attractiveness to migrants, using the characteristics mentioned as a basis, Michigan would not be near the head of the list, and the in-migration from 1940 and 1955 would appear rather unexpected.

If forced to speculate about the future, I would guess that Michigan's migration pattern would, in most years, yield a small net out-migration, balanced perhaps by those exceptionally good years that are sometimes experienced by areas which concentrate in the manufacture of durable goods. To quantify this type of speculation is virtually an impossible task. Therefore, it is being assumed for purposes of the population projections that net migration will be a negligible factor in the growth of total population. Specifically, it is assumed that net migration to the state for the period 1960-80 is zero. A zero net migration assumption means that the future population of the state consists of the survivors of the present population and the survivors of births in the intervening years. It should also be pointed out that in the absence of net migration the projections can be useful in answering the hypothetical but meaningful question, "What future demands and requirements will the present population of the state have in future years?

The combined effect of the mortality, fertility, and migration assumptions results in a total population increase of 14 per cent during the current decade and an additional 15 per cent increase during the 1970's, so that by 1980 the projected Michigan population is 10,204,000 (Table IV-8). These projections of population are considerably lower than those now circulating in literature about the state. The most typically quoted projections for the state are the ones prepared by the Bureau of the Census in 1957, which estimate the 1970 state population at 9.4 to 10.4 million[9] compared to our present projections of approximately 8.9 million. The Census Bureau projections assumed an in-migration of .5 to .9 million persons

[9]U. S. Bureau of the Census, "Illustrative Projections of the Population by States, 1960, 1965, and 1970," *Current Population Reports,* Series P-25, No. 160 (Washington: Government Printing Office, Aug. 9, 1957).

Table IV-8

PROJECTIONS OF THE MICHIGAN POPULATION BY AGE*

Age	1960	1965	1970	1975	1980	Increase 1960-70 (Per Cent)	Increase 1970-80 (Per Cent)
0-4	970	887	867	1,003	1,143	-11	32
5-14	1,623	1,842	1,847	1,745	1,861	14	1
15-24	1,015	1,305	1,612	1,830	1,835	59	14
25-44	2,076	2,004	2,001	2,194	2,581	- 4	29
45-64	1,513	1,649	1,785	1,875	1,857	18	4
65+	626	700	778	847	928	24	19
Total	7,823	8,387	8,891	9,494	10,204	14	15

*Population data in this table are in thousands.

to Michigan between 1955 and 1970. At the time those projections were made, the migration assumption appeared reasonable with respect to Michigan's experience during the previous fifteen years. Today, such a figure seems to be out of the question, an illustration of the continuing need for updated projections utilizing the most recent data available.

The projections shown in Table IV-8 indicate different rates of growth for the various age groups. The number of preschool children (aged 0-4) is expected to decline slightly from 970,000 in 1960 to 867,000 in 1970 and then rise rapidly to 1,143,000 by 1980. The rise between 1970 and 1980 results from the rise in births during the 1970's, a rise due to the larger number of parents rather than to an increase in family size. The population aged 5-14, roughly equivalent to the elementary school population, should continue its increase to 1965 and then remain fairly stable to 1980. By far the greatest change will occur in the population aged 15-24, which will increase from about one million persons in 1960 to more than 1.8 million persons by 1975. The impact of this increase in population on high school and college enrollment as well as on the labor force is shown later. This increase is not speculative. The children have already been born. The population aged 25-64, which constitutes the bulk of the labor force, will increase by about 5 per cent between 1960 and 1970, a much lower growth rate than the 14 per cent rise anticipated for the total population. After 1970, the increase in this group will be more substantial as the larger birth cohorts of the 1940's begin to attain this age level. Persons 65 and over are expected to represent an increasing proportion of the total population throughout the projection period 1960-80. It is possible that the expectation of .8 million and .9 million older persons in 1970 and 1980 represents an overestimate of this population. There is some evidence that the net out-migration of this age group increased between 1940-50 and 1950-60, although inaccurate reporting of ages among the older persons precludes a reliable estimation of movement in this age group.[10] Detailed projections of the Michigan population are contained in the Appendix (Table IV-App. 1).

The projected population of Michigan counties for the years 1965, 1970, 1975, and 1980 is shown in Table IV-Appendix 2.[11]

[10]Censal survival estimates for the age group 65 and older indicate that there was a net out-migration of whites amounting to approximately 14,000 in 1940-50 and 32,000 in 1950-60. During both periods there was a small non-white in-migration at these ages.

[11]The population projections for Michigan counties were divided into two groups:

I. Wayne, Macomb, Oakland, Washtenaw, Ingham, and Genesee counties.

II. All other counties.

The populations of Group I counties were projected on the basis of local characteristics. For example, Washtenaw and Ingham counties were treated as if they were single-industry areas with the future college enrollment serving as a basis of projection for the total population. The population of the Detroit area counties was projected by using an analytic component method, assuming that the three-county area would experience a net in-migration of about 100,000 per decade. Projections for Genesee County were made to fit the pattern of the Detroit area because of the similarity of industrial profile for Flint and Detroit.

The populations of Group II counties (all other counties in the state) were projected with the assumption that the 1950-60 average annual rate of change in the proportion of the state population located in a given county would continue through the 1960-70 decade. For the 1970-80 period, one-half the average annual rate of change 1950-60 served as a basis for the projections. The individual county projections were adjusted to fit the projections of the state population.

These projections are summarized in Table IV-9, which shows the population distribution in metropolitan and nonmetropolitan counties as well as the distribution in selected regions of the state. The future growth of individual counties is expected to continue the trend toward concentration in metropolitan counties of the state. If the population of the state's ten metropolitan areas (14 counties) is traced back to 1900, we find 42 per cent of the state population living within the metropolitan county boundaries. By 1960 these areas had increased their share of the state population to 73 per cent. In 1980 they are expected to include 76 per cent of the state population. The continuing concentration of population in the metropolitan areas of the state is expected to be largely at the expense of the Upper Peninsula and the northern portion of the Lower Peninsula. These two areas represented 9 per cent of the state population in 1960. During the next twenty years, their population should remain fairly stable in number, the net out-migration being expected to balance the natural increase, so that by 1980 their share of the state population will be down to 7 per cent.

Table IV-9

DISTRIBUTION OF POPULATION IN MICHIGAN, 1900–1980
(Percentage of Total State Population)

	1900	1940	1950	1960	1970	1980
All metropolitan areas	41.9	68.8	71.4	73.1	74.8	75.9
Detroit	17.6	45.2	47.3	48.1	48.7	49.4
Other	24.3	23.6	24.1	25.0	26.1	26.5
Nonmetropolitan areas	58.1	31.2	28.6	26.9	25.2	24.1
Southern part of Lower Peninsula	32.8	18.7	18.2	18.0	17.6	17.1
Northern part of Lower Peninsula	14.5	6.4	5.7	5.0	4.4	4.1
Upper Peninsula	10.8	6.1	4.7	3.9	3.2	2.9
Total	100.0	100.0	100.0	100.0	100.0	100.0

The impact that the increase in total population will have on the potential growth of the labor force in Michigan is outlined in Tables IV-10 and IV-11. Past trends and future growth of the national population were already discussed in Chapter II. In Michigan the labor force participation rates differ from the national pattern. Michigan males aged 25-64 have slightly higher participation rates, whereas Michigan females show considerably lower participation rates than is the case nationally. These differences probably reflect the heavy emphasis on manufacturing in the state. In the future it is expected that changes in labor force participation rates will follow the national pattern shown in Chapter II: decreasing levels for men under 25 and over 55, in contrast to increasing rates for women 25 and over.

Table IV-10

LABOR FORCE PARTICIPATION RATES BY AGE AND SEX, MICHIGAN, 1960–80*
(Percentage of Total Labor Force)

Age	Male			Female		
	1960	1970	1980	1960	1970	1980
14–19	42.8	39.0	36.0	30.0	29.0	28.0
20–24	89.4	87.5	86.5	44.0	44.0	44.0
25–34	95.7	95.7	95.7	32.3	33.7	34.2
35–44	96.1	96.1	96.1	39.8	43.8	45.3
45–54	95.0	95.0	95.0	43.9	50.4	52.9
55–64	85.2	83.2	81.2	32.0	37.5	40.0
65+	26.2	23.2	20.2	9.0	10.0	10.3

*1960 labor force participation rates as shown in the U.S. Bureau of the Census, *Census of Population: 1960,* Final Report PC (1)-24C, *General Social and Economic Characteristics, Michigan* (Washington: Government Printing Office, 1962), adjusted to compensate for difference between average total labor force figures for 1960 and those reported in the census for April, 1960.

When the participation rates are applied to the projected population, they yield the labor force projections shown in Table IV-2. The total Michigan labor force is projected to increase from 3.0 million in 1960 to 3.5 million in 1970 and 4.1 million in 1980. Total growth in the labor force will be unevenly distributed through the age groups. Between 1960 and 1970 nearly 62 per cent of the labor force increase will be concentrated in the age group 14-24. Over 300,000 jobs will have to be added for this age group alone. The input of population at the young ages in Michigan is greater than the anticipated national increase because of differences in the demographic pattern for the state—the higher fertility and selective migration during the past two decades. With the high unemployment rates characteristic of this age group, the problems to be faced by the state are even greater than those expected at the national level.

The shock wave produced by young, new entrants into the labor force will be most acutely felt in 1965 when the number of persons becoming 18 years old during the year will represent an *increase* of about 40,000 over the comparable number during 1964. As Sonenblum suggests in Chapter II, if the younger members of the labor force are unable to find employment within a reasonable time, their future productivity may be seriously impaired.

The implied growth of one-half million in the state labor force between 1960 and 1970 would not be an unusual decennial experience for the state. But since there has been relatively little change in the rate of growth of employment opportunities since 1953, an additional half-million in the labor force necessarily means that the state must find a new source of growth if it is to fulfill the needs created by a growing population. The labor force projections should be viewed as a potential which is not automatically achieved for a local area.

To a large extent the educational level of the population will serve as a determinant of the state's ability to meet the demand for jobs created by the increasing population and its associated potential increase in labor force. This form of interaction occurs in several ways. The highly educated groups will contribute the major share of the continuing technological and scientific developments which eventually yield the new products and procedures essential to the growth of new industries. New

Table IV-11

LABOR FORCE PROJECTIONS BY AGE AND SEX, MICHIGAN, 1960–80*

Age	1960*	1965*	1970*	1975*	1980*	Increase 1960–70 (Per Cent)	Increase 1970–80 (Per Cent)
Males:							
14–24	332	432	540	599	612	63	13
25–44	978	930	928	1,027	1,225	- 5	32
45–64	690	732	778	804	780	13	0
65+	77	79	81	81	81	5	0
Total	2,077	2,173	2,327	2.511	2,698	12	16
Females:							
14–24	209	257	311	347	353	49	14
25–44	383	393	401	433	503	5	13
45–64	292	355	412	449	453	41	11
65+	30	37	43	48	54	43	26
Total	914	1,042	1,167	1,277	1,363	28	17
Both sexes:							
14–24	541	689	851	946	965	57	13
25–44	1,361	1,323	1,329	1,460	1,728	- 2	30
45–64	982	1,087	1,190	1,253	1,233	21	4
65+	107	116	124	129	135	16	9
Total	2,991	3,215	3,494	3,788	4,061	17	16

*Data are in thousands.

ideas have a cumulative effect, so that each year we are faced with unprecedented gains in scientific-technological development. The exponential rate of change demands generally applicable skills. In other words, it becomes essential to have a population whose skill level can accommodate the increasing rate of change in activity. The trend toward the clustering of new industries around university centers and the almost permanent unemployability of the less educated is neither accidental nor temporary. With rapid change, even training in the newest skills soon becomes obsolete. The crucial component of training is the adaptability of the skills being taught. Adaptability is necessarily tied to the level of educational attainment within a population.

Several measures of educational level of the Michigan population, as contrasted with that of the United States and the nine other largest states, are presented in Table IV-12. With respect to enrollment of males at ages 16-19, the state appears to be doing an excellent job in continuing the education of persons in their late teens. With respect to these ages, Michigan ranks higher than the nation, and it ranks higher than the other nine states in 32 out of 36 possible comparisons. Similarly, the proportion of "drop-outs" (persons who have not completed high school and who are not currently enrolled) for males aged 17 is lower than the national level and lower than eight of the nine states in the table. A more detailed review of drop-outs at age 17 shows that the Michigan rate of 14.8 per cent ranks sixteenth among the states in conterminous United States.[12] The variation in drop-outs at this age is exceptionally large, ranging from about 9 per cent in Oregon and Utah to more than 25 per cent in eight northern states and one New England state. Additional information on the enrollment status of the population aged 15-19 is given in Table IV-13. These data show that the persons enrolled in Michigan are somewhat

[12]Beverly Duncan, of the University of Michigan Population Studies Center, provided the data on drop-outs which had been compiled under a project, "Family Factors and School Dropout: 1920-1960," supported through the Co-operative Research Program of the Office of Education, U. S. Department of Health, Education, and Welfare.

Table IV-12

SELECTED EDUCATIONAL MEASURES FOR THE TEN LARGEST STATES—1960

	U.S.	Mich.	N.Y.	Cal.	Penn.	Ill.	Ohio	Texas	N.J.	Mass.	Fla.
Percentage of males enrolled at ages:											
16	86.6	89.1	88.3	90.5	88.9	87.6	89.9	83.9	87.4	85.5	85.8
17	76.3	81.9	78.0	76.5	77.7	75.3	81.2	71.6	76.8	75.8	75.5
18	54.6	60.9	57.0	51.2	53.1	52.3	56.1	53.1	50.2	60.5	51.9
19	37.3	40.9	42.7	34.0	37.2	36.0	36.0	37.8	34.9	46.7	33.6
Percentage drop-out for males, 17	19.9	14.8	16.9	20.0	15.8	20.0	14.2	25.7	18.6	17.6	21.7
Percentage of population, 25+ who had completed high school	41.1	40.9	40.9	51.5	38.1	40.4	41.9	39.5	40.7	47.0	42.6
Ratio of college enrollment to population, 18–24	.23	.25	.27	.32	.21	.24	.21	.21	.19	.31	.16
Median education of males, 25–29	12.3	12.3	12.4	12.5	12.1	12.2	12.3	12.3	12.1	12.5	12.2
Percentage of population, 25+ who have completed college	7.7	6.8	8.9	9.8	6.4	7.3	7.0	8.0	8.4	8.8	7.8

Table IV-13

ENROLLMENT STATUS FOR MICHIGAN AND THE UNITED STATES—1960
(Percentage by Age Groups)

Age	Enrolled in			Not Enrolled		
	Elem. School	High School	College	High School Grad.	Drop-Out	Total
United States:						
15	14	79	...	...	7	100
16	6	80	...	1	13	100
17	3	71	2	5	19	100
18	2	30	19	24	25	100
19	1	9	23	38	29	100
Michigan:						
15	11	84	...	...	5	100
16	3	86	...	...	11	100
17	2	77	2	4	15	100
18	1	33	18	26	22	100
19	...	8	24	42	26	100

more advanced in their grade level than the national population and that at each age from 15 through 19 the proportion of drop-outs is lower among the Michigan youths. However, with the large birth cohorts of the late 1940's and early 1950's about to enter the labor force, the fact that more than one-fourth of this population may not have completed high school will pose major problems of employment beginning about 1965. Some recent data on unemployment of young adults in 1962 indicate that the rate of unemployment for persons who have not completed high school is twice as high as the rate for high school graduates.[13]

One of the more perplexing aspects of the data shown in Tables IV-12 and IV-13 is the relatively high educational standing of Michigan youths coupled with the relatively low

[13]U. S. Bureau of Labor Statistics, "Employment of School Age Youth, October, 1962," *Special Labor Force Report,* No. 34, prepared by Carl Rosenfeld.

educational levels of adults in the state. The state ranks lower than the national average in the proportion of adults who have completed either high school or college, particularly the latter, as is shown in the table, where Michigan ranks below eight of the nine states. This is a complete reversal of the picture presented at the younger ages. The switch in the relative educational position of the state must mean either that Michigan has recently experienced a more marked improvement than the other states in the enrollment status of its younger population or that the state is losing its educational advantage through the process of selective migration. The selective migration hypothesis appears to be more likely, given the data shown previously on the educational loss among white males aged 25-29 in the interregional exchange of migrants. Michigan appears to be on an educational treadmill. Its educational efforts for the younger ages are not providing a full payoff at the adult ages. Michigan ranks seventeenth among the states in the ratio of college enrollment to population of the ages of 18-24. An average effort at the college level may be totally inadequate for future economic growth in a state that appears to be losing its better-educated population to other areas of the country.

Projections of future elementary (including kindergarten), high school, and college enrollment for the state are shown in Tables IV-14 and IV-15. It was assumed that the proportion of persons aged 5-14 enrolled in school would remain unchanged between 1960 and 1980. There is little room for change in enrollment rates at these ages. For example, 98 per cent of the population aged 10-14 is enrolled in either elementary or high school. At ages 15-19, the drop-out rates were assumed to decline from the rates shown in Table IV-13, so that by 1980 the drop-out rate for persons aged 18 would be down to 15 per cent from 22 per cent at that age in 1960.[14] Similar declines were projected for all persons aged 15-19. Projections of the college population were keyed into fall, opening enrollment data. For the college age population (17-34 in these projections) it

[14]Lower drop-out rates would not appreciably affect the projections of high school enrollment. A drop-out rate as low as 5 per cent would only add 25,000-30,000 to the projections.

Table IV-14

SELECTED ENROLLMENT RATES FOR MICHIGAN, 1960–80
(Percentage by Age Group)

A. Enrollment Rates for Elementary and High School (Spring)

Age	Elementary			High School		
	1960	1970	1980	1960	1970	1980
5–9	92.4	92.4	92.4	. . .	. . .	. . .
10–14	88.3	88.3	88.3	9.5	9.5	9.5
15–19	3.8	3.8	3.8	61.2	61.9	61.6
20–34	0.3	0.3	0.3	1.5	1.5	1.5

B. Opening Enrollment Rates for College (Fall)

Age	1960	1963	1970	1980
17	8.0	8.5	9.5	10.0
18–19	28.2	29.5	34.0	40.0
20–24	12.9	14.8	17.5	20.0
25–29	5.3	5.3	6.0	7.0
30–34	2.1	2.4	2.9	3.5

was assumed that the increasing enrollment rates characteristic of the 1950 decade would continue into the future, but at slower rates of change than have occurred in the past ten or fifteen years. At ages 18-19 the college enrollment rate is expected to increase from the present 30 per cent to 40 per cent by 1980 and at ages 20-24, to increase from 15 per cent to 20 per cent. The proportion of people who will desire to attend institutions of higher education at future dates is probably much higher than is indicated by the enrollment rates used in the study. National studies of parents' expectations about sending their children to college indicate that about 25-30 per cent of the parents feel that their children are "certain" to go to college, while another 17-34 per cent feel that their children have a "fair chance" of attending.[15] Although expectations of this kind are sometimes unrealistic, parental hopes for sending children to college have become widespread among the population, including the lower income groups. The rates used in these projections correspond approximately with the higher series of college enrollment projections made by the Bureau of the Census.[16]

According to the projections, the pressures on the elementary schools will be reduced after 1965 as enrollment remains relatively constant at about 1.7 million children up to 1980. For the first time in many years, elementary schools will have an opportunity to improve quality rather than expending all of their energies on the burgeoning enrollment. High school experience will be different. Peak enrollment will not be reached until 1975, at which time about 60 per cent more students will be attending Michigan high schools than in 1960. During the 1970's, the annual number of high school graduates is likely to be about 130,000 to 150,000, as contrasted with the 1960 class of 87,000.

At the college level, two sets of projections have been prepared. The first set simply illustrates the magnitude of future enrollment if present enrollment rates remain constant. It shows the effect that population change itself has on enrollment. Even this series indicates an increase of about 10,000 students per year through 1975. The more realistic series, which assumes increasing enrollment rates, shows that college enrollment will double in the next eleven to twelve years and reach 440,000 students by 1980. The anticipated increase in college enrollment facing the state has been described in several publications appearing in the last ten years. Yet the

[15]John Lansing, Thomas Lorimer, and Chukashi Moriguchi, *How People Pay for College* (Ann Arbor: Dept. of Sociology, Institute for Social Research, Univ. of Michigan, 1960).

[16]U. S. Bureau of the Census, "Illustrative Projections to 1980 of School and College Enrollment in the United States," *Current Population Reports,* Series P-25, No. 232 (Washington: Government Printing Office, June 22, 1961).

Table IV-15

ENROLLMENT IN MICHIGAN SCHOOLS, 1950–80

Year	Elementary	High School	College	
			Current Rates	Projected Rates
1950	921,000	292,000	95,000	95,000
1960	1,495,000	439,000	160,000	160,000
1965	1,701,000	568,000	211,000	222,000
1970	1,708,000	660,000	262,000	305,000
1975	1,620,000	706,000	309,000	390,000
1980	1,726,000	662,000	328,000	442,000

response of the state has been rather slow. This inaction can only intensify the continuing loss of the well-educated to other sections of the country.

Automobile Production and Jobs

Any consideration of the future population of Michigan that does not take into account the future of the automobile industry and its relationship to the creation of jobs in the state would be particularly unrealistic. Moreover, the topic is especially tempting because of the similarities between human populations and populations of durables, including cars. The age-number distribution of an automobile population, like the human aggregate, is dependent on the varying sizes of birth cohorts and the appropriate set of mortality rates. As is true for the U.S. human population, there is relatively little movement of automobiles across the national boundaries. The following paragraphs are an attempt to project the future production of automobiles and its probable impact on the state labor force.

The primary reason a demographic analysis of automobiles can be useful in predicting future production levels is that automobile mortality is the major determinant of production. Between 1955 and 1963, passenger car deaths accounted for two-thirds of the new cars introduced into the U.S. economy. Production and automobile deaths (disappearance from the list of registered cars) are correlated. In good years there are many births and many deaths, while in lean years there are few births and few deaths (one of the major differences between populations of human beings and durables).

The basic strategy in predicting future automobile production is to determine the future numbers of registered cars (a function of the future size of population), the net annual increase in registered cars, and the annual deaths. Then:

$$\text{net additions} + \text{deaths} = \text{births (new cars)}.$$

Let us start at the end with automobile mortality. Registration data for cars include data on age (model year). If there are 1.0 million cars aged 8 in 1960 and 0.8 million cars aged 9 in 1961, the probability of dying from age 8 to 9 is .20. With data of this kind it is possible to build a life table for automobiles. Such a life table was constructed from the experience of the 1959-61 period and is shown in Table IV-16. The expectation of life for passenger cars is 11.4 years. About 99 per cent of the cars survive to age 4, but by age 14 only 21 per cent remain. The use of this life table in combination with the age distribution of cars yields the number of deaths in the following year. All that is required to obtain the total number of additional cars in the following year is the net additions in registrations. The relation between the number of registered cars and the number of households is shown in Table IV-17. In 1955 there were 1.09 registered cars per household. By 1963 this ratio was up to 1.22.[17] The future number of households in the United States has been estimated by the Bureau of the Census, taking into

[17]Many cars in the United States are not directly associated with households--company cars, government cars, etc. In this sense the typical U. S. household does not have 1.22 cars available for use.

Table IV-16

SELECTED COMPONENTS OF 1959-61
LIFE TABLE FOR PASSENGER CARS

Exact Age	Probability of Dying within One Year	Survivors to Exact Age	Future Expectation of Life
0	.000	1,000	11.42
2	.002	999	9.43
4	.010	991	7.49
6	.040	962	5.68
8	.125	857	4.24
10	.200	622	3.44
12	.250	386	2.95
14	.287	213	2.59
20	.367	18	1.89
24*	1.000	3	0.50

*The life table has been constructed so that no car survives to age 25, even though there are cars much older than this. The arbitrary truncation at age 25 has virtually no effect on life expectation or expected scrappage rates because of the small proportion of automobiles surviving to that age.

account the recent trend toward more frequent household formation.[18] The ratio of cars per household was projected by assuming that the increase in the ratio of .016 per year for the period 1955-63 would continue to 1970 and increase at a slower pace in succeeding years. In terms that may be more meaningful, the 1970 national pattern of car ownership will approximate the pattern of western states in 1960, where 30 per cent of the households had two or more cars available compared to the national figure of 21 per cent. This implies that between now and 1970 about one out of nine households will have an extra

[18]U. S. Bureau of the Census, "Interim Revised Projections of the Number of Households and Families: 1965 to 1980," *Current Population Reports*, Series P-20, No. 123 (Washington: Government Printing Office, April 11, 1963).

car, in addition to the cars they would normally be purchasing at the current rate for households.

The projections are optimistic with respect to the future role of the automobiles in our society. But the changing distribution of the American population should lead to predictions of rapid increases in the automobile population. Beginning in 1920-30, the growth rates of rings of metropolitan areas exceeded the growth rates of their central cities. In each succeeding decade ring growth played an even more prominent part in metropolitan expansion. During the last decade the growth rate of rings was nearly five times as great as that of the central city rate. The fastest growing areas have gradually shifted outward, so that today the highest rates of growth are in the areas twenty to thirty miles from the central cities. The increasing physical size of metropolitan areas and the dispersal of certain economic functions from the central city means that all trips—work, leisure, shopping—will increase in length and tend increasingly to be lateral rather than centripetal. Given the scattered distribution of population and commercial functions, the possibility that mass transit systems will solve the transportation problem becomes smaller. The spokes of the radial pattern of a mass transit system simply do not come close enough to a large proportion of the population to serve as a substitute for the automobile. Accordingly, the projections of the future automobile populations rise from the present figure of 68 million to 84 million in 1970 and 108 million by 1980.[19] Even a continuation of the present automobile ownership rate would result in 92 million passenger cars by 1980 (as shown in parentheses in Table IV-17).

[19]The projections of the future number of passenger cars in the United States contained here correspond rather closely to the projections prepared by the National Planning Association, in which the basis of projection was the relation between automobile ownership and income. See: U. S. Bureau of Labor Statistics, *Projections to Years 1976 and 2000: Economic Growth, Population, Labor Force, Leisure, and Transportation,* a Report to the Outdoor Recreation Resource Review Commission, prepared by the National Planning Association (Washington: Government Printing Office, 1962).

Table IV-17

HOUSEHOLDS AND PASSENGER CARS IN THE UNITED STATES, 1950-80

Date	Households	Registered Passenger Cars per Household	Registered Passenger Cars
1950	43,554,000	0.93	40,334,000
1955	47,788,000	1.09	52,135,000
1960	52,610,000	1.17	61,684,000
1961	53,291,000	1.19	63,280,000
1962	54,652,000	1.20	65,640,000
1963	56,100,000	1.22*	68,000,000
Projected:			
1964	57,000,000	1.24	70,500,000
1965	58,000,000	1.25 (1.22)†	72,700,000 (70,800,000)†
1966	58,800,000	1.27	74,600,000
1967	59,800,000	1.28	76,800,000
1968	60,800,000	1.30	79,100,000
1969	61,800,000	1.32	81,400,000
1970	63,000,000	1.33 (1.22)†	84,000,000 (76,900,000)†
1975	69,000,000	1.38 (1.22)†	95,200,000 (84,200,000)†
1980	75,000,000	1.44 (1.22)†	108,000,000 (91,500,000)†

*Estimated.

†The number of registered cars shown in parentheses is the estimated number of registered passenger cars which corresponds with the registered passenger cars per household as shown in parentheses in the preceding column. For example, if there are 1.33 registered cars per household in 1970, it is estimated that there would be 84 million registered passenger cars. On the other hand, if there were 1.22 registered cars per household in 1970 we would expect to have about 76,900,000 cars.

The projections of the future number of registered passenger cars and the automobile deaths, derived from the life table, yield the critical components of the total number of passenger cars added to the auto population in future years (Table IV-18). Net additions in cars are obtained by subtracting the number of registered cars in year x from the number of registered cars in year $x + 1$. In 1965, for example, there are 2,200,000 net additions to the auto population and there are 5,350,000 auto deaths (shown as "scrap" in Table IV-18). A total of 7,550,000 new cars will be required to satisfy the replacement and addition needs. The replacement needs rise rapidly in the future—to 6 million by 1970, 7 million by 1975, and 8 million by 1980. A recent trend in the lowering of automobile mortality at the older ages, probably associated with the increase in multiple car ownership, when projected to future years, does not appear to alter the replacement needs appreciably. The rapid increase in the replacement needs may, to some extent, be attributed to the changing age distribution of cars. During the 1950's auto deaths were relatively low because there were few old cars, a result of the absence of production in the 1942-45 period.

The number of new passenger cars required by the U.S. population in future years is expected to rise to nearly 9 million in 1970 and nearly 11 million in 1980. Projections of U.S. auto production at future dates may be estimated by assuming .4 million imports and .2 million exports annually, which was the case in 1962 and 1963 (i.e., if we subtract .2 million from the total passenger car additions in Table IV-18).

Projections for an individual year should be interpreted as part of the long-term demand for automobiles, a demand which is highly income elastic from year to year. One bad economic year followed by a good year usually results in compensating auto production and auto death. But two or more successive recession years may never be fully compensated. These projections implicitly assume no extended periods of recession, and in this sense they are optimistic projections for the industry.

If we assume that truck and bus production is about 17-19 per cent of passenger car production (which was the pattern of the last seven years), then the total motor vehicle production in

Table IV-18

PASSENGER CAR REGISTRATION, SCRAPPAGE, AND SALES, 1950--80*

Year	Total Registered Passenger Cars	Net Additions Registered Passenger Cars	"Scrap"	Passenger Car Additions		
				Total	Domestic Sales	Imports
1950	40.33	3.88	2.64	6.52	6.50	.02
1955	52.14	3.68	4.04	7.72	7.66	.06
1960	61.68	2.12	4.84	6.96	6.52	.44
1961	63.28	1.60	4.07	5.67	5.39	.28
1962	65.64	2.36	4.77	7.13	6.75	.38
1963†	68.50	2.86	4.94	7.80	7.40	.40
Projected:						
1965	72.70	2.20	5.35	7.55	7.15	.40
1970	84.00	2.60	6.15	8.75	8.35	.40
1975	95.90	2.50	7.10 (6.85)	9.60 (9.35)	9.10 (8.95)	.40
1980	108.00	2.60	8.20 (8.00)	10.80 (10.60)	10.40 (10.20)	.40

*All data are reported in millions. Figures in parentheses represent the automobile scrappage and production situation if, by 1970, the expectation of automobile life rises from the current 11.42 years to 11.79 years.

†Estimated.

the United States will amount to approximately 10 million in 1970 and about 12.5 million in 1980.

To summarize, there are clearly several factors at work which will help to sustain a healthy automobile industry. These include more frequent household formation by primary individuals, a continuing increase in the number of households (guaranteed by the large birth cohorts of the postwar years), the outward shift of the residential population as well as of commercial functions from central cities, and a rising income level with its impact on multiple car ownership. The central issue of concern here is how far an expanding automobile industry will contribute to the total number of jobs needed for the increasing population of the state.

Previously it was shown that the state could expect an increase of approximately one-half million in the labor force by 1970. Translated into required additional jobs, the increase in the labor force would mean about 470,000 jobs at the 1960 unemployment rate of 6.9 per cent, 535,000 jobs if the state unemployment rate were comparable to the U.S. unemployment rate (5 per cent), or 570,000 jobs if Michigan is to achieve the unemployment rate of 4 per cent assumed in the projections

[Editors' note: The labor force consists of the unemployed plus the employed. From Table IV-11 we see that the labor force projection in Michigan for 1970 is 3,494,000, which includes the 500,000 decennial increase. If the unemployment rate in 1970 were to be equal to the 1960 unemployment rate of 6.9 per cent, then the number of new jobs created during the interval 1960-70 would be 100 per cent less 6.9 per cent, or 93.1 per cent of the decennial increase in the labor force. This amounts to approximately 470,000 new jobs.

If, however, the unemployment rate drops during the decade to 5 per cent, sufficient new jobs would have had to be created to employ 95 per cent of the 500,000 increment to the labor force in addition to 1.9 per cent (6.9 per cent minus 5 per cent) of the original labor force before the increment was added. This amounts to about 535,000 new jobs (95 per cent of 500,000 plus 1.9 per cent of 2,990,000). By similar calculation a drop in the rate of unemployment to 4 per cent by 1970 would require approximately 570,000 new jobs (90 per cent of 500,000 plus 2.9 per cent of 2,990,000).]

contained in Chapter II. Given the projections of motor vehicles, it is possible to estimate the contribution of the auto industry to the creation of new jobs in the state.

Three factors determine the additional number of jobs in the automobile industry for Michigan: future production levels, the number of motor vehicles produced per person in the industry, and Michigan's share of the national industry. By 1970 it is expected that the annual production of motor vehicles will be 10.1 million.

The number of vehicles produced per worker is a highly variable item influenced by total production for a given year as well as by technological advance. In 1955, a good auto year, there were 2.7 more vehicles produced per worker than in 1952, a poor year for the industry. In more recent years, we find that in 1960 there were 9.3 vehicles produced per industry worker and that in 1962 and 1963 the ratio was approximately 10.2 Future output per worker is dictated by the demand for the product and by the introduction of automated equipment. Some writers have argued that the auto industry will be a particular target of automation because of the high wage rates in the industry. However, as others have noted, the nature of particular operations and the emphasis on frequent restyling will inhibit increased automation in the industry. Even with modest increases in per capita output, the production of 11 cars per worker per year appears to be only a few years away. With high demand, the industry may be capable of approximating the figure today. The industrial projections shown in Chapter II imply an output of about 11.3 vehicles per worker by 1976.

Michigan's share of employment in the automobile industry has declined from 63 per cent of the national employment in 1940, to 55 per cent in 1950, and to 45 per cent in 1960. Since 1960 its share has fluctuated between 43 and 45 per cent. Many of the advantages of size which the state earlier possessed because the industry was founded here have gradually been lost. The westward movement of population and subsequent development of new large markets required that the product be shipped greater distances. In addition, there is some evidence showing that value added per production man-hour in the industry has been advancing more rapidly in Michigan than in other parts of the country. That is, the substitution of other factors of production for labor has been carried out at a more rapid rate in the state.[20] These trends argue for a continuation of the long-term decline of Michigan's share of the automobile industry—occasional announcements of the establishing of new small plants in the state, such as we have just heard from General Motors, notwithstanding.

The number of new jobs in Michigan likely to be created in the automobile industry by 1970 is shown in Table IV-19. All figures in the table are based on the assumption that production will amount to 10.1 million vehicles. Each cell of the table represents an additional pair of assumptions about Michigan's share of the industry and vehicles per worker. If Michigan's share of the industry by 1970 were 45 per cent, and if there were 10 vehicles produced per worker (less than the current levels), then we could expect the state to have a net increase of 77,000 jobs in the industry between 1960 and 1970. Focusing on what now appears to be a pair of more realistic assumptions, 10.5 cars per worker and 42.5 per cent of the industry, we should expect that 32,000 additional jobs would be created. One combination which cannot be ruled out implies a decline in the number of auto industry jobs, even with the high production anticipated for 1970.

Table IV-19

ADDITIONAL AUTOMOBILE INDUSTRY JOBS IN MICHIGAN—1970
(Assumed Production of 10.1 Million Vehicles)

Michigan's Share of National Employment (Per Cent)	Motor Vehicles Produced per Worker		
	10.0	10.5	11.0
45.0	77,000	56,000	36,000
42.5	52,000	32,000	13,000
40.0	27,000	8,000	-10,000

[20]Stephen Sobotka, *Profile of Michigan* (Glencoe, Ill.: The Free Press, 1963).

With a state requirement of well over a half-million jobs by 1970, it should be clear that we cannot rely on a healthy auto industry to solve the job problem facing the state. A net addition of 30,000 to 40,000 jobs is well under 10 per cent of the number of jobs needed by 1970.

There is no simple multiplier for estimating the total number of jobs which will be created as a result of the net additions to the auto industry. In 1960 the state had a total of 6.23 other kinds of jobs for every job in the auto industry. Obviously, it does not require six additional jobs to support each additional auto worker. When one considers the indirect effects of additions to the auto industry, one needs to take into account other manufacturing activities which act as suppliers to the industry, and service functions required to support the manufacturing population. Unfortunately, the available manufacturing data are not tabulated in the detail required to segregate suppliers of the auto industry. In gross terms it would appear that less than two other types of jobs are necessary to support the addition of each worker to the auto industry.[21] Given the poor multiplier estimates, it is still apparent that only a small fraction of the required growth in jobs will come directly or indirectly from the automobile industry. Any tendency of state leaders to think that because the future of the auto industry appears secure they can relax in their efforts to attract new industry represents poor judgment.

If not through the auto industry, how does a state create more than a half-million jobs required by its population? In an attempt to answer this question, let us return to the conditions that existed in 1940. At that time, Michigan was in an unusually

[21]For each auto worker it is estimated that the number of manufacturing suppliers is .25. For every person engaged in manufacturing activity in Michigan there are 1.27 persons engaged in nonmanufacturing activity. The estimate of the number of service workers generated by each addition to the auto industry is $1.25 \times 1.27 = 1.59$. Adding the .25 manufacturing suppliers yields a total of 1.84 jobs associated with the creation of each job in the auto industry. The apparent precision of the figures should not mislead the reader. A firm estimate of the number of manufacturing supplier workers cannot be made with the available data. Moreover, all service activity is not directed at the local population.

advantageous position with respect to developments for the next fifteen years. The state's heavy commitment to the motor vehicle industry, metals, and nonelectrical machinery was ideally suited to the events of the period, including the two wars and the consequent backlog of demand for autos. Between 1940 and 1953 more than 150,000 jobs were created by the auto industry alone. To understand developments in this period more clearly, we will use the technique of dividing local growth, in terms of the number of people employed, into three additive components: (1) the national all-industry growth element; (2) the industrial composition element; and (3) the competitive element. This type of division is frequently called shift analysis and is the subject of Chapter V by Lowell Ashby.[22] To explain these three components, one more term will be introduced, *expected growth*. The expected growth in the number of jobs for a local area, say Michigan, is simply the sum of the national growth rates of individual industries applied to the number of persons employed in those industries in Michigan. If the state consisted of two industries, one employing 60 persons and one employing 40 persons, and if the national growth rates for those industries were 40 per cent and 15 per cent, then the expected growth rate for Michigan would be 30 per cent (60 x .40/100 + 40 x .15/100 = .30).

The three growth components can now be defined. The national all-industry growth element is the rate of growth for the total civilian employment. For example, between 1950 and 1960 the number of civilians employed in the United States grew by 14.5 per cent. The industrial composition element is the expected growth rate for a local area minus the national growth rate. When a local area has its labor concentrated in high-growth industries, this element is positive, reflecting an advantageous mix of industry. The competitive element is the actual rate of growth minus the expected rate of growth. If this

[22]The use of "shift analysis" as a means of describing economic change is becoming a frequently used tool in analysis. For example see: Raymond Vernon, *Metropolis 1985* (Cambridge, Mass.: Harvard Univ. Press, 1960); and Harvey Perloff *et al.*, *Regions, Resources, and Economic Growth* (Baltimore, Md.: Johns Hopkins Univ. Press, 1960).

element is positive it means that, given the industrial composition of the local area, more jobs have been created than would be expected on the basis of national trends within individual industries.

It can be seen how the actual growth rate of an area can be divided into its three components:

ACTUAL	=	NATIONAL	+	COMPOSITION	+	COMPETITION
	=	(national)	+	(expected minus national)	+	(actual minus expected)

Each of the three growth components has been derived for the periods 1940-50 and 1950-60, and projected for 1960-70, the projections being based on the projections of industry growth shown by Sonenblum in Chapter II. This type of analysis, done in greater detail and applied to local areas of the state as well as to selected industrial sectors, is fully developed in Chapter V. The industrial classification used in the analysis presented here is taken from the Census Bureau's two-digit classification system. It involves the use of thirty-four industry categories as follows:

Primary Industry	Secondary Industry		Tertiary Industry
	Durable	Nondurable	
Agriculture, forestry, fishing	Stone, clay, glass	Food	Transportation
Mining	Metals	Tobacco	Communication
Construction	Nonelectrical machinery	Textiles	Utilities
	Electrical machinery	Apparel	Wholesale
	Motor vehicles	Lumber	Retail
	Other transportation	Furniture	Finance, insurance, real estate
	Instruments	Paper	Business services
	Other manufacturing	Printing and publishing	Private household service
		Chemicals	Other service
		Petroleum	Public administration
		Rubber and plastic	Industries not reported
		Leather	

When this category system is used to analyze the three components of growth in the number of civilians employed in the state, the following results are obtained:

	1940-50	1950-60
National all-industry	+459,000	+348,000
Composition	+162,000	+ 17,000
Competition	- 51,000	- 30,000
Total	570,000	335,000

Of primary interest are the results dealing with the competitive and compositional effects. In both decades Michigan lost about 9 per cent of the increase in employed through competition with other areas. When the loss for 1940-50 is examined in detail by industry, it is found that there were actually some competitive gains in tertiary industry while the competitive losses were concentrated in manufacturing. The small gains in the service sector indicate that the state was slowly changing in the direction of an economy more comparable to the national economy. But since the competitive gains in these activities amounted to only 20,000 jobs, the state was not moving at a very rapid rate. In the manufacturing industries Michigan's experience was extremely varied. Most durable goods industries gained competitively, whereas most nondurable industries lost competitively. The exceptions to this pattern were major ones, however. Competitive losses in the auto industry were very large, as were losses in electrical machinery. The former loss reflects the decentralization of the industry, which perhaps cannot be prevented. All told, losses in the auto industry were greater than the total competitive loss of the state. The competitive loss pattern of 1950-60 was almost identical with that of the previous decade—competitive gains in service industries, losses in the nondurables, and gains in the durables with the same two exceptions of autos and electrical machinery. Again, autos could more than account for the entire competitive loss of the state. Michigan's failure to attract nondurable industries is probably related to the relatively low wage rates in those industries, coupled with the generally high wage rates in the state. This is a mixed blessing. Nondurable manufacturing was a relatively slow-growing industry during the 1950's, and it is expected to continue to grow at a slow pace in the future.

The compositional dimension of the shift analysis is also revealing with respect to the changing conditions in the state. In 1940-50, the industry mix accounted for more than 28 per cent of the job increase during the decade. By the following decade, the mix had deteriorated to the point of accounting for only 5 per cent of the job increase. This means that in 1940 the state had a very favorable industrial distribution with respect to those industries which experienced rapid growth during the decade. Michigan's heavy concentration in durable goods manufacturing turned out most satisfactorily because the growth rate of employment in durables was twice the growth rate of all civilian employment. In particular, the rapid growth rate of the auto industry (50 per cent) contributed to the favorable composition. In the 1950-60 decade the number employed in the auto industry actually declined nationally, so that concentration in this industry was largely responsible for the decline in the favorable composition of the state. As of 1950, in terms of composition, Michigan was about at par with the nation although its industrial profile was very different from the nation's. The concentration in autos and the relatively small proportions in services produce negative balances in the ledger of composition, while the concentration in other durables and the relatively small numbers in agriculture and nondurables produce positive balances.

In reviewing these data, one is certainly given the impression that the favorable industry mix of 1940 was artificial, linked as it was to the war and the delayed demand for cars. In other respects it is also apparent that the industry mix of the state is not as poor as is sometimes suggested. What has happened between 1940 and 1960 is that the industrial profile of the state has remained fairly stable (see Table IV-20), whereas the U.S. profile has been subject to greater change, and the industries identified as growth industries have shifted. Perhaps the cries of the pessimists are related more closely to relative than to absolute stagnation.

An evaluation of Michigan's current industry mix can be obtained by assuming that some model of industry growth will yield accurate predictions of the future. For this purpose, I have relied on the industry projections to 1976 provided in Chapter II. These projections of growth rate by industry have

Table IV-20

INDUSTRIAL DISTRIBUTION OF EMPLOYED LABOR FORCE IN MICHIGAN, 1940–60

Industry	1960 (Per Cent)	1950 (Per Cent)	1940 (Per Cent)
All primary	4.1	7.5	13.0
All secondary	44.0	46.6	43.3
Construction	4.7	5.0	4.1
Durable manufacturing	29.8	32.6	29.6
Nondurable manufacturing	9.5	9.0	9.6
All tertiary	51.9	45.9	43.7
Transportation and public utilities	5.9	6.5	5.6
Wholesale and retail	18.4	17.7	16.2
Finance, insurance, real estate	3.4	2.7	2.7
Other services	20.6	15.9	16.5
Public administration	3.6	3.1	2.7
Total	100.0	100.0	100.0

been applied to the 1960 industrial distribution of the United States and Michigan. The results indicate that expected growth in Michigan during 1960-70 is virtually identical with expected national growth. If these data are converted to the dimensions of shift analysis, they indicate that the 1960 Michigan industry mix will provide a compositional benefit of only 12,000 jobs, or roughly 2-3 per cent of the total jobs added.[23] It appears that

[23]An alternative industry growth model was also used in the shift analysis for 1960-70. The major industry projections currently being used by the Bureau of Labor Statistics show that expected growth in Michigan is about the same as expected growth in the nation, the same results obtained by using the industry projections of Chapter II. See U. S. Bureau of Labor Statistics, "Employment Projections by Industry and Occupation, 1960-1975," *Special Labor Force Report* No. 28 (Washington: Government Printing Office, March, 1963).

the compositional advantage which was enjoyed by the state in 1940 and which disappeared by 1950 will also be nonexistent during the coming decade.

It is impossible to obtain a measure of the competitive dimension for 1960-70, because such a measure involves a comparison of the actual and the expected growth in jobs. If the state follows the pattern of the past two decades, by losing about 9 per cent of the total jobs created, then the competitive loss could amount to 40,000 - 50,000 jobs. Given a need for approximately 60,000 jobs beyond the national growth level to close the gap in unemployment between the state and the nation, the state would require a compositional advantage of about 100,000 jobs to keep unemployment no higher than the national level and fill the jobs required by a population subject to net migration of zero.

The picture sketched at this point begins to bear an almost perverse resemblance to the middle years of the last decade. The auto industry has had two good years and is likely to experience an even better one this year. If this results in a heavy in-migration, the state may again find itself in economic difficulties. During the past several years, migration has functioned as a safety valve. The labor force has remained relatively constant in number, and unemployment has been reduced. From the projections it appears that the industrial profile of the state cannot bear the burden of in-migration.

Next year will be, for the state, the key year of the decade. After three successive high-production years in the auto industry and low levels of unemployment, we may have the first heavy in-migration in nearly ten years. It appears to me that current production levels in the auto industry are somewhat higher than the long-term demand would suggest. In this case, the 1965 production of vehicles may be adjusted downward. Add to this an unprecedented number of 18-year-olds attempting to enter college and the labor market. In combination, these more or less probable events represent a major obstacle in the economic future of the state. If we survive 1965, then we will approach Michigan in the mid-seventies with our most difficult problems solved.

Table IV-Appendix 1

DETAILED PROJECTIONS OF POPULATION OF MICHIGAN BY AGE AND SEX, 1965–80
(In Thousands)

Age	1965			1970			1975			1980		
	Male	Female	Total	Male	Female	Total	Male	Female	Total	Male	Female	Total
0–4	452	435	887	442	425	867	511	491	1,002	583	560	1,143
5–9	491	475	966	450	433	883	440	424	864	509	490	999
10–14	448	428	876	490	474	964	449	433	882	439	423	862
15–19	378	365	743	446	427	873	488	473	961	447	432	879
20–24	276	286	562	375	364	739	443	426	869	484	472	956
25–29	208	239	447	274	285	559	372	363	735	439	425	864
30–34	229	243	472	207	238	445	271	284	555	369	361	730
35–39	264	271	535	227	242	469	205	237	442	269	282	551
40–44	268	280	548	260	269	529	223	239	462	201	235	436
45–49	242	254	496	261	275	536	253	264	517	217	235	452
50–54	221	226	447	231	247	478	249	268	517	242	257	499
55–59	187	192	379	205	217	422	215	238	453	232	257	489
60–64	162	166	328	167	181	348	184	204	388	192	224	416
65–69	124	133	257	137	151	288	142	164	306	155	186	341
70–74	95	109	204	97	114	211	106	130	236	110	141	251
75–79	60	74	134	66	86	152	67	90	157	74	102	176
80–84	29	41	70	35	49	84	38	57	95	39	60	99
85+	13	23	36	16	28	44	19	34	53	21	40	61
Total	4,147	4,240	8,387	4,386	4,505	8,891	4,675	4,819	9,494	5,022	5,182	10,204

Table IV-Appendix 2

PROJECTIONS OF POPULATION IN MICHIGAN COUNTIES, 1960-80

	1960	1965	1970	1975	1980
Michigan	7,823,194	8,387,000	8,891,000	9,494,000	10,204,000
Alcona	6,352	6,400	6,100	6,400	6,500
Alger	9,250	8,600	7,800	7,700	7,700
Allegan	57,729	61,300	64,000	67,000	70,900
Alpena	28,556	31,300	33,400	35,600	38,200
Antrim	10,373	9,900	9,200	9,000	9,100
Arenac	9,860	9,600	9,200	9,100	9,300
Baraga	7,151	6,500	5,800	5,600	5,500
Barry	31,738	33,600	35,100	36,700	39,000
Bay	107,042	113,500	118,100	123,500	130,600
Benzie	7,834	7,400	6,800	6,600	6,600
Berrien	149,865	164,400	176,900	188,300	202,500
Branch	34,903	36,100	36,800	38,200	39,700
Calhoun	138,858	143,400	145,400	150,100	156,700
Cass	36,932	40,700	44,100	47,000	50,700
Charlevoix	13,421	12,900	12,200	12,200	12,200
Cheboygan	14,550	14,400	14,100	14,200	14,700
Chippewa	32,655	33,200	33,300	34,200	35,400
Clare	11,647	11,900	12,100	12,400	13,000
Clinton	37,969	40,300	42,100	44,100	46,700
Crawford	4,971	5,300	5,400	5,600	5,900
Delta	34,298	33,600	32,500	32,800	33,600
Dickinson	23,917	22,600	21,100	20,900	21,000
Eaton	49,684	53,300	56,200	59,100	63,000
Emmet	15,904	14,900	14,100	13,800	13,900
Genesee	374,313	413,400	450,800	494,600	540,000
Gladwin	10,769	11,100	11,200	11,600	11,900
Gogebic	24,370	22,300	20,000	19,600	19,300
Grand Traverse	33,490	34,800	35,700	37,000	38,900
Gratiot	37,012	37,500	37,300	38,200	39,500
Hillsdale	34,742	34,900	34,500	35,100	36,200
Houghton	35,654	32,400	29,200	28,600	28,100
Huron	34,006	33,200	31,800	32,000	32,400
Ingham	211,296	238,000	267,000	298,600	331,900
Ionia	43,132	44,200	44,400	45,700	47,400
Iosco	16,505	19,500	22,800	25,300	28,400
Iron	17,184	16,300	15,200	15,200	15,200
Isabella	35,348	37,700	39,300	41,200	43,600
Jackson	131,994	140,700	147,100	154,200	163,500
Kalamazoo	169,712	189,200	207,100	216,000	234,400
Kalkaska	4,382	4,100	3,700	3,700	3,700

Table IV-Appendix 2 *(Continued)*

	1960	1965	1970	1975	1980
Kent	363,187	392,700	416,900	440,500	470,500
Keweenaw	2,417	2,200	1,800	1,700	1,700
Lake	5,338	5,200	4,900	4,900	5,000
Lapeer	41,926	43,700	44,700	46,400	48,700
Leelanau	9,321	9,300	9,100	9,200	9,500
Lenawee	77,789	82,200	85,300	89,100	94,000
Livingston	38,233	44,100	50,000	54,600	60,200
Luce	7,827	7,400	6,800	6,800	6,800
Mackinac	10,853	11,300	11,600	12,000	12,600
Macomb	405,804	532,100	669,300	829,800	1,003,900
Manistee	19,042	18,600	17,800	17,900	18,300
Marquette	56,154	58,700	60,300	62,700	65,800
Mason	21,929	21,800	21,300	21,600	22,200
Mecosta	21,051	21,400	21,200	21,700	22,400
Menominee	24,685	23,600	22,000	21,800	22,000
Midland	51,450	59,500	67,700	74,100	82,000
Missaukee	6,784	6,100	5,600	5,600	5,400
Monroe	101,120	112,500	123,100	132,100	143,300
Montcalm	35,795	37,100	37,700	39,100	40,700
Montmorency	4,424	4,400	4,400	4,500	4,600
Muskegon	149,943	160,400	168,700	177,300	188,400
Newaygo	24,160	24,700	24,600	25,300	26,200
Oakland	690,259	808,200	905,500	1,014,100	1,132,000
Oceana	16,547	16,200	15,500	15,600	15,800
Ogemaw	9,680	9,600	9,200	9,200	9,400
Ontonagon	10,584	10,300	9,900	9,900	10,100
Osceola	13,595	13,000	12,300	12,200	12,200
Oscoda	3,447	3,500	3,500	3,500	3,700
Otsego	7,545	7,900	8,100	8,400	8,800
Ottawa	98,719	110,000	120,500	129,200	140,300
Presque Isle	13,117	13,200	13,200	13,500	13,900
Roscommon	7,200	7,700	8,000	8,400	8,900
Saginaw	190,752	204,800	216,000	228,500	244,400
St. Clair	107,201	111,600	114,200	118,500	124,300
St. Joseph	42,332	44,900	46,600	48,700	51,500
Sanilac	32,314	31,800	30,900	31,100	31,800
Schoolcraft	8,953	8,600	8,000	8,100	8,000
Shiawassee	53,446	55,400	56,700	58,600	61,400
Tuscola	43,305	44,500	44,700	46,000	47,900
Van Buren	48,395	51,900	54,500	57,300	60,900
Washtenaw	172,440	196,200	227,600	261,400	292,200
Wayne	2,666,297	2,716,600	2,755,800	2,819,800	2,908,800
Wexford	18,466	17,700	16,600	16,600	16,700

V

MICHIGAN: PROLOGUE AND PROSPECT[1]

Lowell D. Ashby

The Michigan economy, like those of other states, is a complex of interrelated industrial commitments. These commitments, past and present, constitute a prologue to as yet unwritten chapters of economic change. But just as a man's past acts condition what he will be able to do, so the industrial prologue helps to shape Michigan's industrial future.

Michigan has been an industrial leader in a national economy which for a century and a half has undergone an acceleration in its pace of technological change. It is evident today that this acceleration will itself be accelerated. The outlook is for an era of radical change without precedent which transcends mere quantitative interpretation.

Many are justly concerned about whether men and their institutions can accommodate so much change. Men, after all, require some measure of order and security. There must remain both ethical and aesthetic norms for distinguishing those changes which are tolerable from those which are not.

Whether a change is tolerable or not, good or bad, large or small is often determined by its setting or background. For example, the industrial environment for the manufacture of motor vehicles has long been national in scope. In the 1940's the total national employment (all industries) surged upward by

[1]The technical discussion and empirical applications in this chapter as well as in the Appendix are largely drawn from Lowell D. Ashby, "Regional Change in a National Setting," Staff Working Paper in Economics and Statistics, No. 7, U. S., Department of Commerce (Washington, April, 1964). As with the staff paper, the views, techniques, and terminology do not necessarily represent those of the Department of Commerce.

Although they do not necessarily share my views, I wish to thank John M. Mattila, Robert E. Graham, Jr., and Edgar S. Dunn, Jr. for their critical reviews and comments.

nearly 27 per cent. But in this same interval employment in the manufacture of motor vehicles and motor vehicle equipment increased by more than 51 per cent. In this industry Michigan's growth rate amounted to nearly 34 per cent, or about 17 percentage points below the industry pace for the nation as a whole. (This experience is graphically summarized in Figure V-1.) In the 1940's Michigan was able to increase its employment from 355,700 to 474,900 despite the fact that Michigan's growth lagged within the motor vehicle industry. The increase came about because the state was heavily committed to an industry which was gaining on an entire economy, and the economy itself was in a rapid expansion phase. The net effect was a large growth of 119,200 in Michigan's employment in the manufacture of motor vehicles and motor vehicle equipment, as shown in the left-hand panel of the chart.

Employment Shift Analysis, 1940–60

The question naturally arises: "What would have happened to employment in motor vehicles in Michigan if the national growth pace had been slower and if the motor vehicle industry nationally had been a slow-growth industry?" The decade of the 1950's answers this question for us. In over-all national employment the growth pace declined from 27 per cent for the decade of the 1940's to 15 per cent for the decade of the 1950's. And while the pace of national growth for motor vehicles in the 1940's had been 51 per cent, in the decade of the 1950's it dropped below zero to a negative 3 per cent. Michigan again fell behind the national growth rate in motor vehicles employment--and again by about 17 percentage points. In the second decade Michigan registered more than a 20 per cent decline in motor vehicle employment, or a decline of 97,800, as shown in the middle panel of Figure V-1.

The 119,200 gain of the 1940's, less the 97,800 loss of the 1950's, left Michigan with a modest 21,400 net gain for the 1940-60 period, as shown in the right-hand panel. This increase was not as large, however, as it would have been had the employment in the motor vehicle industry in Michigan increased at the national rate in this industry over the two decades. In summary,

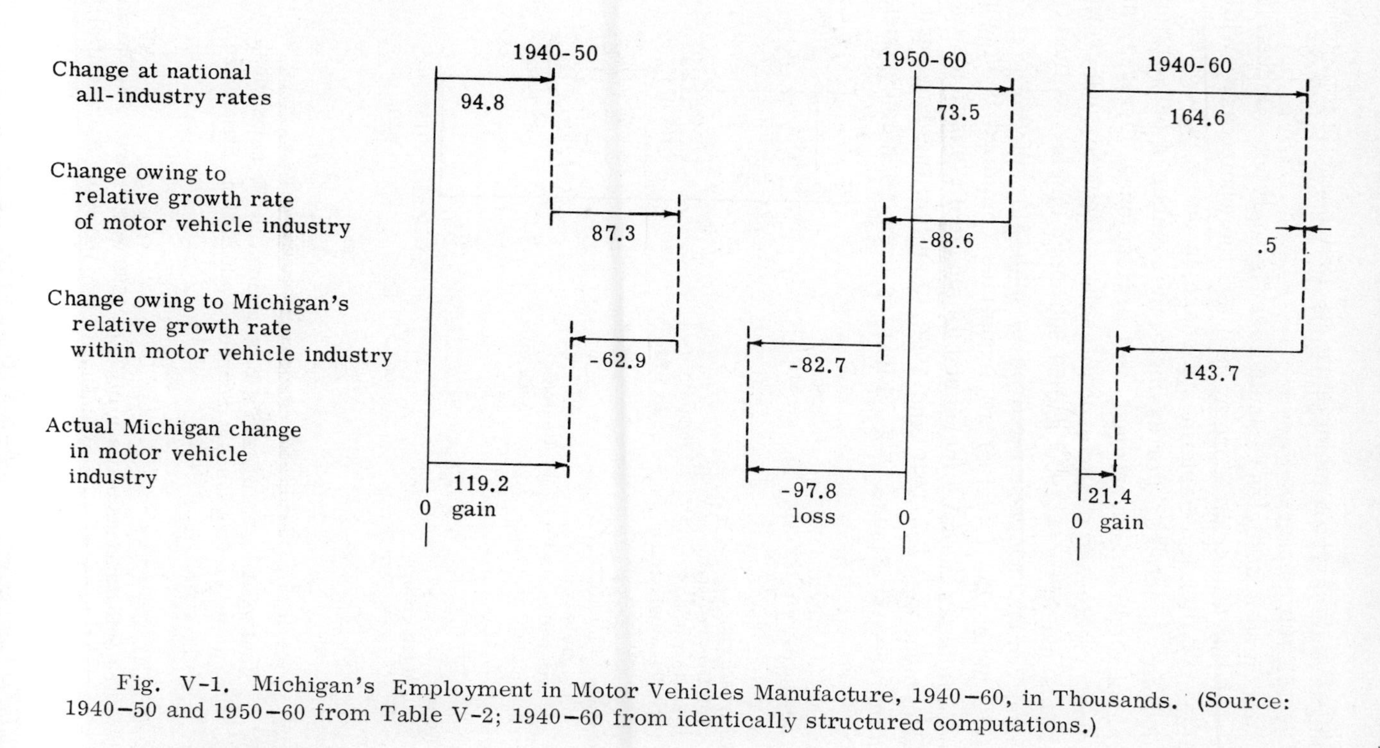

Fig. V-1. Michigan's Employment in Motor Vehicles Manufacture, 1940–60, in Thousands. (Source: 1940–50 and 1950–60 from Table V-2; 1940–60 from identically structured computations.)

Michigan fell short of maintaining its 1940 share in the industry by 143,700 employees.[2]

But motor vehicles manufacture is only one industrial layer of the Michigan economy and not the whole cake. While Michigan failed to maintain its share in some industries, it made gains in others. For example, the number of persons engaged in medical, educational, and professional services (including private and public school teachers) showed such growth that this category in 1960 had 50,300 more employees than the number which had been required to maintain Michigan's 1940 share. When the effect of all industries combined is considered, Michigan actually increased its share of the nation's total employment between 1940 and 1960. Just how this happened is summarized in Figure V-2. First, if each Michigan industry

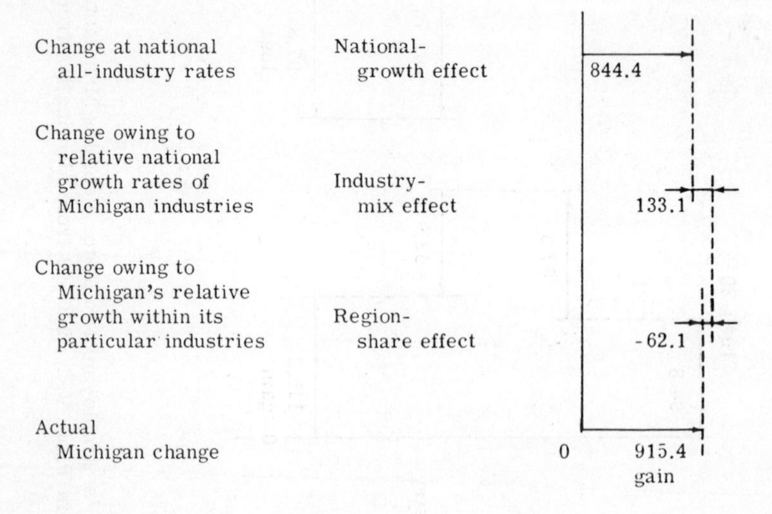

Fig. V-2. Michigan's Employment in 31 Industries, 1940–60, in Thousands. (Source: Computations Structured as in Table V-2.)

[2]The actual change between 1940 and 1960 was 21,400. The change at the national industry rate would have been 165,100. The shortfall was 143,700. This is explained by the difference between the Michigan rate of increase in the industry (6.0 per cent) and that in the nation (46.4).

had grown at the national rate of growth for all industries combined, employment would have increased by 344,400. Second, Michigan was fortunate in that over the two-decade period its economy happened to be specialized in industries whose national growth rates were higher than the national rate for all industries combined. This happy industry mix accounted for an added 133,100 employees. Third, within its industries, Michigan's growth rate was often slower than the national rate for those industries. On balance Michigan lost employees because of failure to maintain the growth pace characteristic of the industries to which it was committed. This failure cost Michigan about 62,100 employees.

Considering all of the elements of change, Michigan's actual employment growth over the two decades was 915,400. The industry mix gains were stronger than the competitive or region-share losses. Thus, on balance, Michigan had 71,000 (915,400 less 844,400) employees in excess of the number required to maintain its 1940 share of the nation's total.[3]

After looking at Michigan as a complex of industries, it is instructive to view it as a group of communities each with its own complex or industry mix.

Michigan is logically divisible into four large economic communities or areas:

Area 1. Three counties in the Detroit Standard Metropolitan Statistical Area (S.M.S.A.)[4]

[3]The following tabulation shows the performance of each state in the Great Lakes region for the 1940's, the 1950's, and the two-decade span. Employment excesses (+) or shortages (-) in terms of the number required to maintain beginning-of-period share are shown.

	1940-50	1950-60	1940-60
Michigan	+92.4	- 35.8	+ 71.0
Ohio	+97.5	- 20.8	+ 91.7
Indiana	+62.0	- 29.7	+ 41.8
Illinois	-59.6	-194.7	-263.7
Wisconsin	+14.0	- 94.0	- 77.7

[4]As of 1960, as defined in U. S., Executive Office of the President (Kennedy), Bureau of the Budget, *Standard Metropolitan Statistical Areas* (Washington: Government Printing Office, 1961).

Area 2. Eleven counties in other S.M.S.A.'s

Area 3. Fifty-four counties in Lower Peninsula, nonmetropolitan (non-S.M.S.A.) areas

Area 4. Fifteen counties in the Upper Peninsula

The analysis of the 20-year growth in employment for these Michigan county clusters is set out in Figure V-3. Not surprisingly, since it accounted for nearly half of the state's employment, the Detroit area's growth behavior over the period had features that were characteristic of the entire state: positive industry-mix effects and negative competitive or share-of-industry effects. The three other communities were different in their growth response. Area 2 exhibited both industry-mix and competitive gains; Area 3 showed negative industry-mix and positive competitive response; and Area 4 lost ground because of its industry mix, based largely on agriculture, forestry and fisheries, and mining, as well as its competitive performance within this mix.

The separate industries of a state (or for that matter the separate industries of its counties or other areas) can be given similar analytical treatment. The areas and industries of Michigan are placed on common analytical ground for both the 1940's and the 1950's in Table V-2 below.

As will be seen, each of Michigan's areas increased its employment in the 1940's. In the 1950's each showed an increase, with the exception of the Upper Peninsula. Turning to major industry groups, only agriculture, forestry and fisheries, and mining showed employment losses in both decades. The only other identified loss in Table V-2 is that for motor vehicles and motor vehicles equipment manufacture in the decade of the 1950's. Losses in this industry in the 1950's, however, are more than made up by gains in manufacturing industries which supply the parts, materials, and services needed to produce motor vehicles. Among the products which are indirectly involved in the production and marketing of motor vehicles are other transportation equipment, machinery, metals, chemicals, rubber products, and petroleum products.

For every area and every industry it is possible to pose the same questions concerning the make-up of the measured change.

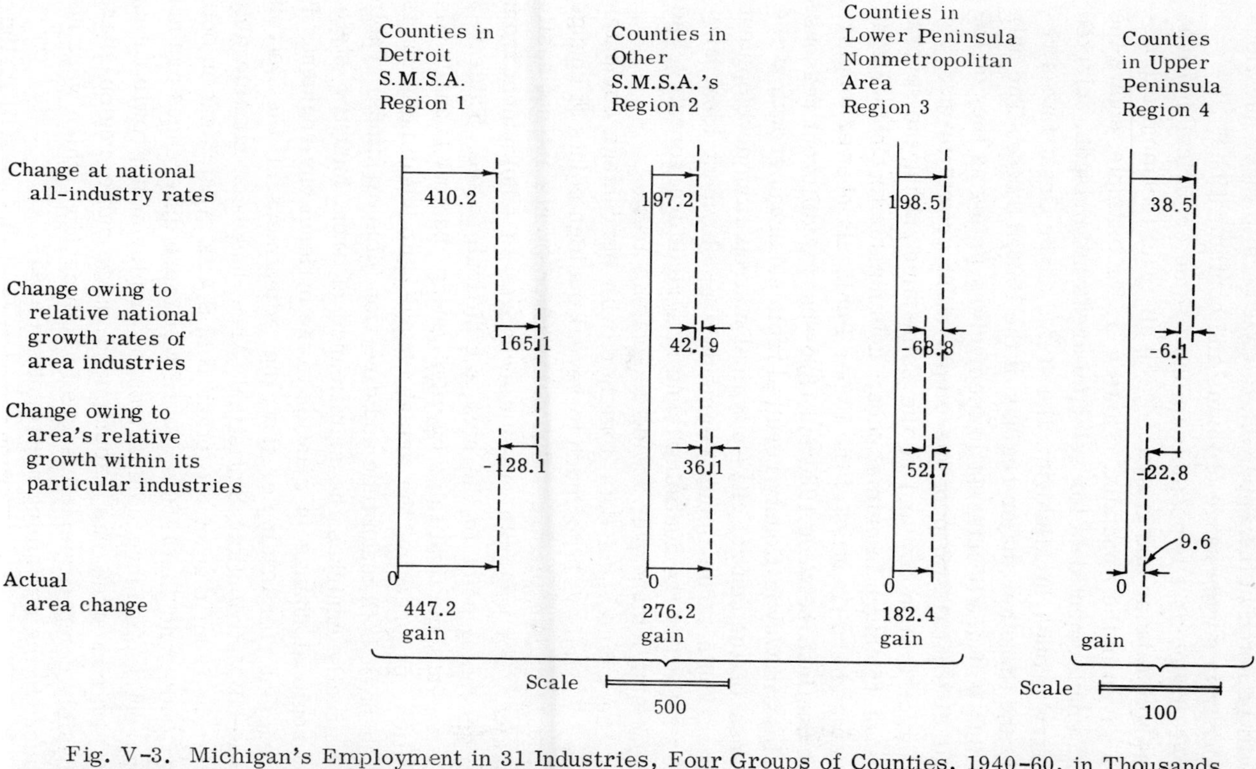

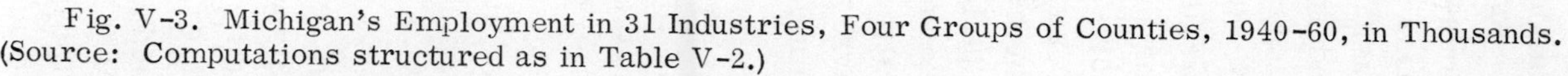
Fig. V-3. Michigan's Employment in 31 Industries, Four Groups of Counties, 1940–60, in Thousands.
(Source: Computations structured as in Table V-2.)

As will be noted in the Appendix, the answers to these questions can occur in a wide range of forms and configurations.

At this point it is possible to show some empirical applications, both tabular and graphic, of the abstract technical expositions given in the Appendix. Table V-1, for example, shows the basic employment data for selected areas in Michigan, selected industry groups in Michigan, the states of the Great Lakes region, and the other major regions of the United States. The data of Table V-1 are of interest in themselves, giving as they do the broad historical sweep of the employment growth process for the nation's economy and at the same time putting the several parts of Michigan in prime focus. It is notable that both Wayne County and the counties of the Upper Peninsula showed employment declines between 1950 and 1960—but for different reasons. The loss in Wayne County resulted from suburban growth at the expense of the central city--a typical metropolitan development in the 1950's. The Upper Peninsula's employment loss, however, reflected the declining trend in agriculture, forestry, and mining employment over a wide geographic area.

The employment data together with percentage computations in Table V-1 do much to reveal the high points of change in the Michigan picture. But some finer points are not easily detected. For example, absolute changes in employment from one decennial point to the next are difficult to see. Table V-2 supplements the first table by highlighting absolute changes. In addition, by breaking the actual change into meaningful parts which have both magnitude and direction (plus or minus), Table V-2 greatly enriches the significance of area, industry, state, and regional change in relation to the national environment. It is evident, for example, that the adjustment of the Detroit Standard Metropolitan Statistical Area has been considerably different from that of the other S.M.S.A.'s in Michigan in both the 1940's and the 1950's. Moreover these differences are not apparent from mere comparison of employment growth rates. The Detroit area has experienced unfavorable region-share (possibly competitive) influences in both decades which were not evident in the remaining metropolitan areas.

Graphic devices sharpen the picture of change still further. Figure V-4 shows how the elements of region share and industry mix can be viewed as a single point with a definite orientation in relation to the performance of the nation as a whole. Thus, points to the right and left of the vertical line represent positive and negative region-share performance, while points above and below the horizontal line represent positive and negative industry-mix adjustments. The intersection of the two major axes is at a zero, zero reference point which signifies any region with zero region share and zero industry-mix adjustment. The nation itself is always represented by such a reference (or vector) point when it is used as the standard of growth reference. This use of the nation corresponds to the zero entries for region-share and industry-mix effects on the last line of Table V-2.

Figure V-4 is also characterized by two sloping lines through the origin. The first of these is the positively sloped line marked *E*. This line represents the locus of all vector points representing equal region-share and industry-mix effects. The second is the negatively sloped line marked *O*. This line represents the locus of all vector points where the region-share (sometimes called "competitive") effect and the industry-mix effect sum to zero.

The lines described divide the chart space into eight octants centered at the zero, zero point. These octants are numbered 1 through 8 and provide a classification system of some utility for regions, states, counties, or combinations of such areas. Thus the single vector point for Michigan conveys two pieces of information previously shown in Figure V-2. It represents a negative region-share effect of 62,100 and a positive industry-mix effect of 133,100 for the twenty-year span, 1940 to 1960. Over this long period, then, Michigan was oriented to national growth in about the same way as all other regions whose vector points fell into octant 4.

In Figure V-4 every vector point above and to the right of the *O* line represents a region with a positive net total effect (sometimes called net total shift), while points below and to the left represent regions with negative net total effects. A corollary fact is that the horizontal (or vertical) distance of any vector point from the *O* line is a measure of the net total effect for the corresponding region. Thus the net total effect for Michigan

Table V-1

EMPLOYMENT AND PERCENTAGE CHANGE, UNITED STATES AND SELECTED AREAS, 1940, 1950, AND 1960

		Employees* (In Thousands)			Change (Per Cent)		
		1940	1950	1960	1940–50	1950–60	1940–60
Wayne County†		764.8	984.4	955.7	28.7	- 0.0‡	25.0
Oakland County†		86.5	147.1	241.2	70.1	64.0	178.8
Macomb County†		35.5	66.3	137.2	86.8	106.9	286.5
Detroit S.M.S.A.‖	(3 Cos.)	886.8	1,197.8	1,334.1	35.1	11.4	50.4
Other S.M.S.A.'s	(11 Cos.)	426.2	580.5	702.4	36.2	21.0	64.8
Lower Pen., nonmetropolitan	(54 Cos.)	428.8	531.5	611.2	24.0	15.0	42.5
Upper Peninsula	(15 Cos.)	83.2	94.2	92.7	13.2	- 0.0§	11.4
Michigan	(83 Cos.)	1,825.0	2,404.0	2,740.4	31.7	14.0	50.2
Agric., forestry, fisheries		216.1	162.0	93.7	- 25.0	- 42.2	- 56.7
Mining		15.9	15.5	15.3	- 1.9	- 1.3	- 3.2
Construction		73.1	118.4	125.6	61.9	6.0	71.7
Mfg., motor vehicles and equipment		355.7	474.9	377.1	33.5	- 20.6	6.0
Mfg., other		344.3	503.4	658.7	46.2	30.9	91.3
Railroads, trucking, other utilities		114.8	172.7	173.3	50.4	0.3#	50.9
Wholesale and retail trade		295.8	421.2	484.0	42.4	14.9	63.7
Services and professional (including education)		330.8	419.9	614.7	26.9	46.4	85.8
Public admin. and armed forces		55.1	84.3	108.4	52.9	28.7	96.8
Industry not reported		23.4	31.7	89.6	35.3	182.8	282.7

Table V-1 *(Continued)*

	Employees* (In Thousands)			Change (Per Cent)		
	1940	1950	1960	1940–50	1950–60	1940–60
Ohio	2,344.9	3,067.7	3,521.8	30.8	14.8	50.2
Indiana	1,151.7	1,520.8	1,726.5	32.0	13.5	49.9
Illinois	2,874.4	3,581.2	3,940.9	24.6	10.0	37.1
Wisconsin	1,060.8	1,357.6	1,473.8	28.0	8.6	38.8
Great Lakes states	9,256.8	11,931.3	13,403.4	28.9	12.3	44.8
New England states	3,060.1	3,661.2	4,137.9	19.6	13.0	35.2
Mideast states (includes Dist. of Columbia)	10,876.2	13,363.2	14,892.1	22.9	11.4	36.9
Plains states	4,513.5	5,378.9	5,683.3	19.2	5.7	25.9
Southeast states	9,878.3	11,913.4	13,414.1	20.6	12.6	35.8
Southwest states	3,087.5	4,091.5	5,055.6	32.5	23.6	63.7
Rocky Mountain states	929.4	1,264.1	1,558.3	36.0	23.3	67.7
Far West states (includes Alaska and Hawaii)	3,774.0	5,871.3	8,227.9	55.6	40.1	118.0
United States total	45,375.8	57,474.9	66,372.6	26.7	15.5	46.3

*Data are the result of summation across 31 temporally comparable industries.

†Since employment is indicated by place of residence rather than by place of work, changes in employment in small areas such as a county do not necessarily indicate accurately changes in the level of production within the area.

‡-0.029.

‖Standard Metropolitan Statistical Area as of 1960 as defined in accordance with criteria established by the Bureau of the Budget of the Executive Office of the President.

§-0.016.

#0.357.

Source: Employment data from the *U.S. Census of Population.*

Table V-2

COMPONENTS OF EMPLOYMENT CHANGE, UNITED STATES AND SELECTED AREAS, 1940–50 AND 1950–60*
(Thousands of Employees)

	1940–50					1950–60				
	Change at Natl. Rate	Industry Mix	Region Share	Actual Change	Code†	Change at Natl. Rate	Industry Mix	Region Share	Actual Change	Code†
Wayne County	203.9	124.7	-109.0	219.6	4	152.4	16.5	-197.6	28.7	5
Oakland County	23.1	11.5	26.0	60.6	1	22.8	1.3	70.0	94.1	1
Macomb County	9.5	5.9	15.4	30.8	1	10.2	1.4	59.2	70.8	1
Detroit S.M.S.A.	236.5	142.1	- 67.6	311.0	4	185.4	19.2	- 68.4	136.2	4
Other S.M.S.A.'s	113.6	35.3	5.4	154.3	1	89.9	12.4	19.6	121.9	1
Lower Pen., nonmetropolitan	114.3	- 33.2	21.6	102.7	6	82.3	- 19.5	17.0	79.8	8
Upper Peninsula	22.2	- 0.1	- 11.1	11.0	7	14.6	- 8.8	- 7.3	- 1.5	8
Michigan	486.6	144.1	- 51.7	579.0	4	372.2	3.3	- 39.1	336.4	5
Agric., forestry, fisheries	57.6	- 95.7	- 16.0	- 54.1	8	25.1	- 87.1	- 6.3	- 68.3	8
Mining	4.2	- 4.0	- 0.6	- 0.4	8	2.4	- 7.0	4.4	- 0.2	6
Construction	19.5	29.6	- 3.8	45.3	4	18.3	- 6.0	- 5.1	7.2	8
Mfg., motor vehicles and equipment	94.8	87.3	- 62.9	119.2	4	73.5	- 88.6	- 82.7	- 97.8	8
Mfg., other	91.8	58.3	9.0	159.1	2	77.9	57.6	19.8	155.3	2
Railroads, trucking, utilities	30.6	18.3	9.0	57.9	2	26.8	- 18.3	- 7.9	0.6	8
Wholesale and retail trade	78.9	37.2	9.3	125.4	2	65.2	- 17.3	14.9	62.8	6
Services and professional (including education)	88.2	- 15.2	16.1	89.1	3	65.0	94.2	35.6	194.8	2
Public admin. and armed forces	14.7	29.4	- 14.9	29.2	4	13.1	14.3	- 3.3	24.1	4
Industry not reported	6.3	- 1.1	3.1	8.3	1	4.9	61.5	- 8.5	57.9	4

Table V-2 *(Continued)*

	1940–50					1950–60				
	Change at Natl. Rate	Industry Mix	Region Share	Actual Change	Code†	Change at Natl. Rate	Industry Mix	Region Share	Actual Change	Code†
Ohio	625.3	148.7	- 51.2	722.8	4	474.9	124.1	- 144.9	454.1	5
Indiana	307.1	32.1	29.9	369.1	2	235.4	17.5	- 47.2	205.7	5
Illinois	766.4	213.3	- 272.9	706.8	5	554.4	166.9	- 361.6	359.7	5
Wisconsin	282.8	- 22.4	36.4	296.8	3	210.2	- 35.1	- 58.9	116.2	7
Great Lakes states	2,468.2	515.8	- 309.5	2,674.5	4	1,847.1	276.7	- 651.7	1,472.1	5
New England states	815.9	216.9	- 431.8	601.0	5	566.8	199.3	- 289.4	476.7	5
Mideast states	2,900.0	812.5	-1,225.5	2,487.0	5	2,068.8	754.0	-1,293.9	1,528.9	5
Plains states	1,203.5	- 309.9	- 28.2	865.4	8	832.6	- 320.3	- 207.9	304.4	8
Southeast states	2,634.0	-1,306.1	707.2	2,035.1	6	1,844.2	-1,057.3	713.8	1,500.7	6
Southwest states	823.3	- 218.8	399.4	1,003.9	3	633.4	- 101.4	432.1	964.1	3
Rocky Mountain states	247.8	- 32.0	119.0	334.8	3	195.8	- 64.7	163.1	294.2	3
Far West states	1,006.4	321.6	769.4	2,097.4	1	909.0	313.7	1,133.9	2,356.6	1
United States total	12,099.1	0.0	0.0	12,099.1	*i*	8,897.7	0.0	0.0	8,897.7	*i*

*Entries are the result of summation across analytical results for each of 31 industries. See also notes on Table V-1.

†Octant code designations are usually by number. Where vector points fall on lines separating octants, designations are by letter. Where the vector point falls at the intersection of the major axes, as for the United States when it is the analytical universe, the letter designation *i* is given.

Source: Basic data are from U.S. Bureau of the Census, *Census of Population* as indicated in Table V-1. Analytical results are from a computer production run on a one, zero base.

is illustrated graphically by the dotted horizontal line having a positive length of 71,000.

The nature of the analytical technique is such that if a vector were drawn for every one of the nation's constituent regions, then such vectors would graphically sum to the zero,

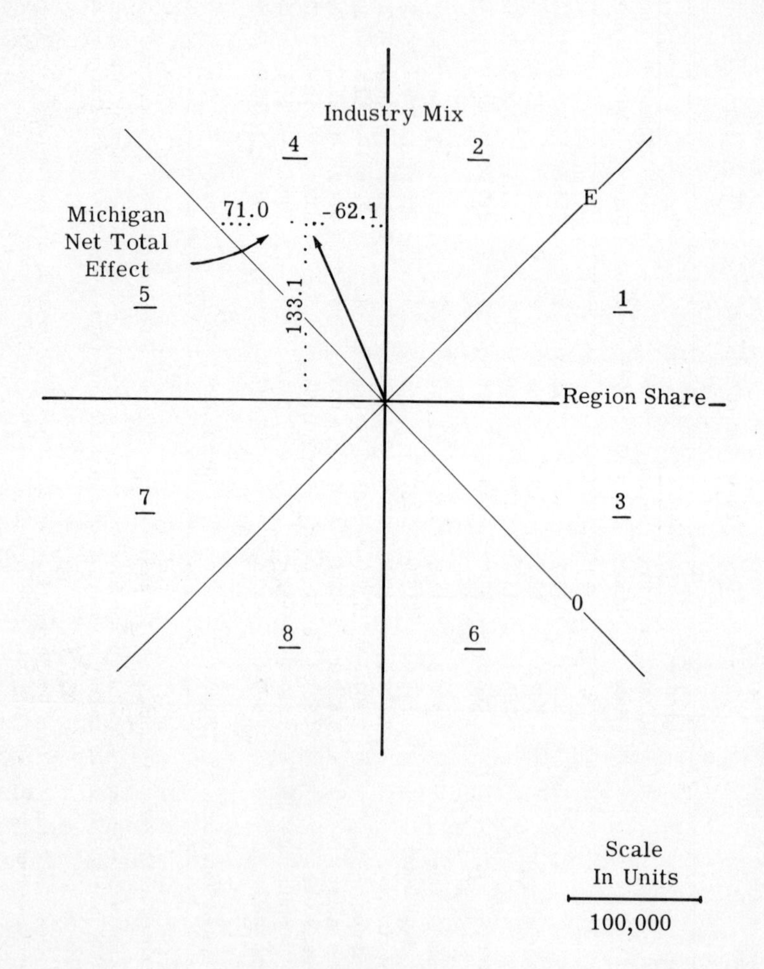

Fig. V-4. Octant Chart and Michigan Employment Effects, 1940-60, in Thousands. (Source: Fig. V-2.)

zero point. Likewise, if a vector were drawn for every one of the nation's constituent industries, such vectors would sum to the zero, zero point.

The summation of a comprehensive region set to the zero, zero point is illustrated both in Table V-2 and in panels A and B of Figure V-5 for the two periods of the 1940's and the 1950's. The configuration of region-share and industry-mix effects is seen to be similar in the two decades. There are, however, displacements. The displacement for the Great Lakes region, for example, is computed by subtracting its two-dimensional vector values for the first decade from those of the second:

$$\begin{bmatrix} -651.7 \\ 276.7 \end{bmatrix} - \begin{bmatrix} -309.5 \\ 515.8 \end{bmatrix} = \begin{bmatrix} -342.2 \\ -239.1 \end{bmatrix}$$

(1950–60) (1940–50) Displacement

Thus the situation of the Great Lakes region worsened somewhat with respect both to region share and industry mix from one decade to the next. The displacement vectors for a comprehensive region set, like the parent basic adjustment vectors, have the zero, zero sum property. This is evident in panel C of Figure V-5. Just as employment effects vectors show national growth adjustment between two points in time, so displacement vectors show the direction and magnitude of change in the type of adjustments made in two different periods.

The remaining charts further highlight the significance of the analytical elements in Table V-2.

Figure V-6, for example, shows the region-share—industry-mix position of the states for the Great Lakes region. Only Wisconsin and Indiana displayed positive region-share effects in the 1940's (panel A), and only Indiana was positive in relation to both major axes. Michigan and Ohio occupied about identical positions in the 1940's, while Illinois showed relatively larger region-share losses.

In the 1950's all states in the Great Lakes region showed region-share losses and industry-mix gains except Wisconsin, which had losses in both dimensions.

In the matter of change of orientation between the two decades, all the states except Michigan were displaced negatively

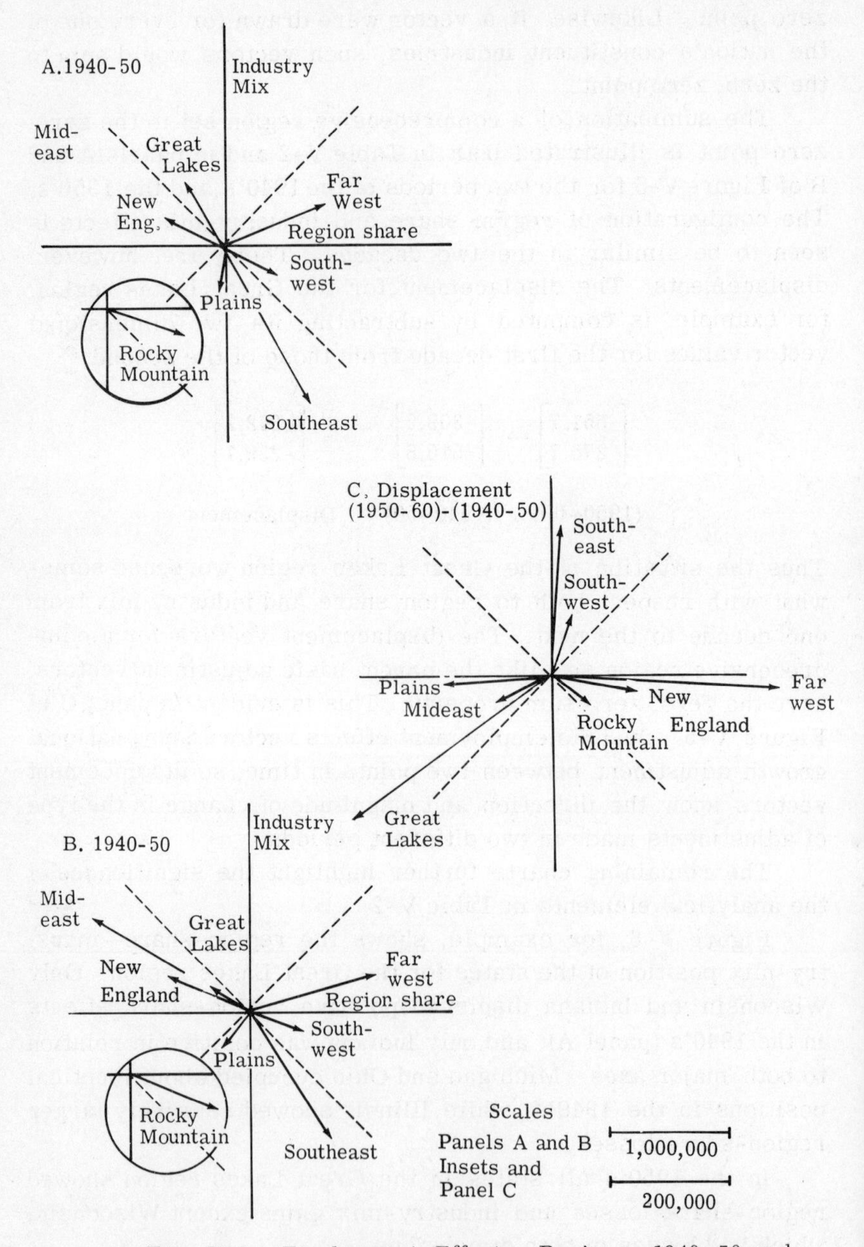

Fig. V-5. Employment Effects, Regions, 1940–50 and 1950–60, and Displacements, 1940–50 to 1950–1960. (Source: Table V-2.)

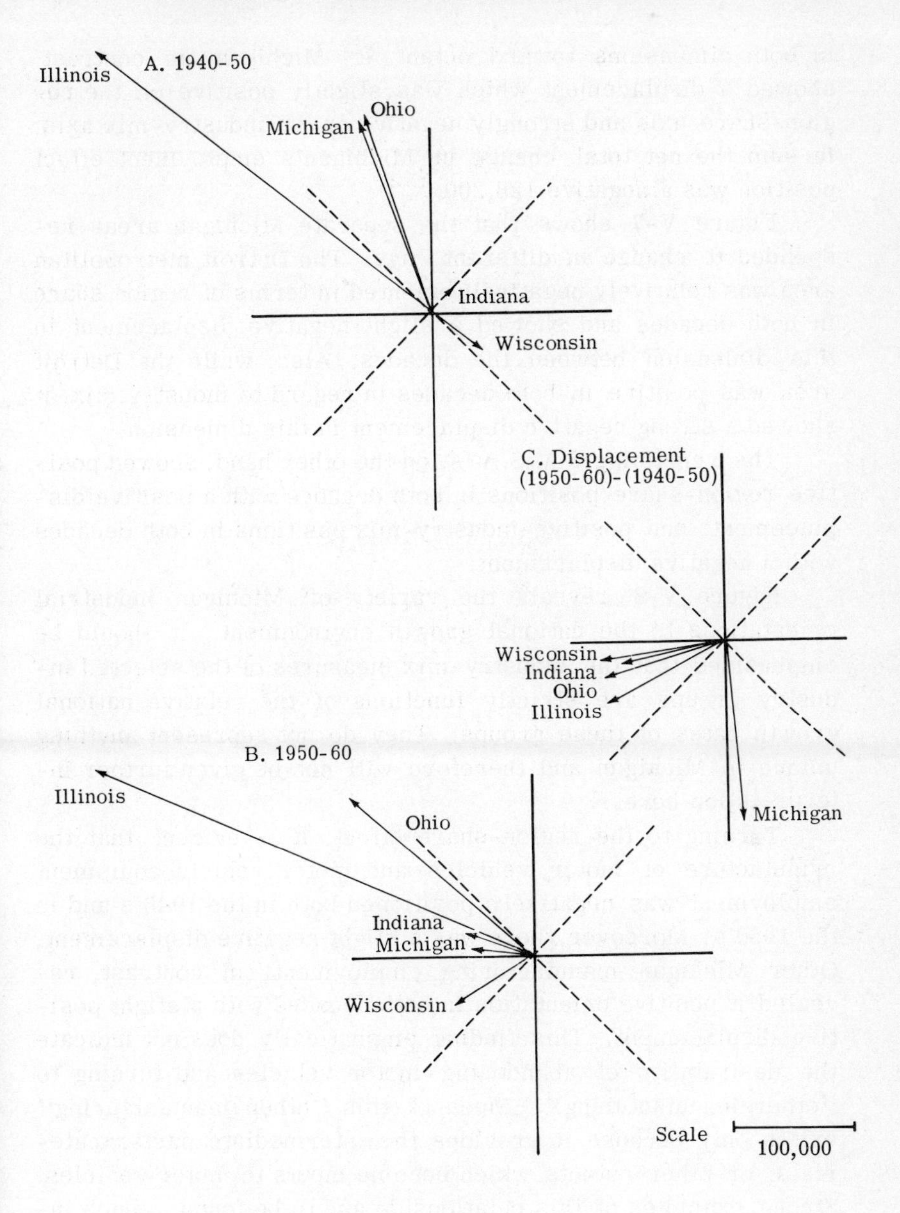

Fig. V-6. Employment Effects, Great Lakes States, 1940–50 and 1950–60, and Displacements, 1940–50 to 1950–60. (Source: Table V-2.)

in both dimensions toward octant 7. Michigan, in contrast, showed a displacement which was slightly positive on the region-share axis and strongly negative on the industry-mix axis. In sum the net total change in Michigan's employment effect position was a negative 128,200.

Figure V-7 shows that the separate Michigan areas responded to change in different ways. The Detroit metropolitan area was relatively negatively oriented in terms of region share in both decades and showed a slight negative displacement in this dimension between the decades. Also, while the Detroit area was positive in both decades in regard to industry mix, it showed a strong negative displacement in this dimension.

The remaining S.M.S.A.'s, on the other hand, showed positive region-share positions in both decades with a positive displacement, and positive industry-mix positions in both decades with a negative displacement.

Figure V-8 reveals the variety of Michigan industrial orientations to the national growth environment. It should be emphasized that the industry-mix measures of the selected industry groups are strictly functions of the relative national growth rates of these groups. They do not represent anything unique to Michigan and therefore will not be given further interpretation here.

Turning to the region-share effect, it is evident that the manufacture of motor vehicles and motor vehicle equipment employment was negatively positioned both in the 1940's and in the 1950's. Moreover, there was a slight negative displacement. Other Michigan manufacturing employment, in contrast, revealed a positive orientation in both decades with a slight positive displacement. This finding emphatically does not indicate the desirability of abandoning motor vehicles and turning to "other manufacturing." Much of this "other manufacturing" exists only because it provides the intermediate parts, materials, or other outputs which become inputs to motor vehicles. Strong examples of this relationship are to be found in such industry groups as those producing other transportation equipment, machinery, metals, chemicals, rubber products, and petroleum products. Any major dislocation or decline in motor vehicle production and employment must also affect these other

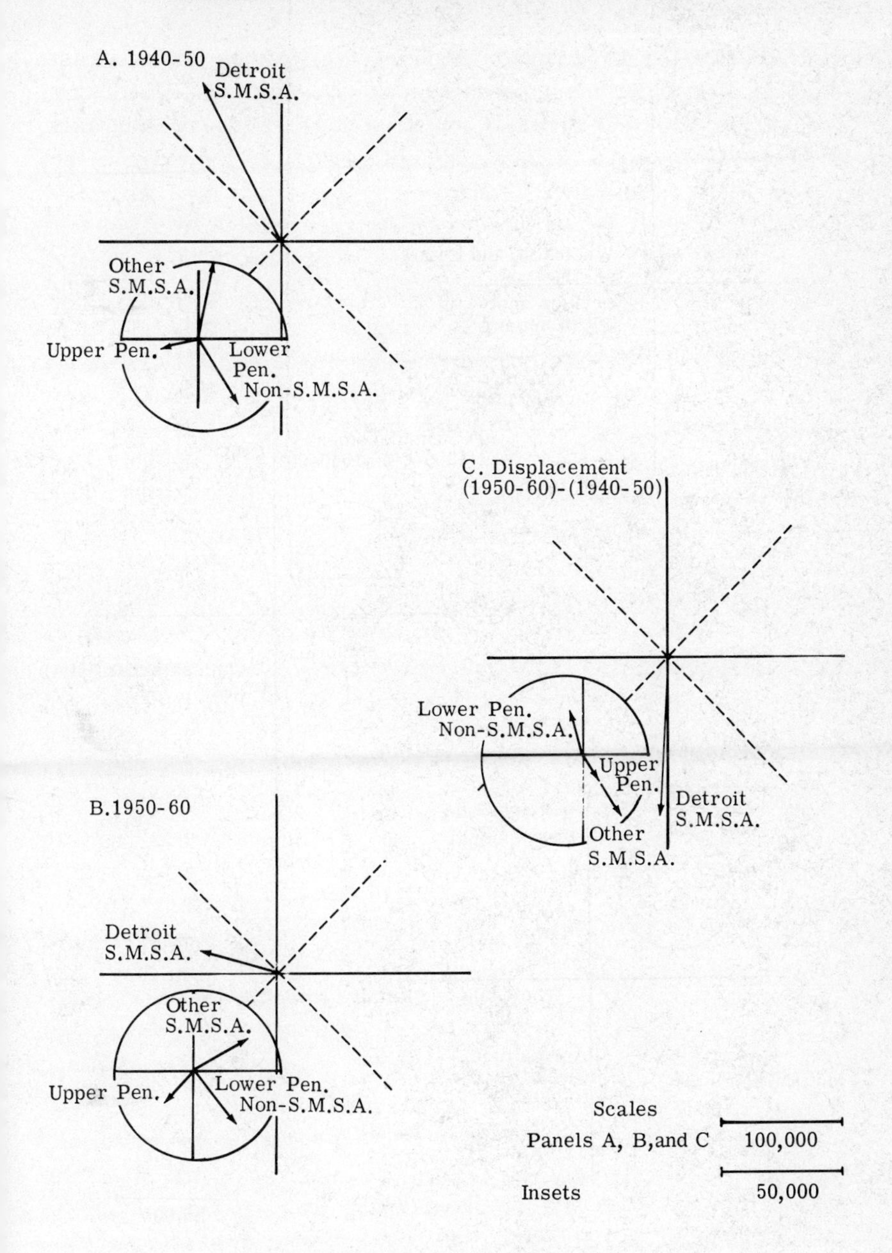

Fig. V-7. Employment Effects, Michigan Areas, 1940–50 and 1950–60, and Displacements, 1940–50 to 1950–60. (Source: Table V-2.)

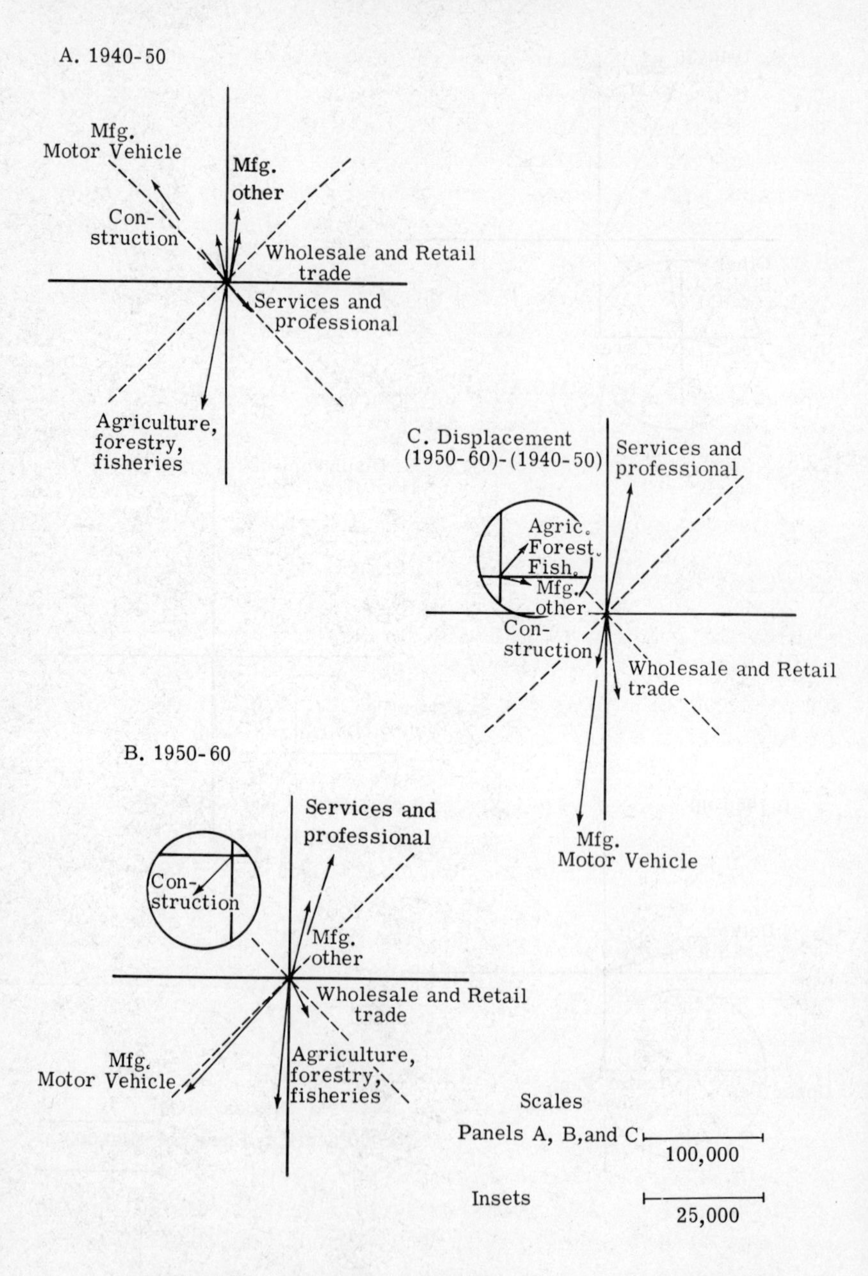

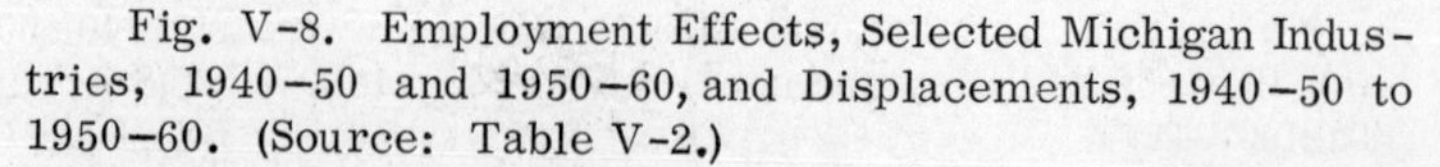

Fig. V-8. Employment Effects, Selected Michigan Industries, 1940–50 and 1950–60, and Displacements, 1940–50 to 1950–60. (Source: Table V-2.)

industry groups rather quickly. No sudden change in Michigan's orientation to some form of heavy industry which uses these auxiliary industry groups can be contemplated.

Along with other manufacturing, both the services and professional sectors and the trade industry sector showed positive region-share effects in both decades with a moderate positive displacement.

Finally, in reference to Figure V-8, it must be pointed out that not all of the information in the Michigan industry portion of Table V-2 is plotted. Moreover, the data in this table represent aggregations of analytical results from a finer industrial sectoring scheme, namely thirty-one separate industry sectors.

The 1960's and Beyond

At this writing it is no doubt difficult for concerned observers to see current economic performance and prospects in their proper context. As we have said, Michigan's motor vehicle industry gained 119,200 jobs in the 1940's and lost 97,800 in the 1950's. But currently the auto industry is in the third year of a boom phase whose termination is not yet in sight. No one doubts that this industry is securely grounded in our way of life—that, short of some disastrous national emergency, its output constitutes a necessity. Nor does anyone doubt that the inexorable processes of motor vehicle consumption and scrapping will maintain a huge and growing market for the foreseeable future. However, David Goldberg presents persuasive evidence that the approximately 500,000 new jobs needed in Michigan by 1970 cannot be derived from motor vehicle industry alone—even when both direct and indirect employment are considered. The entire industrial spectrum requires attention if the employment problem is to be seriously confronted.

In appraising Michigan's prospects in the current decade we refer to the projections of total national and total Michigan employment prepared by Sidney Sonenblum (Chapter II). The actual Michigan projection indicates an increase in excess of 400,000 workers in the 1960's. However, if Michigan were to duplicate the national projected rate, its increase would exceed the required 500,000[5].

A clear issue is posed. Can Michigan maintain the employment growth pace of the nation during the current decade? Taken together, the Sonenblum projections for Michigan and the nation imply that Michigan is not maintaining its share of the national total employment in the 1960's and that the shortfall is something more than 100,000. There is corroborating evidence in the Bureau of Labor Statistics' measured employment for the period 1960 to 1963, which indicates that Michigan is losing its place with respect to national share. However, these results as well as the Sonenblum projections were arrived at before our present period of optimism about the economy at state and national levels.

The best judgment we can make in the light of the last two decades is that the advantage deriving from the industry mix of the 1940's has been largely dissipated[6]. Consequently the actual

[5]The following employment values are linearly derived from the data for 1957 and 1976 presented in Table II-16.

	1960	1970
United States	71,691,000	86,634,000
Michigan	3,002,400	3,417,100

Michigan projected change:	
1960 to 1970	414,700
At national rate	542,000
Based on BLS	351,000*

*This last projected change is drawn from the Bureau of Labor Statistics' measured employment (established basis) as follows:

	1960	1963
United States	54,020,000	56,263,200
Michigan	2,350,700	2,382,600
Michigan share (per cent)	4.3515	4.2347
Michigan share (per cent), linearly projected to 1970	3.9623	

[6]The dissipation of the industry-mix effect could be traced to either of two causes: (1) that the rates of growth of the several industries are

success the state of Michigan will achieve in closing the projected employment gap may depend largely on its competitive position or more generally its share of industry.

Will employment expand as rapidly in Michigan as in the nation at large in the industries where Michigan has its major commitment? On this question, our judgment is that Michigan will do well if it can generally maintain its share of present industry involvements. In summary, industry-mix effects of zero and industry-share effects of zero constitute a worthy Michigan objective for the 1960's. Taken together they imply that to meet its employment objectives the state will have to grow as fast as the nation in these times of an expanding economy.

Success in maintaining or increasing the employment share of an industry depends upon access to markets on the output side and access to the appropriate managerial, capital, and manpower components on the input side. The interplay between output acceptance and input availabilities is continuous.

It is important to realize that in two employee groups of equal size and in the same industry the growth potential may be widely different. One thousand operatives in a given manufacturing line may represent few or no possibilities of the entrepreneurial activity that brings about growth. Another group of a thousand in the same industrial line may include many professional people in technical, legal, and managerial fields—some possibly endowed with genius. This group may have an enormous power as catalysts to hasten growth. Entirely new industries serving entirely new markets have sprung from such combinations. The presence of such a core of organizing and creative talent provides a solid economic footing for the general work force.

We are merely reiterating an old American theme in a new

becoming more alike, or (2) that the industry structures of the several regions (in this case, Michigan) are becoming more like that of the nation. The evidence through the 1940's and the 1950's points definitely to the latter explanation. For example, the chief declining sector, agriculture, is by definition becoming less weighty in the nation's economy. This means that the national economy in this respect is moving toward the structural orientation displayed by some of the older industrial areas such as Michigan.

setting. Benjamin Higgins, an authority on economic growth, points out that our western frontier was a "small man's" frontier in contrast to the "big man's" frontier of Brazil, Australia, and to some extent Canada. He finds that economic development has been more firmly established and more salutary on the American "small man's" frontier where government policy and the institutional framework enabled individuals, partnerships, or small corporations to make their way alone. Small firms have acted as organizing nuclei for industries and the development of entire regions. The American frontier of the nineteenth century is now a strong part of the economic whole and stands in contrast to the hollow frontiers found in many other countries, which make little or no contributions to the total economy.

Benjamin Chinitz has pointed out that in 1870 the population of the Chicago industrial area exceeded that of the Pittsburgh industrial area by a factor of 1.2, while in 1960 the factor of excess was 2.8. Some of this growth disparity between the two industrial areas is attributed by Chinitz to large steel firms' monopoly of legal, technical, and managerial skills in the Pittsburgh area. As a consequence, such skills were not readily available to small firms. Pittsburgh was a "big man's" frontier. In Chicago, however, small firms could and did attain an economic foothold, and they formed the organizing impetus to develop the groundwork for a great labor force and population[7].

The concern shown by these writers is shared by Wilbur Thompson with respect to the metropolitan area of Detroit

[7]The Pittsburgh area is defined by Chinitz to include the counties of Alleghany, Beaver, Washington, and Westmoreland. The Chicago area is defined to include the counties of Cook, DuPage, Cane, Lake, and Will in Illinois and Lake in Indiana. The basic population data are:

	1870	1960
Pittsburgh	405,554	2,405,435
Chicago	482,108	6,649,972

Similar views concerning the roots of industrial area growth are expressed by Edgar M. Hoover in "Pittsburgh Takes Stock of Itself," *Pennsylvania Business Survey*, Vol. V, No. 1 (January, 1964), 1-6.

(Chapter VI). In the early days Detroit may have been a "small man's" frontier, but success in a few lines has made it a "big man's" frontier. Today the outlook and the state of mind of Detroit, and possibly of all Michigan, depend on the current cyclical phase of motor vehicle production. Thompson points out that a broader diversification, a more metropolitan character with a broader spectrum of industrial pursuits—even at some cost in terms of immediate average wage levels—would better serve the cause of economic stability and qualitative growth in the long run.

The United States, fortunately, remains an area where the man of limited means may move around freely. But the nature of the movement has changed radically since 1890, when the westward movement of the frontier ended. New opportunities today are created by ideas which serve an ever-changing technology, rather than by movement to undeveloped regions. Limitations to movement are not only geographic but also educational. Given the accelerating rate of change, education becomes the prime vehicle by which people may improve their adaptive capacity. Therefore, the retention of people with high levels of educational endowment offers the greatest hope for the economic health of a state or region. Since the occupational distribution may be crucial, it follows that an area's educational institutions may be its most effective means of enabling the population to adapt to change. The importance of the state's educational system, not merely for growth but for better development of human resources, is re-emphasized by the acceleration in the rate of change. This will be true in 1970 as well as the years that follow, when the competition among regions is likely to intensify and the need for growth is compounded with the problems that such growth engenders.

[Editors' note: In the light of Ashby's statements here, the reader may wish to reconsider evidence on the results of interregional exchange of population by educational level, as shown in Goldberg's chapter.]

TECHNICAL APPENDIX

The analytical process used in the foregoing article reveals the underlying components which comprise the change in an economic variable (such as employment) in a particular sector (such as industry) for a particular region (such as a state or county). These components are three in number:

1. Change at national all-sector rates for sector i in region j (g_{ij}, change at national rate).
2. Change owing to relative growth of national sector i for sector i in region j (k_{ij}, industry-mix effect).
3. Change owing to relative growth of region j in sector i for sector i in region j (s_{ij}, region-share effect).

Where d_{ij} represents the actual change in a variable between two points in time for sector i of region j, there emerges the simple relation:

$$g_{ij} + k_{ij} + s_{ij} = d_{ij}$$

All that is required to compute these basic elements is two data matrices representing an initial and a terminal point in time. Let X_t represent the initial and X_{t+1} the terminal data matrix. These matrices are in general of dimension M by N. M equals the number of sectors indexed by $i = 1, 2, 3, \ldots M$. N equals the number of regions indexed by $j = 1, 2, 3, \ldots N$.

A particular numerical illustration where there are two sectors ($M = 2$) and three regions ($N = 3$) is assumed here. While the basic data can be specified in an M by N matrix, an $(M + 1)$ by $(N + 1)$ array is more convenient for exposition as below.

	X_t					X_{t+1}			
	All Reg. 0	Reg. 1	Reg. 2	Reg. 3		All Reg. 0	Reg. 1	Reg. 2	Reg. 3
All Sect. 0	83	33	30	20	All. Sect. 0	108	47	45	16
Sector 1	33	3	10	20	Sector 1	41	15	20	6
Sector 2	50	30	20	0	Sector 2	67	32	25	10

The d_{ij} elements (forming the D array) arise from the simple subtraction of X_t from X_{t+1}. That is, every element in X_t is subtracted from the corresponding element in X_{t+1} with the result shown below.

$D = d_{ij}$

	All Reg. 0	Reg. 1	Reg. 2	Reg. 3		All Reg. 0	Reg. 1	Reg. 2	Reg. 3
All Sect. 0	25	14	15	-4	All Sect. 0	d_{00}	d_{01}	d_{02}	d_{03}
Sector 1	8	12	10	-14	Sector 1	d_{10}	d_{11}	d_{12}	d_{13}
Sector 2	17	2	5	10	Sector 2	d_{20}	d_{21}	d_{22}	d_{23}

For a particular example, this array shows that the variable in sector 2 of region 1 has increased by 2 between the initial and terminal dates under consideration.

In order to explain the elements g_{ij}, k_{ij}, and s_{ij}, it is necessary to define base elements and rate elements.

The base element for any particular sector in a particular region is some combination of the values in that sector-region cell for the initial and the terminal points in time. In general these combinations are appropriately considered as convex. That is, $B = b_{ij} = aX_t + (1\text{-}a)X_{t+1}$ where $0 \leqq a \leqq 1$. Thus matrix B is an average of the initial and terminal point values with specified weights.

The most conventional base combination is the one where the initial value of the cell has a weight of unity and the terminal value has a weight of zero. This would mean, in terms of the above expression, that $a = 1$ and the base matrix becomes simply X_t as follows:

$$B = b_{ij}$$

	All Reg. 0	Reg. 1	Reg. 2	Reg. 3		All Reg. 0	Reg. 1	Reg. 2	Reg. 3
All Sect. 0	83	33	30	20	All Sect. 0	b_{00}	b_{01}	b_{02}	b_{03}
Sector 1	33	3	10	20	Sector 1	b_{10}	b_{11}	b_{12}	b_{13}
Sector 2	50	30	20	0	Sector 2	b_{20}	b_{21}	b_{22}	b_{23}

The rate matrix, R, is made up of elements r_{ij}. Every such element is a ratio d_{ij}/b_{ij}. In the particular case being considered (with a one-zero base) the result is as shown below.

$R = r_{ij}$

	All Reg. 0	Reg. 1	Reg. 2	Reg. 3
All Sect. 0	0.30121	0.42424	0.50000	-0.20000
Sector 1	0.24242	4.00000	1.00000	-0.70000
Sector 2	0.34000	0.06667	0.25000	*

	All Reg. 0	Reg. 1	Reg. 2	Reg. 3
All Sect. 0	r_{00}	r_{01}	r_{02}	r_{03}
Sector 1	r_{10}	r_{11}	r_{12}	r_{13}
Sector 2	r_{20}	r_{21}	r_{22}	r_{23}

* Undefined rate

It is now possible to compute the change in a particular sector of a particular region on several alternative assumptions. Thus:

$$b_{ij}r_{00} = \text{change at national all-sector rate,}$$
$$b_{ij}r_{i0} = \text{change at national sector rate,}$$
$$b_{ij}r_{ij} = \text{change at region sector rate.}$$

From these elements may be constructed the three terms originally mentioned:

$$b_{ij}r_{00} = g_{ij} = \text{change at national rate,}$$
$$b_{ij}r_{i0} - b_{ij}r_{00} = k_{ij} = \text{industry-mix effect,}$$
$$b_{ij}r_{ij} - b_{ij}r_{i0} = s_{ij} = \text{region-share effect.}$$

Also in general

$$b_{ij}\,[r_{00} + (r_{i0} - r_{00}) + (r_{ij} - r_{i0})] = b_{ij}(r_{ij}) = d_{ij}.$$

In the particular numerical illustration at hand, it is simple to work out the values for an example, say sector 2 of region 1. Thus:

$$b_{21}r_{00} = (30)(0.30121) = 9.03636$$
$$b_{21}r_{20} = (30)(0.34000) = 10.20000$$
$$b_{21}r_{21} = (30)(0.06667) = 1.99998$$

and

$$b_{21}r_{00} + (b_{21}r_{20} - b_{21}r_{00}) + (b_{21}r_{21} - b_{21}r_{20}) = d_{21}$$

or

$$(9.03636) + (1.16364) + (-8.20002) = (1.99998).$$

The results in the foregoing chapter were rounded to the nearest tenth of a thousand. Here the results rounded to the nearest integer would be:

$$g_{21} + k_{21} + s_{21} = d_{21}$$
$$(9) + (1) + (-8) = (2).$$

The interpretation of this result may be simply stated. The second sector of the first region would have expanded by 9 units at the national all-sector rate of expansion.

This change, however, was in fact adjusted upward because the national second-sector rate was greater than the national all-sector rate.

Finally, the change was in fact adjusted downward because the first region's second-sector rate was smaller than the national second-sector rate.

In summary, the hypothetical change at the national all-sector rate, when adjusted for both the sector-mix and region-share effects, precisely equaled the actual change.

The present technical exposition is in terms of data matrices of dimension 2 by 3. The trial run from which the empirical results of the preceding chapter are drawn involved data matrices of 31 by 3,101 (that is, 31 industry sectors of employment for each of 3,101 local areas, mostly counties).

Thus, if the present technical exposition is to show results similar to those of Table V-2 and Figure V-2 it must summarize results across all industry sectors for each region. The requisite rounded industry-sector results for the current illustration are as follows:

	g_{ij}	k_{ij}	s_{ij}	d_{ij}
Region 1				
Sector 1	1	0	11	12
Sector 2	9	1	-8	2
Region 2				
Sector 1	3	-1	8	10
Sector 2	6	1	-2	5
Region 3				
Sector 1	6	-1	-19	-14
Sector 2	0	0	10	10*

*It will be recalled that since the one-zero base element for sector 2 of region 3 was zero, the rate, r_{23}, was undefined. Either of two approaches can be taken in this case.

One of these is that any change arising on a zero base be defined, by convention, as wholly composed of share effects.

The other is that the logic of the matter be pressed further than it is possible to press the arithmetic. Thus, the known rates cannot generate any change on a zero base. Hence:

$$b_{23}r_{00} = 0(0.30121) = 0 = g_{23}$$

and

$$b_{23}r_{20} = 0(0.34000) = 0 = k_{23}$$

but since

$$g_{23} + k_{23} + s_{23} = d_{23} = 10$$

it follows that

$$s_{23} = d_{23} = 10.$$

It is as if the undefined rate generated the entirety of the change on the zero base. Thus it is as if

$$b_{23}(* - r_{20}) = s_{23} = 10 - 0 = 10.$$

The two approaches thus lead to the same result.

Thus a summary across the two industry sectors is made to arrive at a summary line tabulation:[8]

Region	Change at National Rate	Sector-Mix Effect	Region-Share Effect	Actual Change
1	10	1	3	14
2	9	0	6	15
3	6	-1	-9	-4
Total	25	0	0	25

When the sector-mix effects (summed across all sectors) are added to the region-share effects (summed across all sectors) the result is the net total effect or net total shift for a region. In the case of region 1 this is 4. This number, however, may be computed directly without regard to computations for sector mix and region share for the separate sectors in the region. This number can be obtained as the regional all-sector rate minus the national all-sector rate as applied to the regional total base employment. In the case of region 1 it is (0.42424 - 0.30121) times (33) equals 4.05999 which rounds to 4. This computation (applied to regional total base employment) is strictly analogous to the procedure for computing the region-share effect for a particular sector. Thus what has been termed the "net total effect" may just as properly be called the region-share effect for the region as a whole.

With an operational computer program from which empirical results are to be drawn, certain parameter settings must be made. These parameter settings will determine, among various other options, the following:

1. The geographic combinations (particular clusters of the available regional data).

[8]It is well to emphasize again that the results in this technical example, like the empirical results summarized here and in the chapter itself, are drawn from one-zero base computations.

2. The sectoral combinations (particular groupings of the available sectoral data).
3. The base computation (any combination of initial and terminal data matrices from one-zero to zero-one).

In this, as in any other technique, the analytical outputs are affected by the nature of the data inputs. The following summary concerns how a particular parameter setting will affect the numerical analytical results as summarized across *M* sectors for a particular region.

1. Any results for a particular region will be invariant in all respects, whether these results are obtained by analyzing such a region (say, the state of Michigan) as a unit or as the sum of component regions (say, the counties in Michigan).
2. Any results for a particular region will be affected in terms of the sector-mix and region-share elements by the level of sector aggregation under analysis. However, the sum of the sector-mix and region-share effects (net total effect) is invariant no matter how aggregated or disaggregated the sector detail under analysis may be within a given total. Since the net total effect is invariant, neither the change at national rate nor the actual change is affected.
3. Any results for a particular region will be affected by the particular base chosen for rate computations in respect to change at national rate, sector-mix effect, and region-share effect. However, the sum of the three elements ($g_{ij} + k_{ij} + s_{ij}$) is invariant. Hence the actual change, d_{ij} is unaffected.

VI

THE FUTURE OF THE DETROIT METROPOLITAN AREA[1]

Wilbur R. Thompson

The Role of Exports in Urban Growth

The economy of an urban area can be analyzed and an attempt made to tell its fortune in a number of different ways. Although urban-regional economic analysis is a relatively new art, it has already become traditional to depict the community as a small nation engaged in foreign trade. In this figurative view the outside world begins at the outer edges of the nearby hinterland, which the city serves as a trade and service center, and extends to distant cities in the nation and overseas—wherever sectors of the local economy trade their manufactured goods. The urban area becomes, above all, a local labor market, a primary unit of employment and income generation. The locality is buffeted by changes in demand for its "export" products and in the "derived demand" for local labor, changes that originate outside the local economy and over which it has little or no control. Even those workers employed by local business that sells largely or entirely to local households depend on "foreign" demand, since the customers for such business are, in the last analysis, employees of the local export industries. Or, viewed from a slightly different angle, the community can buy from outsiders—food, clothing, gasoline, and other necessities—only by selling to outsiders, in other words, exporting.

[1]The terms "Detroit area" or "Detroit metropolitan area," as used throughout this chapter, refer to the Detroit Standard Metropolitan Statistical Area (S.M.S.A.), consisting of Macomb, Oakland, and Wayne counties.

The literature of urban-regional growth, largely written by such non-economists as economic geographers, economic historians, and city or regional planners, characteristically projects the future size and shape of the whole urban economy from the anticipated size and shape of its export sector. The format is simple and direct. The export base of most urban economies is dominated by a relatively small number of manufacturing activities; therefore, one simply estimates the number of export manufacturing workers that would be employed locally at the target date and then adds the number of local service employees needed to accommodate the export industry workers and their families (and, of course, to serve each others' families). Finally, if the projected total number of export and service industry workers is multiplied by the average number of dependents per worker, the future total population of the area falls neatly into place.

Following this logic, we could proceed here by analyzing the growth prospects of the automobile industry. Such an analysis would, of course, concern itself both with the output and employment trends for the industry as a whole and with these trends in the Detroit area's share of that industry. The effort would, in fact, consist essentially of coming up with the likely national employment in automobile production in the target year and the likely local employment share. The product of the two quantities is the projected local export base. All that would be left, then, would be to link export employment to total employment and the latter to total population, through the estimated future labor force participation rate.

Certainly this would be the best way to predict the future of a small urban economy, but there are a number of reasons why a simple export base projection is not entirely appropriate for judging the economic prospects of the Detroit area. First, the leading industry here is a mature one; moreover, it has recently been decentralizing. A moderately optimistic projection of employment for the local automobile industry would show it remaining constant during the next two decades. To predict a constant local export base (and thereby a constant total size) would contradict the clear trend toward concentration of an ever larger share of the national population in the very large metropolitan areas, the class into which the Detroit area falls. This is not to say that the automobile industry will not continue to be the principal employer in the area for decades to come, only that it will probably not provide the significant *marginal changes* that will be the key to local development.

Second, the golden age of manufacturing seems to have run its course in the sense that the *share* of manufacturing in total employment has begun what threatens to be a long-term decline. True, manufacturing will probably not experience as precipitous a decline in its share of employment as that which characterized agriculture during the past century. The income elasticity of demand for manufactured goods is generally much greater than for foods and fibers, and this condition ensures a growth in per capita consumption of manufactured goods which will take much of the bite out of the rapidly increasing productivity per worker. The situation is therefore unlike that of farming, where labor displacement has made a severe impact. Still, manufacturing in general and production employment in particular would not seem to hold the key to the pattern of employment growth in the age of automation, especially in an already overspecialized manufacturing economy such as that of Detroit.

Third, for reasons developed at some length in the pages to follow, the large metropolitan area seems to have a life of its own, and its growth pattern is far more subtle and complex than can be explained simply by magnifying the growth pattern of its principal export industries. A second broad approach, then, would be to see the Detroit area as a potential metropolis and, by observing the trends in economic structure and performance of the other major metropolitan areas of the nation, to seek some regularities in the behavior of these very large urban economies to which this local economy might tend to conform. This latter approach will be stressed in this paper, although the intention is not to deny in any way that Detroit is both a metropolis—potentially, at least—*and* an automobile city. Because a full understanding of Detroit would patently call for a study of the automobile industry in depth, and because that ambitious work is beyond this brief effort, the choice was made to turn instead to a less appreciated local growth dynamic—the growth momentum of the large metropolis.

Again, nothing that has been said above denies the critical role, in fact the overpowering dominance, of the automobile industry in the local business cycle. As long as auto-making is the principal source of local employment and a very unstable industry as well, the Detroit business cycle will continue to be a virtual mirror image of the automobile cycle. But the issue here is not year-to-year fluctuations in local employment and income, but rather decade-to-decade shifts in the structure of the local economy.

The Growth Pattern of a Metropolis

We turn now to view the Detroit area economy not on the basis of its export industries but rather as a metropolis whose growth may be to some extent independent of export industries. A strong case can be made, in fact, for choosing a hybrid economic-demographic approach in the case of very large urban areas. While a small urban area may rise and fall with the fortunes of its principal export industries, urban areas having, say, a population of a half-million and over ordinarily achieve considerable stability (through industrial diversification) and thereby acquire considerable holding power. For any city there seems to be some critical size. Short of this point, continuing growth is not inevitable, and even the city's very existence is not assured. Beyond that particular size, however, although the rate of growth may slacken at times even to zero, absolute contraction is highly unlikely. Some process or mechanism, like a ratchet, seems to come into being, locking in past growth and preventing contraction.[2]

[2]A deductive rationalization of the "ratchet effect" has been developed at some length by the author in another place. An abridged version of that argument is as follows:

> With growth and size comes industrial diversification, and even a random blending of young, mature, and decadent industries tends to stabilize local growth at a rate roughly equivalent to the national average rate or the rate

Some empirical support for this hypothesis is offered in Figure VI-1. This scatter diagram relates the logarithm of 1950 population size of the full census of 212 standard metropolitan statistical areas (S.M.S.A.) to their respective percentage changes in population during the period 1950-60. Clearly, the smaller metropolitan areas show great variation in growth rate, ranging widely from decade gains of over 100 per cent to absolute losses in excess of 10 per cent. Our sample, moreover, reaches down in population size only to places of a little less than 50,000 people (the minimum size for an S.M.S.A.), and the smaller urban places exhibit an even greater range of growth rates. But, more relevant to present interests, as we

applicable to some broad, surrounding region (e.g., New England, the Southwest) . . . . A second possible basis for irreversible urban growth after some threshold size has been achieved is simply power politics . . . . To the extent that Federal and state financial aids and public works projects can revive faltering urban economies, the bigger urban areas are in a position to press harder for government support. Thirdly, somewhat related, is the fact that tremendous amounts of fixed capital have been sunk in social and private overhead in the very large urban area—streets, sewers, schools, stores and housing—so that even if the area's (export) productive facilities are worn out or obsolete, it is economically and politically unthinkable to abandon so much immobile capital. No nation is so affluent that it can afford to throw away a major city. Fourth, a larger and larger proportion of industrial activity is customer-oriented. . . . A large local economy becomes almost self-justifying as a rich product market. New industries, born elsewhere, establish branch plants . . . . Finally, a large urban area is more likely to give birth to new industries at critical points in its life cycle than is a small urban area; a surer and steadier supply of invention, innovation and promotion is to be expected in larger places. Suppose that an entrepreneurial genius occurs only once in every ten thousand births, then a fifty-thousand-population urban area with, say, one thousand births per year will produce this key person only once every ten years, on the average. This area may not have a new industrial savior ready at the time of critical need, whereas the five-hundred-thousand-population urban area, spawning a genius a year, almost certainly will. Sheer size may stabilize the supply of the key human resources necessary to economic growth and development. (Wilbur R. Thompson, *A Preface to Urban Economics: Toward a Conceptual Framework for Study and Research* [Washington: Resources for the Future, Inc., 1963], p. 13. [Preliminary, Multilith].)

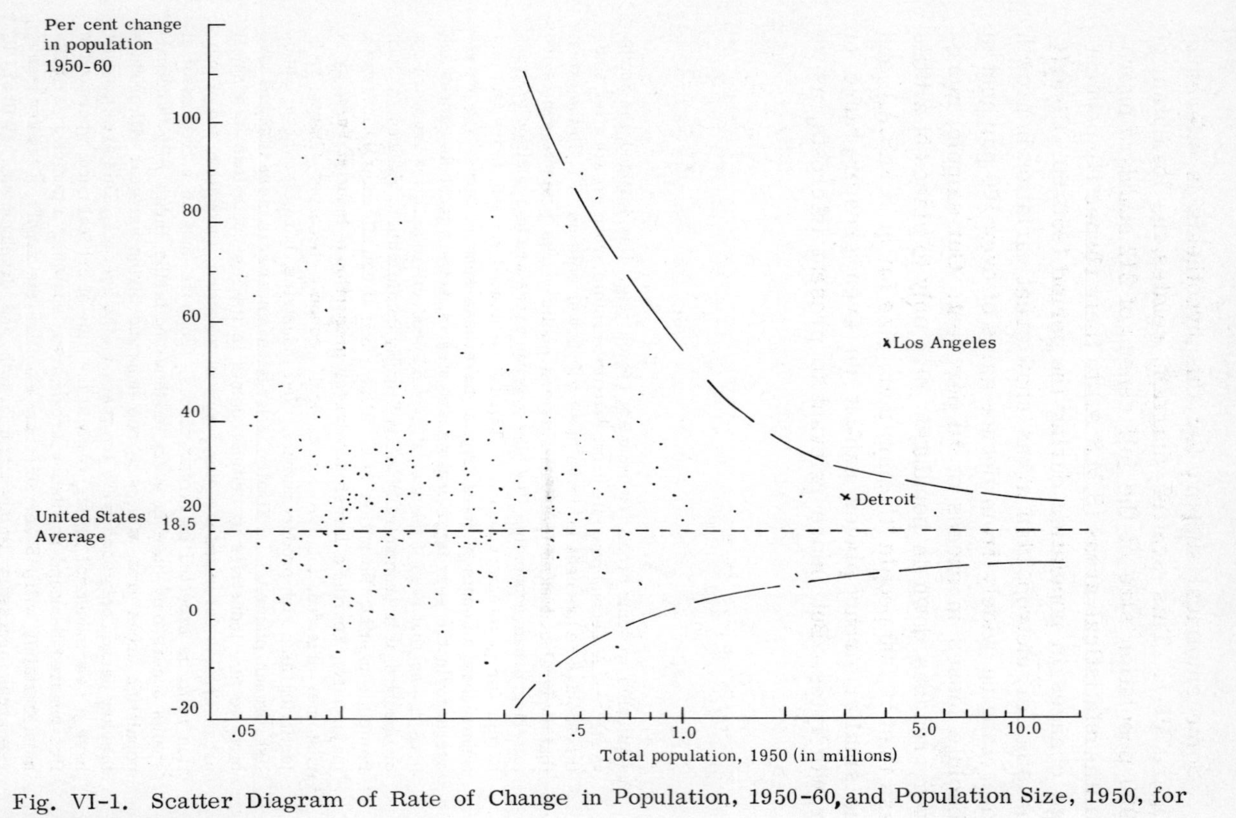

Fig. VI-1. Scatter Diagram of Rate of Change in Population, 1950-60, and Population Size, 1950, for 212 Metropolitan Areas.

move upward in city size, inter-urban variation in growth rate narrows dramatically. By the time we reach a population of one-half million all the absolute declines have been eliminated, except in the case of Newark, New Jersey (which is a special illustration of a decaying central city of the New York area economy), and except for one decade gain of over 60 per cent in Los Angeles. Beginning at the one-million population mark, the aggregate growth experience of the various metropolitan areas becomes quite similar, generally ranging between 10 and 25 per cent per decade. (See also Table VI-2, below.) A similar graph, not shown, was constructed for the 1940-50 decade, and a similar pattern was found.

Not only does a given large metropolitan area tend to exhibit a growth rate very much like that of other very large metropolitan areas, but its growth rate also tends to be very much the same as in the preceding decade. Support for this hypothesis is presented in Figure VI-2, a scatter diagram linking the population size of an urban area with its "growth stability." Growth stability is defined as the maintenance of a given rate of growth, shown by a linear trend on a logarithmic chart, and is quantified by expressing the ratio of 1950-60 population change to the 1940-50 change. A coefficient of one denotes a constant rate of growth, while both higher and lower values indicate inter-decade variation in growth rate—growth instability.

Again, the smaller metropolitan areas exhibit marked variation in growth stability, some growing as much as 40 per cent faster (1.4) in the later decade than in 1940-50, others growing only 75 per cent as fast (0.75) from 1950 to 1960 as they did between 1940 and 1950, and others exhibiting the inertia of a constant rate of movement. Once again, as we move upward in city size, inter-urban variation narrows. With only two major exceptions, the growth stability ratio varies only moderately, from .9 to 1.1, for metropolitan areas of one-half million population and over. That is, these larger areas exhibit trend lines on logarithmic paper that do not change slope by more than 10 per cent, decade by decade. To the degree that the growth rate of the very large urban area is more stable than that of smaller areas, it is more predictable.

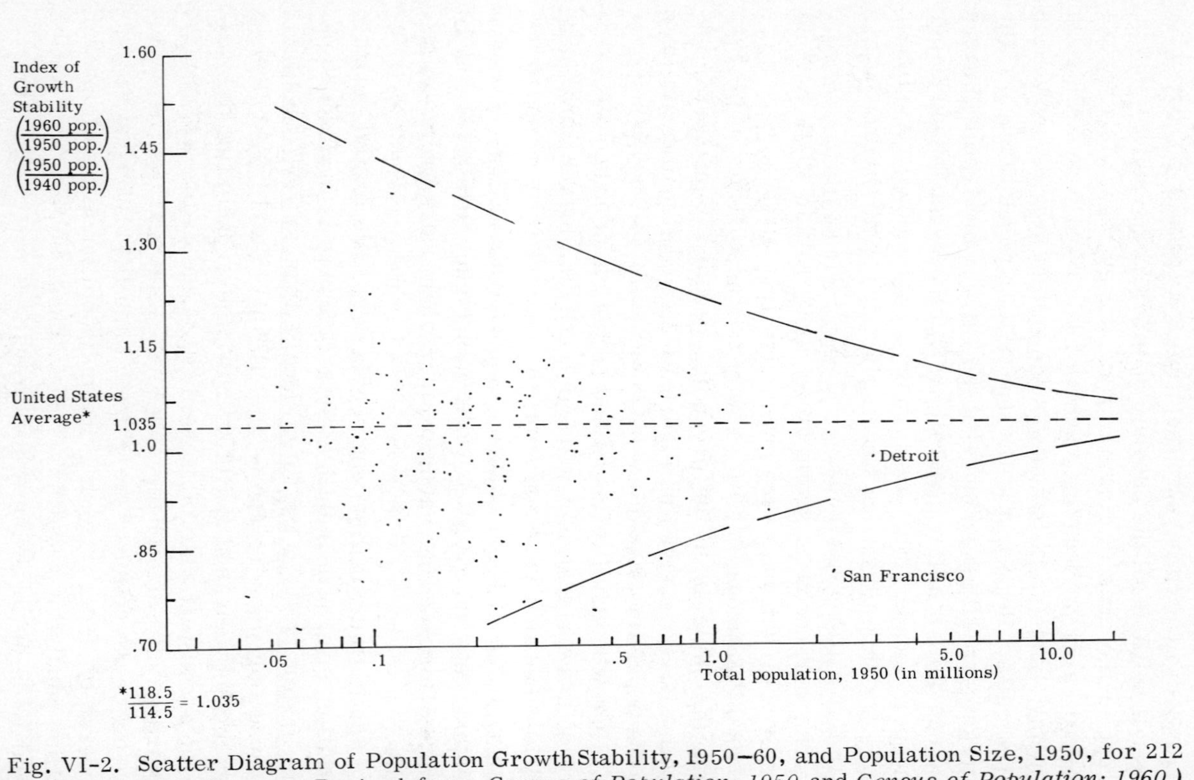

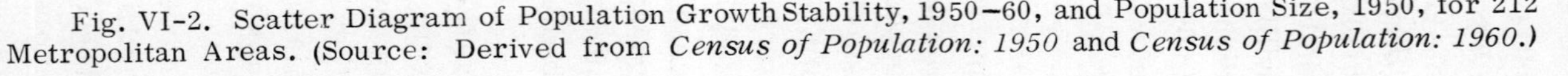
Fig. VI-2. Scatter Diagram of Population Growth Stability, 1950–60, and Population Size, 1950, for 212 Metropolitan Areas. (Source: Derived from *Census of Population: 1950* and *Census of Population: 1960*.)

Surely, we should not be too surprised to find that big cities are more alike than small ones—in growth rate or almost anything else. A small urban economy may be concentrated on the manufacture of beer or furniture or steel, but a large urban economy probably includes all three commodities. With increasing size comes greater industrial diversification and thereby greater homogeneity with other industrial areas. And with a blending of young, mature, and decadent industries comes a growth performance more like the average of all other industrial areas. Further, as our major metropolitan areas, now large, become ever larger, we might expect them to exhibit even more similarity in their industrial structures and growth rates.[3]

While a careful comparative analysis of the economies of the major metropolitan areas of the country is far beyond the scope of this paper, a quick marshaling of the industrial data of the *Census of Population* for 1950 and 1960 does suggest that a process of inter-urban industrial homogenization is, in fact, going forward in the very largest urban areas. The proportion of total local employment for both 1950 and 1960 in each of thirteen broad industrial classes (and two subclasses) was computed for each of the fifteen largest metropolitan areas in the country. Then the standard deviation of the percentages employed in a given industry class in the fifteen areas was divided by the arithmetic mean of these percentages, yielding a common measure of dispersion, the "coefficient of variation." The coefficient of variation of the fifteen manufacturing percentages for 1950 was .224, and for 1960 it was .179, an indication that manufacturing became a less heterogeneous (more standardized) component in the industrial structure of major urban areas over the past decade. Turning to Table VI-1, we note that between 1950 and 1960 the coefficient of variation fell

[3]An exception to this would occur if the optimum size of plant (the size required to produce at least cost) were to increase faster than the population size of these urban areas, so that a situation developed in which two major metropolitan area markets were required to support a plant which now requires only one, and plants now in every large urban area were to be located in only half of the areas, and so forth.

Table VI-1

INTER-URBAN VARIATION IN PROPORTION OF TOTAL LOCAL EMPLOYMENT IN FIFTEEN BROAD INDUSTRY GROUPS AMONG FIFTEEN LARGEST METROPOLITAN AREAS OF THE UNITED STATES—1950 AND 1960

Broad Industry Class	Average Percentage of Total Employment		Standard Deviation of Employment Percentages		Coefficient of Variation of Employment Percentages		Converging (C); Diverging (D)
	1950	1960	1950	1960	1950	1960	
Construction	5.66	5.07	0.96	0.58	.169	.115	C
Manufacturing	33.75	32.94	7.57	5.89	.224	.179	C
Durables	20.44	20.98	9.17	7.14	.449	.340	C
Nondurables	13.00	11.84	4.04	3.04	.311	.257	C
Transportation	6.18	4.74	1.31	1.00	.212	.211	C
Communications	1.36	1.39	0.24	0.21	.176	.150	C
Utilities	1.54	1.39	0.14	0.14	.088	.103	D
Wholesale trade	4.33	3.91	0.98	0.72	.226	.185	C
Retail trade	16.49	14.52	1.05	0.46	.064	.032	C
Finance, insurance, real estate	4.57	5.01	1.24	1.18	.271	.235	C
Business and repair services	2.69	2.73	0.49	0.61	.183	.222	D
Personal service	5.84	4.84	1.06	0.66	.182	.137	C
Entertainment	1.17	0.88	0.54	0.32	.458	.367	C
Professional service	8.78	11.86	0.12	1.40	.142	.118	C
Public administration	4.59	4.68	1.26	1.09	.275	.234	C

Source: Derived from U.S. Bureau of the Census, *Census of Population: 1950* and *Census of Population: 1960*.

for eleven of the thirteen broad industry classes and for both subclasses of manufacturing, in most cases very markedly. Only "business and repair service" and "utilities" showed an increasing variation among the giant urban areas, and these are both relatively small sectors of the economy (tenth and twelfth in size among the thirteen in 1960). This evidence from the *Census of Population* strongly supports the hypothesis of growing similarity in industrial structure among the major metropolitan areas of the country.

We argued above that very large urban areas resemble each other more than small urban areas do and that these very large urban areas are becoming more alike in industrial structure. It would seem to follow then that their growth rates should become more alike, and some evidence of this is found in Figure VI-3. A significant narrowing of the growth rates characterizes thirteen of the fifteen largest urban areas over the past decade. Only Los Angeles and, to a lesser extent, Minneapolis-St. Paul move against the general trend toward inter-urban homogeneity. The ten areas in the middle, that is, those with middle-range growth rates, converge from a range of roughly 14 to 28 per cent increase in population per decade to the much reduced spread of about 18 to 25 per cent, a narrowing from about 2 to 1 to about 4 to 3. More formally and inclusively, the coefficient of variation of these fifteen growth rates fell from 0.66 to 0.48 during the past decade.

If Los Angeles is due to come down to earth over the next decade—and it is hard to see how a growth rate in excess of 50 per cent per decade can be maintained—and given the recent industrial rebirth of Boston and signs of renaissance in Pittsburgh, which should pull their growth rates up, the coefficient of variation of major metropolitan area growth rates will almost certainly decrease again in the coming decade. In sum, the evidence presented strongly suggests that the major metropolitan areas are likely to grow at roughly similar rates throughout the near future.

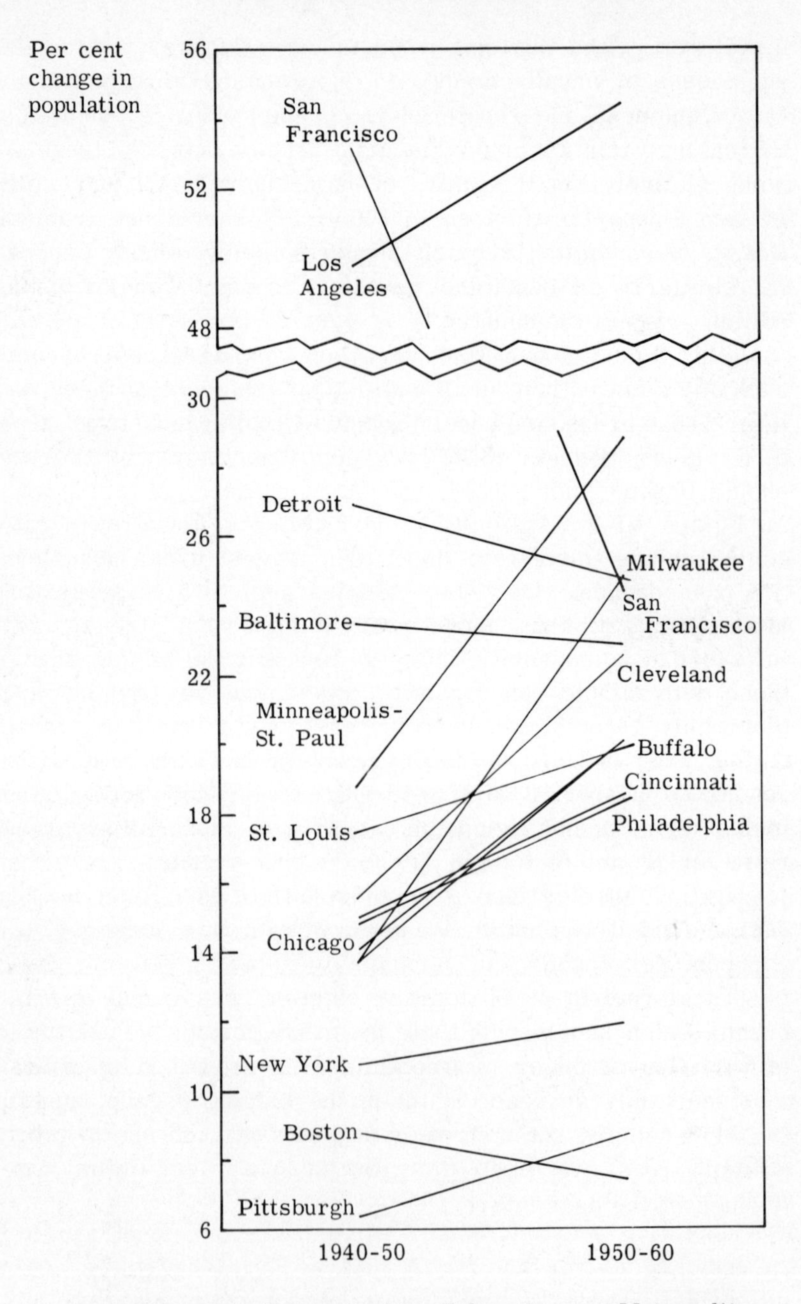

Fig. VI-3. Rate of Growth of the Fifteen Largest Metropolitan Areas in the United States, 1940 to 1960. (Source: See Table VI-2.)

A growth projection for the Detroit metropolitan area

On the basis of this evidence, a decennial rate of population increase for the Detroit metropolitan area of somewhere between 10 and 20 per cent is expected. This growth rate range for large urban areas has been cut back from the 10 to 25 per cent shown during the 1950-60 decade (see Table VI-2) because the constraining expected national rate of population growth for the 1960-70 decade is only a little over 14 per cent, in contrast to the 18.5 per cent national increase from 1950 to 1960. Accordingly, for the current decade the expected average decennial population growth rate for large urban areas is about 15 to 16 per cent, down sharply from the more than 20 per cent experienced in the previous decade.

There is a gap between the average growth rate of population in large urban areas and that of the national population. However, this gap has been reduced from about three percentage points in the 1950-60 decade to between one and two percentage points through the current decade, a phenomenon which reflects the fact that the nonmetropolitan area share of population is declining and that net migration cannot provide as large a share of metropolitan growth in the future as it has in the past. (As a greater and greater share of total national population comes to reside in the larger metropolitan areas, these areas increasingly influence the national population averages. Therefore the average growth of population in these metropolitan areas must converge on the national average rate of population growth.)

The average is one of the key statistics by means of which a distribution is described, and the average is thereby likely to be *the* predictive value. But other good reasons can be adduced to support the projection of a 15 per cent decennial population increase for the Detroit metropolitan area. The automobile industry is no longer growing so vigorously that it can be expected to support heavy in-migration to the local area. Nor is it a declining industry which threatens to force contraction in the local economy. The rapid postwar decentralization of the automobile industry seems to have about run its course, an indication that at worst the Detroit area's participation in the auto industry should suffer only a slow decline. Again, automation of automobile production came early because of the large volume and high degree of standardization of the product, and this fact suggests that the rate of displacement of labor by machines will also be appreciably slower in the future.

Finally, we may draw some consolation from another demographic parameter—the age distribution of the nation's total population. The proportion of the national population between the ages of 20 and 24 moved up very slightly over the past five years, from 6.3 per cent in 1957 to 6.4 per cent in 1962. But this share is destined to increase rapidly during the next decade to 8.0 per cent by 1973 (as estimated in Chapter II). This is the age group whose members come into the new-car market for the first time, bachelors with their first full-time job, and couples with both husband and wife working. The bulge in the birth rate at the close of World War II is even now having its delayed effect on the new-car market. (The smaller 1942-43 bulge is probably at least partly accountable for the current surge in automobile demand. The boys and girls born then were twenty and twenty-one years old in 1962 when the present auto boom began.) Thus, a favorable age distribution of the population could rescue the economy of Michigan and Detroit by providing a stable export base during this difficult period of industrial transformation. A second element of strength is the secular increase in multiple-car families. In sum, the automobile industry will probably provide a large fixed retainer for the Detroit area which, while not quite big enough to support an expanding labor force, will furnish minimum sustenance while the area hustles for new business.

To choose an average growth rate is, of course, roughly equivalent to assuming a near-zero rate of net migration. Thus we should not be surprised to see our projected 15 to 16 per cent decennial rate of population increase yielding figures very close to those offered in the purely demographic projection of Chapter IV. To assume a near-zero rate of net migration, as was done in the demographic work, is to assume implicitly that the local economy is neither especially attractive nor unattractive; this hypothesis is roughly analagous to, or at least compatible with, our assumption that the growth pattern in the automobile industry over the next couple of decades will approximate the average for all industry. (We must either assume this or make the implicit assumption that people are very immobile between regions, or do a little of both.) The neutral work-place assumption should be coupled with the complementary assumption that the local community is neither an especially attractive nor unattractive place to live, for migration today is as much motivated by the amenities of life in the community as it is by prospective job opportunities.

All in all, we would accept here the bland assumption that the Detroit metropolitan area will neither attract nor repel workers in appreciable measure. We would, therefore, accept a zero net migration population projection (i.e., a simple, natural increase population projection) for the Detroit metropolitan area as basically compatible with the growth pattern indicated by this hybrid economic-demographic analysis.[4]

Trends in Income Characteristics of Largest Urban Areas

With increasing size of urban areas and with industrial structures becoming more similar, economic performance

[4]By way of contrast, the sluggish growth of the steel industry is almost certain to keep the Pittsburgh metropolitan area near the lower limit of the observed 10 to 20 per cent large metropolis population growth range. A "moderately pessimistic" prediction of a 10 per cent growth in population over the next decade, coupled with a natural rate of increase of about 15 per cent, implies that the Pittsburgh area economy will have to "export" about one-third of the natural increase in its labor force. We do not expect this to be in the offing for the Detroit area economy because the automobile industry is not nearly so far along its "growth curve" as is steel. That is, the demand for automobiles is more income elastic than the demand for steel; in other words, it will benefit more from our rising per capita income; and the creation of substitute products through technological advance is less threatening at this stage of industrialization and urbanization. (The day may come when the shift to other transportation forms, especially in densely populated areas, does threaten the automobile industry; but certainly this will not occur by 1970 and probably not until 1980 or later.)

characteristics other than growth rate exhibit more homogeneity. The assembling of a wide range of industries and occupations brings a mixing of high- and low-paying jobs. We would be surprised if local industrial diversification did not cause a strong tendency for the Detroit area income level to move closer to the large metropolitan area average. Turning next to Figure VI-4 and Table VI-2, we see that the fifteen largest metropolitan areas are indeed developing more similarity in their income characteristics.

In the third and fourth columns of the table and the first panel of the figure, we note a general tendency toward convergence in median family income. Only Pittsburgh and Los Angeles provide glaring exceptions to the pattern of convergence. Pittsburgh dropped precipitously from second lowest to well below the other areas, a reflection of its severe unemployment problem. The high degree of specialization of the Pittsburgh economy, considering its large size, makes more plausible its exceptional behavior—size has not brought the usual degree of industrial diversification, and without industrial diversification the convergence argument is weakened. Los Angeles, an exception throughout, seems to be an over-size, over-age frontier town, at least in economic characteristics. Rapid growth has made for a tight labor market, in which overtime, second jobs, and second income-earners in the family are prevalent. We can summarize the trend in inter-urban variation in income level among the major metropolitan areas by noting that the coefficient of variation fell from 0.69 to 0.57, a substantial decrease for a single decade. In sum, the very large urban areas seem to be converging toward very similar levels of material well-being.

Homogenization of the industrial structure should not only bring similar income levels but also like degrees of income inequality. As they grow ever larger, Boston, Detroit, and St. Louis should come to have similar mixtures of rich and poor. The degree of inequality of family income in each of the fifteen largest metropolitan areas for each of the two census years, 1950 and 1960, was computed by the use of both the first and third quartiles and the first and ninth deciles (tenth and ninetieth percentiles). The second panel of Figure VI-4 shows the

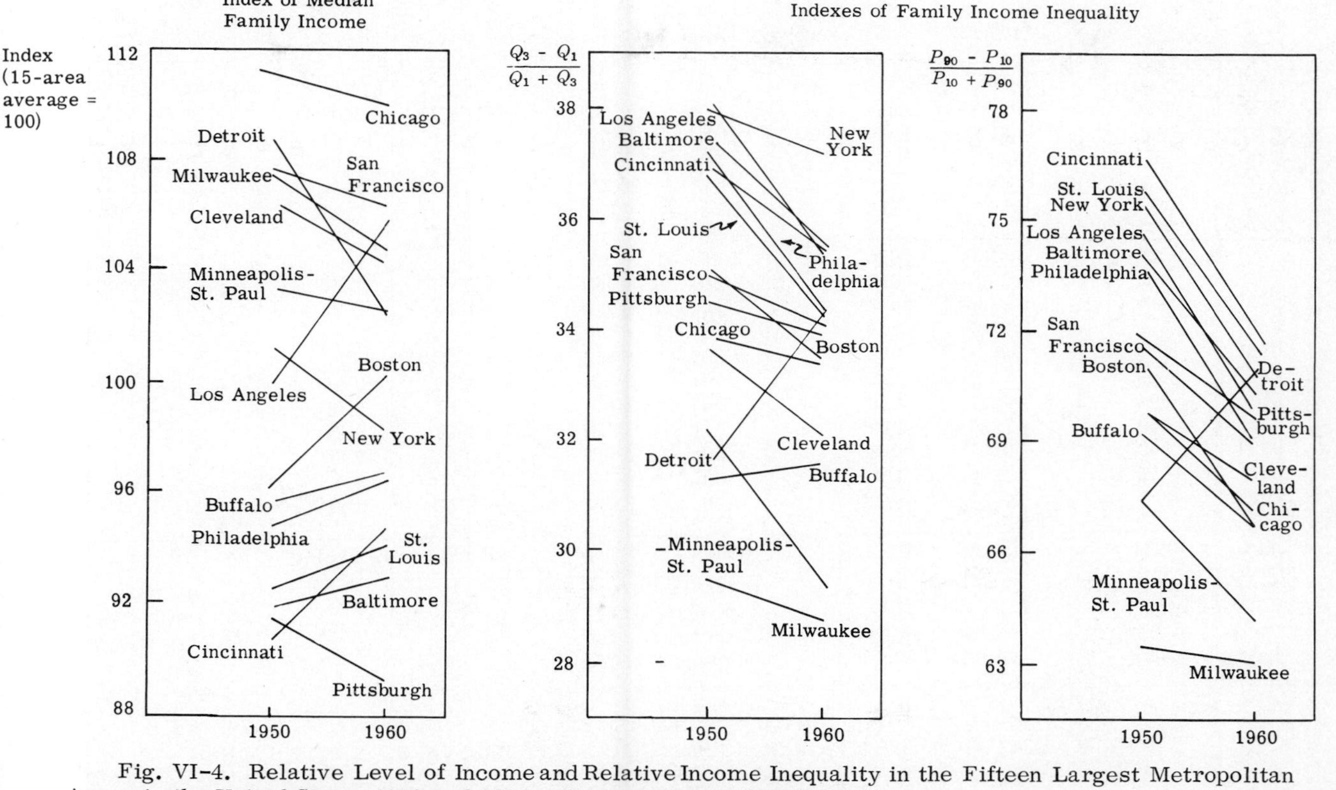

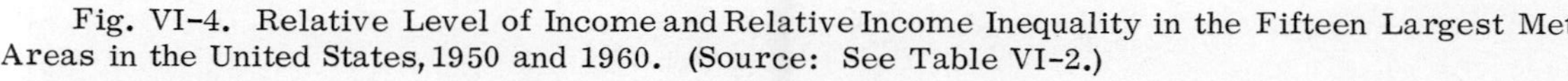

Fig. VI-4. Relative Level of Income and Relative Income Inequality in the Fifteen Largest Metropolitan Areas in the United States, 1950 and 1960. (Source: See Table VI-2.)

Table VI-2

PERFORMANCE CHARACTERISTICS OF FIFTEEN LARGEST METROPOLITAN AREAS IN THE UNITED STATES—1950 AND 1960

Standard Metropolitan Area	Rate of Growth (Percentage Change in Population)		Index of Median Family Income (Percentage of 15-Area Average)		Index of Family Income Inequality $\left(\frac{Q_3-Q_1}{Q_1+Q_3}\right)$		Index of Family Income Inequality $\left(\frac{P_{90}-P_{10}}{P_{10}+P_{90}}\right)$	
	1940-50	1950-60	1950	1960	1950	1960	1950	1960
Baltimore	23.5	22.9	91.9	93.0	.375	.356	.742	.703
Boston	8.8	7.4	96.3	100.3	.351	.336	.713	.666
Buffalo	13.6	20.0	95.7	96.8	.313	.316	.693	.666
Chicago	13.9	20.1	111.2	110.1	.339	.334	.699	.672
Cincinnati	14.9	18.5	90.7	94.8	.370	.355	.769	.720
Cleveland	15.6	22.6	106.6	104.4	.337	.321	.699	.677
Detroit	26.9	24.7	108.9	102.4	.315	.343	.674	.710
Los Angeles	49.8	54.4	99.9	106.0	.382	.354	.747	.698
Milwaukee	13.6	24.8	107.5	104.9	.295	.288	.635	.631
Minneapolis–St. Paul	18.7	28.8	103.4	102.6	.322	.295	.674	.642
New York	10.7	11.9	101.2	98.2	.380	.372	.756	.708
Philadelphia	14.7	18.3	94.9	96.5	.372	.344	.739	.690
Pittsburgh	6.3	8.7	91.6	89.3	.345	.339	.719	.697
St. Louis	17.4	19.8	92.6	94.1	.368	.343	.759	.717
San Francisco	53.3	24.2	107.7	106.4	.350	.341	.717	.689
Standard deviation	13.31	10.48	6.89	5.69	.0264	.0219	.0362	.0256
Arithmetic mean	20.11	21.81	100.0	100.0	.3477	.3358	.716	.686
Coefficient of variation	0.66	0.48	0.69	0.57	.076	.065	.051	.037

Source: Derived from U.S. Bureau of the Census, *Census of Population: 1950* and *Census of Population: 1960.*

"quartile deviation" of family income for each of the fifteen largest metropolitan areas for both 1950 and 1960. Ten of the fifteen areas converge sharply from a range of roughly .31 to .38 to the much tighter spread of .335 to .355, a reduction in separation from .07 to .02. But Minneapolis–St. Paul, Milwaukee, and, to a lesser degree, Cleveland break the pattern by starting low and falling still lower. New York and Buffalo support the general tendency toward convergence but close in at much slower rates.

All in all, the coefficient of variation of inter-urban family income inequality, as measured by the first and third quartiles, fell significantly from 0.69 to 0.57 between 1950 and 1960. To be quite clear, the point being made here is not that large metropolitan areas are becoming more egalitarian with respect to income distribution although they may be doing so, since our inequality coefficients fall for every area except Detroit and Buffalo. The point here is that they are all coming to exhibit about the same degree of inter-family income inequality.

Detroit as a Coming Metropolis—A More Direct View

The degree to which the industrial structure of the Detroit area economy resembles those of her sister metropolises can be assessed more directly and specifically by ascertaining the proportion of total local employment represented in each of thirteen broad industry classes and two subclasses of manufacturing and comparing the figure for each with the 15-area average proportion in that class. Part A of Table VI-3 summarizes this relationship in index form. For example, in 1950 construction's share in total local employment in the Detroit area was only 88 per cent as large as the average in other large metropolitan areas. And Detroit had moved farther away from the typical economic structure of large metropolitan areas by 1960, when the construction index fell to 82. This was, however, the only broad industry class of the thirteen-plus-two which exhibited a diverging movement over the past decade. And eleven of these broad classes, accounting for about 92 per cent of Detroit area employment, exhibited strong trends toward

Table VI-3

CHANGE IN STRUCTURE AND PERFORMANCE OF THE DETROIT AREA ECONOMY RELATIVE TO AVERAGE OF FIFTEEN LARGEST METROPOLITAN AREAS IN THE UNITED STATES—1950 AND 1960

A. By Structural Characteristics

	Index of Relative Proportion of Total Employment in Detroit Metropolitan Area (Avg. of 15 largest areas = 100)		
	1950	1960	Converging (C) Diverging (D)
Construction	88	82	D
Manufacturing	143	129	C
Durables	217	178	C
Nondurables	44	56	C
Transportation	62	69	C
Communications	82	83	...
Utilities	109	108	...
Wholesale trade	64	78	C
Retail trade	91	103	C
Finance, insurance, and real estate	64	69	C
Business and repair services	84	86	C
Personal services	79	91	C
Entertainment	75	74	...
Professional services	79	93	C
Public administration	71	81	C

B. By Performance Characteristics

	Index of Detroit Metropolitan Area (Avg. of 15 largest areas = 100)		
	1950	1960	Converging (C) Diverging (D)
Rate of Growth in Population	134	113	C
Median Family Income	109	102	C
Income Inequality			
Quartiles	91	102	C
Deciles	94	103	C

Source: Derived from U.S. Bureau of the Census, *Census of Population: 1950* and *Census of Population: 1960*.

the "normal" metropolis proportions. No attempt is being made to obscure the fact that the Detroit area is still very atypical, as inspection of the 1960 indexes in the second column so clearly reveals. But the current trend toward a more typical metropolis structure is unmistakable and significant in strength and direction.

As Detroit becomes a more and more conventional metropolis in industrial structure, the local economy should acquire more typical performance characteristics. Part B of Table VI-3 displays the index numbers which link the Detroit area growth rate, income level, and income inequality to the norm of the large metropolitan area average.

The rate at which the Detroit area economy has converged on the 15-area average is breathtaking. For example, median family incomes moved from 109 to 102 (where 100 is the average for the fifteen largest areas), and income inequalities indexes in quartiles moved from 91 to 102 (where, again, 100 represents the average for the fifteen largest areas). So striking is this movement that we must exercise great caution against drawing unwarranted inferences. Since the Detroit area moved from a very abnormal industrial structure only part-way toward an average one, the almost complete convergence of the Detroit area income level (109 to 102) and income inequality index (91 to 102) on these two averages of 100 must reflect other forces at work. Because 1950 was a prosperity year in Detroit, good even in relation to other areas, and 1960 was a year of recession, in general worse in Detroit than in other areas, some of the apparent convergence in income characteristics is probably attributable to cyclical not secular causes. That is, the 1960 Detroit area income was temporarily lower and income inequality temporarily greater than ordinary because of the relatively high level of unemployment in Detroit in 1960. Still, the movement of the Detroit area growth and income pattern toward a more metropolis-like character has been much too dramatic to be explained away solely as a cyclical or chance phenomenon, especially in the light of the clear trend its industrial structure has similarly shown.

The manufacturing base of the Detroit area

Another way to assess trends in the degree of industrial diversification shown by the Detroit area economy is to examine at closer range those sectors in which it has greater than average employment. A simple calculation has been used to identify the industries of greatest local specialization. The fifteen largest metropolitan areas of the country were adopted as a norm, and the average proportion of total employment in each of the 149 "detailed industries" (as defined in the *Census of Population*) was calculated. These averages were then applied to the total employment of the Detroit metropolitan area to determine the "expected" number of workers, industry by industry. These hypothetical employment totals were then subtracted from the actual Detroit area employment figures, leaving the number of "surplus" workers. The results were then edited to separate those figures which probably reflected local specialization due to export orientation and those where local specialization was probably due to distinctive local taste patterns. (An example of such patterns would be the existence in the Detroit area economy of about 500 more workers in bowling alleys than we would expect in a typical metropolitan area of its size—surely a matter of local taste in recreation.) The estimated number of export-oriented "surplus" workers, by industry, is presented in Table VI-4 for the years 1940, 1950, and 1960. (These are estimates of *net*, not gross, export employment.)

What these figures tell us is that in 1940 the export base of the Detroit area economy embraced very little outside of the automobile industry. About 90 per cent of the *net* export employment in the area was in automobile manufacturing, and most of the rest was in related work. Only about 2 per cent of the export base was independent of the pervasive influence of that industry, and this part was engaged principally in the manufacture of office machines. A decade later the local economy was still dominated just as much by automobile manufacturing, and the proportions directly and indirectly engaged in automobile production were almost unchanged, about 90 and 8 per cent, respectively. (The crash effort after the war of filling the huge backlog demand for automobiles was enough to keep Detroit busy.) Again, only about 2 per cent of the export base was inde-

Table VI-4

EXPORT BASE OF THE DETROIT METROPOLITAN AREA, 1940–1960

Industry	Estimated Number of "Surplus" Workers*	
	(In Thousands)	(Per Cent)
1940:		
Automobiles and automobile equipment	170.0	90.14
Misc. machinery	6.1	3.23
Rubber products	3.6	1.91
Office and store machines, equipment, and supplies	2.6	1.38
Misc. nonferrous metal products	1.6	.85
Other iron and steel products	1.4	.74
Nonferrous metals and their products	1.2	.64
Dairy products	.8	.42
Nonferrous metal primary products	.4	.21
Cut stone and stone products	.4	.21
Paints, varnishes, and colors	.3	.16
Cement, concrete, gypsum, and plaster products	.2	.11
Total	188.6	100.00
1950:		
Motor vehicles and equipment	299.0	89.52
Misc. machinery	15.6	4.67
Fabricated structural metal products	5.3	1.59
Office, computing, and accounting machines	4.0	1.20
Rubber and misc. plastic products	3.7	1.11
Primary nonferrous industries	2.7	.81
Other primary iron and steel products	1.5	.45
Drugs and medicines	1.2	.36
Misc. nonmetallic mineral and stone products	.4	.12
Motor vehicles and equipment—wholesale	.3	.09
Nonmetallic mining and quarrying	.2	.06
Nonspecified metal industries	.1	.03
Total	334.0	100.00
1960:		
Motor vehicles and equipment	216.5	75.52
Misc. machinery	32.0	11.16
Misc. fabricated metal products	11.2	3.91
Office, computing, and accounting machines	8.8	3.07
Newspaper publishing and printing	4.6	1.60
Cutlery, hand tools, and other hardware	3.2	1.12
Rubber products	2.9	1.01
Trucking service	2.1	.73
Drugs and medicines	1.1	.38
Primary nonferrous industries	.9	.31
Motor vehicles and equipment—wholesale	.8	.28
Blast furnaces and steelworks	.8	.28
Pottery and related products	.6	.21
Engineering and architectural service	.6	.21
Farm machinery and equipment	.6	.21
Total	286.7	100.00

*Number of workers in the Detroit metropolitan area in excess of the number who would have been employed if the area had the same average industry mix as the fifteen largest metropolitan areas in the United States.

Source: Derived from U.S. Bureau of the Census, *Census of Population: 1950* and *Census of Population: 1960.*

pendent of the automobile industry; the manufacture of office machines continued to occupy this smaller group, with drugs and medicines taking an added share.

But now, another decade later, we find that the proportion directly engaged in auto-making has fallen sharply from nine-tenths to about three-quarters of total export employment. Again, much of the remainder is linked to the automobile industry, but not quite so much. A few new minor (net) export specialities have broken through—printing and publishing, tools and hardware, engineering and architectural services, and farm machinery—which are at least semiautonomous. But close inspection of the 1960 list of industrial specialities suggests that it is primarily in the industries related to automobile manufacturing that the Detroit area economy has expanded—or rather, deepened.

The significant development in the export sector of Detroit's economy in the past decade does not appear to be the doubling of the independent manufacturing share, from about 2 to 4 per cent of the total, so much as the doubling, from about 8 to 18 per cent, of that portion which is linked to automobiles. Within the confines of a considerably smaller total export employment, miscellaneous machinery and various metal-fabricating industries have doubled, and the previous steel-making deficit has been turned into a surplus employment for the local economy. While a much more subtle and incisive analysis would be necessary before we could precisely identify and quantify the changing pattern of the export sector, in a broad way we might say that the increasing vertical integration of the export complex has been the paramount economic development in the Detroit area, at least in the manufacturing export sector.

But can we characterize vertical integration as industrial diversification? If we make more and more of the components which go into automobiles and more and more of the tools and equipment used in automobile-making, are we really becoming more diversified? Surely, we will experience cyclical swings in automobile production just as much as before, and if so the local cycle characteristics may remain unchanged. But in the long run we stand to gain new skills and production experience in primary metals, metal-fabricating, machinery production, and so forth. The base is being put in place from which first excursions into new products can be launched.

A number of observers of the local industrial scene have noted the relatively underdeveloped state of nondurables manufacturing in the Detroit area and have speculated that the making up of this lag may be one of the principal directions that industrial growth will take in the coming years. True, the vertical integration of the Detroit area automobile complex has pushed the area into a few nondurable lines, such as paperboard panels and textile floor coverings in cars. Still these gains are small beside the vertical growth in durables referred to above. A few nondurables do show signs of such marked expansion that it might significantly affect the structure of the local economy. A comparative analysis of the employment trends in manufacturing in the fifteen largest metropolitan areas from 1940 to 1960 suggests patterns of local change which could easily raise printing and publishing from its current figure of 1.9 per cent share of total local employment to perhaps 2.25 per cent by 1975; and manufacturing of food products seems likely to rise similarly from 2 to about 2.25 per cent by 1975.

In sum, the net expansion in nondurables will probably increase their share of total employment from the current 7 per cent to somewhere around 7.5 per cent by 1975 (an appreciable increase only in the light of the general decline in manufacturing's share). The judgment here is that this area is unlikely to become a major center for nondurable goods, partly because of its relatively high local wage rates and partly because urban areas, however large, seldom specialize in more than a quarter to a third of the full range of manufacturing activity.

Still, an even modest increase in nondurable goods manufacturing in the Detroit area—stimulated by the transportation cost advantage in local production for the local market—will probably provide an important source of local employment growth. The "modest increase" from 6.9 to 7.5 per cent of total employment, suggested above, when multiplied by a 1975 level of total employment which will probably be about 28 per cent greater than in 1960, yields a 36 per cent increase in nondurable goods employment, or an absolute employment gain of some 34,000 jobs, assuming about the same percentage of unemployed in 1975 as in 1960. This projected figure can be compared to the estimated gain of 52,000 jobs in durable goods manufacturing, a 12 per cent increase, which we have derived by projecting a decline in the durable goods share from 33.7 per cent in 1960 to about 29.5 per cent in 1975 (multiplied by the 28 per cent increase in total employment). Thus, we expect that a small increase in the small share held by nondurable goods manufacturing will create about two-thirds as many new jobs as will be generated out of a slowly declining share in the huge durable goods sector. In more general terms, increased production for the local market, i.e., a trend toward greater local self-sufficiency in nondurable manufactures, will probably provide a local growth stimulus of a magnitude almost equivalent to the growth of the durable goods manufacturing *export* base.

Detroit as an industrial entrepreneur

The long-run prospect is for new products to emanate from this industrial environment as it grows richer. One should, in fact, recognize that as a city grows larger its role changes from producer to creator. Rather than simply disgorging volumes of standardized products *(à la* Flint), Detroit has been and must continue to be the center of automotive technology and design. But Detroit must become something more than just a center of automotive technology; it must emulate New York and Boston and Chicago by finding its very reason for being in invention and innovation that strike out in many and diverse directions. The economic history of New York is instructive at this point and indicates an important moral for the Detroit area economy and its leaders.

> The New York metropolitan area grew by incubating new functions, nurturing them and finally spinning them off to other sections of the country, all the while regenerating this cycle. The flour mills, foundries, meat-packing, textiles and tanneries of the post-Civil War period drifted away from New York, their place taken by less transport-sensitive products—garments, cigars, and office work. Currently, New York is losing the manufacturing

> end of many of its most traditional specialties, as garment sewing slips away to low-wage Eastern Pennsylvania leaving only the selling function behind, and as printing splits away from immobile publishing. But New York's growth never seems to falter as the new growth industries are much more than proportionately regenerated in its rich industrial culture.[5]

Because it is almost inevitable that a substantial amount of decentralization will occur with the maturing of the local growth industries, the big city in particular should spend less time worrying about losing a share of some existing industry and more time working to cultivate new replacement industries. The city that aspires to be a true metropolis should pattern its actions on the executive image, delegating tasks readily as they become routine and keeping itself free to take on the new and sophisticated work in which it has a comparative advantage over smaller places. In taking this direction the big city often has no choice, for the smaller community offers lower costs of production for routine operations and will often maneuver desperately to underbid for the work that its survival demands; tax concessions, rent-free plants, low-interest loans, and the like are lures used mainly by small urban areas. The small, isolated manufacturing town is much less able than its larger counterpart to compete in research and development work or even in manufacturing operations in the early stages of the "learning curve."

The very large metropolitan areas of the country do, in fact, show some evidence of resembling each other in the business of inventing and innovating. The estimated number of scientists and engineers per thousand manufacturing workers and per thousand total employees for nine metropolitan areas was computed and expressed as a percentage of the 9-area average. (It is not obvious whether manufacturing employment or total employment is the appropriate deflator. Is research and development generated largely from manufacturing activity, or is it rather a function of total activity?) In either case, a

[5]Thompson, pp. 19-20. See Raymond Vernon, *Metropolis 1985* (Cambridge, Mass.: Harvard Univ. Press, 1960), especially chap. iii, for the material from which the summary and closing inference were drawn.

clear tendency toward convergence is exhibited, as shown in Figure VI-5 and Table VI-5. The coefficient of variation of the nine index numbers decreased by about one-third between 1945 and 1955, in both the manufacturing and total employment forms. The tentative conclusion is that research and development work—industrial entrepreneurship in its highest and most dynamic expression—must be assumed as a *routine* function by the aspiring metropolis.

To the extent, moreover, that the critical urban problem of the day is to find ways to provide full employment, industrial entrepreneurship has much more to recommend it than straight production work. The sophisticated job of creating more and more new products and processes is almost sure to use more labor than the routine work of running standard manufacturing operations, especially in this age of automation. Technical discussion, experimentation, setting up pilot plants, and other such work is the big city's forte. Much of this is professional service work rather than manufacturing activity as we have known it in the past, however the Bureau of the Census may classify it. This is especially true of contract research in university laboratories, proliferating market survey activities, consulting, patenting, financing, and so forth. A true metropolis must be fully as much a center of business and technical services as of consumer and personal-family services.

Detroit as a major professional and personal service center

The coming diversification of the Detroit area economy will probably be accomplished through a broadening and deepening of the service industry even more than through vertical integration of the automobile industry. This seems to follow from both the nationwide trend toward an expanded service sector share and the fact that Detroit is relatively underdeveloped in this area of activity.

One can adduce a number of reasons why a substantial expansion of the service sector is in the offing. First, many services, though not all, are income elastic—they are "luxury goods"—and so the demand for them will rise more than would

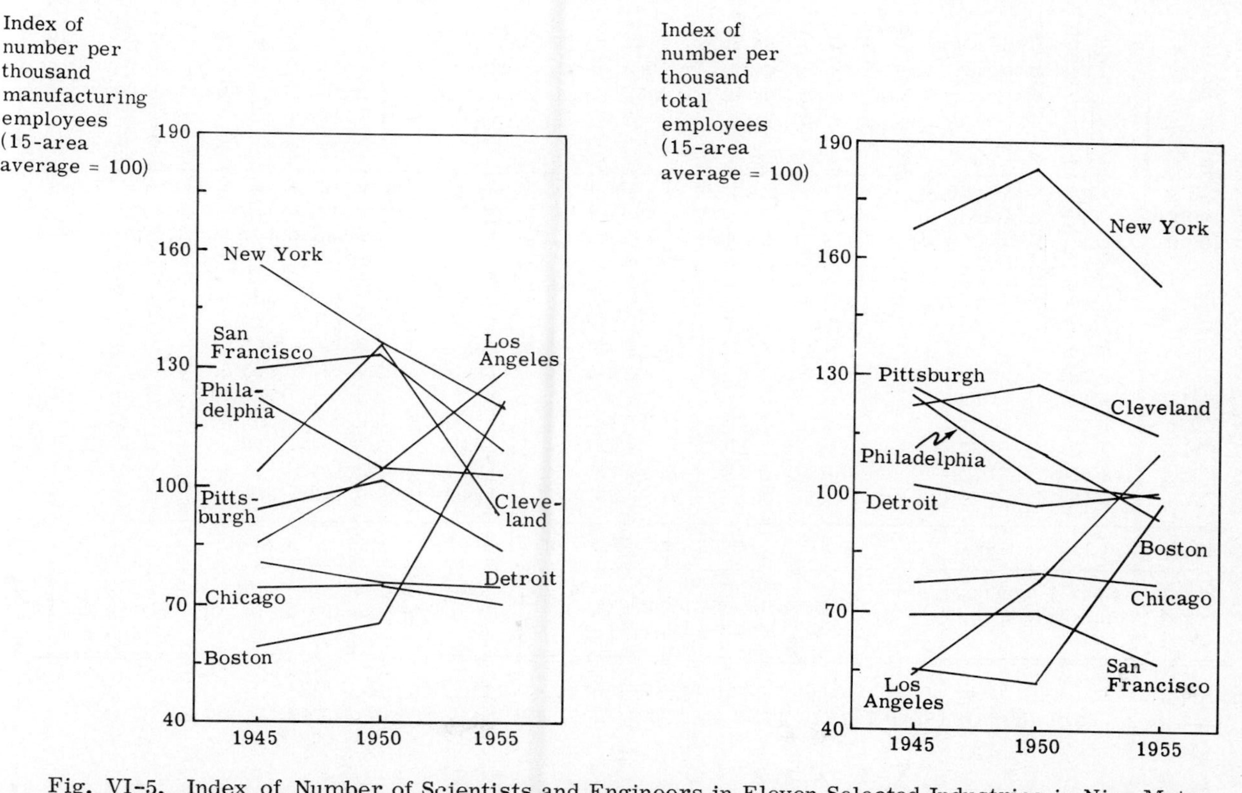

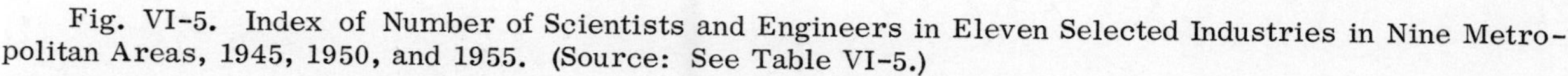
Fig. VI-5. Index of Number of Scientists and Engineers in Eleven Selected Industries in Nine Metropolitan Areas, 1945, 1950, and 1955. (Source: See Table VI-5.)

Table VI-5

NUMBER OF SCIENTISTS AND ENGINEERS IN ELEVEN SELECTED INDUSTRIES IN NINE METROPOLITAN AREAS—1945, 1950, 1955

Metropolitan Area	Number of Scientists and Engineers			Index of Number Per Thousand Manufacturing Employees*			Index of Number Per Thousand Total Employees*		
	1945	1950	1955	1945	1950	1955	1945	1950	1955
Boston	778	1,135	3,544	53.9	65.8	120.3	55.5	51.9	95.1
Chicago	3,403	4,483	7,191	74.3	74.5	70.3	77.5	79.5	76.6
Cleveland	1,345	1,875	2,897	103.5	135.7	91.1	122.0	127.6	114.8
Detroit	2,190	2,762	4,891	81.2	75.3	74.5	102.1	97.1	100.8
Los Angeles	1,494	3,124	9,159	85.9	103.4	128.9	54.2	77.4	110.4
New York	12,074	14,325	22,582	155.9	136.0	119.4	167.4	182.8	153.2
Philadelphia	3,134	3,531	5,909	121.6	104.5	103.0	124.2	102.9	99.5
Pittsburgh	1,541	2,146	2,943	94.2	101.3	83.4	126.7	110.9	93.2
San Francisco	1,025	1,434	2,111	129.5	133.1	109.0	69.5	69.5	56.6
Standard deviation of number per thousand				1.43	1.44	2.03	0.856	0.871	0.967
Arithmetic mean of number per thousand				4.84	6.20	10.14	2.36	2.39	3.85
Coefficient of variation				0.295	0.233	0.200	0.363	0.364	0.251

*15-area average = 100.

Source: Derived from George Perazich, "Growth of Scientific Research in Selected Industries, 1945-1960," Contract Research Report of Galaxy, Inc., to the National Science Foundation, Oct. 14, 1957, table VI, p. 36. (Mimeographed.)

be proportionate to our increasing per capita income. Examples are: financial counseling, psychiatric treatment, restaurant services, and theatre performances. Second, we should expect an increasingly affluent society to demand not only much more of *almost all* kinds of professional services but more of *many* kinds of personal services; moreover, rapid employment growth in these directions can also be expected because services are, on the whole, less subject to automation. Even if we should come to employ machines in medical diagnosis and to automate insurance offices from top to bottom, some services are extremely resistant to automation whereas almost no manufacturing is.

Third, we may find that, as a direct by-product of the process of automation in manufacturing, new service work is created. The need for much more intensive and personal treatment of the displaced factory worker, through vocational testing, psychological analysis, counseling, retraining, relocation, and so forth, could become one of the principal sources of new jobs in the next decade. (There is hardly need to mention other social services related to child care and such kinds of social pathology as alcoholism, crime, and delinquency.) And these new "personnel" jobs could prove to be ones we desperately need: semiprofessional work suited to the abilities and training of the deluge of C+ to B- students due to pour out of our expanded colleges in a few years. We may expect continued rapid growth in the local public sectors and in the private, nonprofit sectors of our economy, especially in the many social service sectors (e.g., social case work).

Fourth, a growing and diversifying Detroit area economy will almost certainly exercise increasing influence over its hinterland—the rest of Michigan, excepting perhaps the southwestern corner of the state which is economically oriented to Chicago. Now that Detroit has reaped the easy harvest of a wealthy and expansive automobile industry, it will become necessary and profitable to go back and glean the fields for unexploited opportunities in service industries. And more than casual evidence does exist that Detroit is growing up and blossoming out in finance, education, and wholesale trade. Witness the new buildings downtown, Wayne State University's growing graduate programs, and the proposed new Detroit merchandise mart.

Objection has been raised to so rosy a view of Detroit's potential as a service center for an extended region. Some observers doubt that Detroit can reach a point where it will not only fill more of its own service needs but even begin to export a significant amount of service. The counterargument is advanced that Detroit's position on a peninsula, constrained by the existence of Chicago to the west and Cleveland to the east, so constricts its potential service market that major status as a metropolis, a "mother city," is not a real developmental choice for this area. One needs only to peruse a set of maps, however, to appreciate that Detroit's near monopoly of Michigan provides fully as rich a hinterland as Boston's *share* of New England, Cleveland's *share* of Ohio (some portion of which goes to Pittsburgh and Cincinnati), Milwaukee's sparsely populated Wisconsin hinterland (for whose trade Milwaukee competes with Chicago), or Philadelphia's cramped market wedged between New York and Baltimore-Washington.

Moreover, with the continued drift to the large metropolitan areas, each metropolitan area becomes increasingly its own region. That is, the next couple of decades will probably see the Detroit area pulling its hinterland customers right into its immediate environs, or expanding to absorb its satellites like Ann Arbor at least as much as it reaches out to provide them with services where they are. In sum, the Detroit economy has already amassed a more or less captive market of over 4 million people, whose per capita income is above the average and larger than that of all but four other metropolitan areas. And, for reasons argued in the first section of this paper, this area is likely to keep all or most of its natural increase. This prospect alone ensures substantial growth and further economic development, at not much below the national average rate, in all but the most adverse circumstances.

The Detroit Area Economy, 1975
A Reluctant Projection

Brief reference was made above, in the section on the manufacturing base of the Detroit area, to the expected level of durable and nondurable manufacturing employment in 1975. While forecasting the future is a most hazardous business, the fun of free-wheeling speculation—writing "poetry" like that above—should carry with it the obligation to be reasonably explicit about the relative magnitudes involved. That is to say, it is now time to round out the manufacturing projections shown above with estimates, however rough and tentative, of future employment across the board.

Assuming again the near-zero rate of net migration argued above, we begin with an expected rate of population increase of 15 per cent per decade; and, because of the current bias in the age structure of the local population toward young adults, we project an increase in the local labor force at the decennial rate of about 18 per cent. A decennial rate of 18 per cent extrapolates to about 28 per cent in fifteen years, and so we have projected an increase in total employment in the Detroit area from 1,329,000 in 1960 to about 1,700,000 in 1975. We have, therefore, roughly 371,000 additional jobs to be distributed by industry.

The underlying analysis of the industry projections which follow was simple and direct in technique. The share of total local employment engaged in each of the 150-odd "detailed industries" reported in the *Decennial Census of Population* was derived for the Detroit metropolitan area and for the other fourteen largest metropolitan areas for the last three census years, 1940, 1950, and 1960. (The 1940 data are not strictly comparable because of significant changes in many industry definitions and also because "metropolitan areas" were not delineated until 1950; in 1940 we have the roughly comparable "industrial areas" at the "two-digit" Standard Industrial Classification level but must descend to the much less satisfactory central cities only at the "three-digit" Standard Industrial Classification level.)

By working both with three points in time and with fifteen areas, we have achieved a combined time series and cross-section analysis. Following the main thesis of this chapter, that the Detroit area is becoming a more typical metropolis, we have projected the time series of local employment shares (1940-60) not only with an eye to the past—to the slope of the line—but also with an eye to whether the Detroit area line is above or below that of other very large metropolitan areas. Time is weighted heavily, however, because even under the hypothesis of the "metropolization" of Detroit, it is not the current industrial structure of the typical metropolis that the local economy should approach, but rather the structure of employment that is coming into being in very large urban areas. Accordingly, the trend of the 15-area average was plotted and extrapolated to 1975, and the Detroit area share projection was (often, not always) bent to approach the *expected, typical* large metropolitan area industrial structure. (For example, a currently rising trend in some share of local employment might be reversed if the other metropolitan areas were exhibiting rapidly falling shares in that activity, even if the Detroit area were still below average in 1960.)

In general, the share of total local employment in a given industry in the Detroit area was projected upward to 1975 if: (1) the trend since 1940, or even just since 1950, has been upward; or (2) the local share is appreciably below the level in other metropolitan areas, and the activity is not one characterized by locational concentration; or (3) a strongly rising national trend is expected (e.g., for a good whose demand is income elastic, an urban service that becomes more in demand with increasing population density, a service rendered to the elderly in an aging population, and so forth).

While a full reporting on this research, comprising some 150-odd share projections and the supporting arguments, is well beyond the scope of this study, a brief summary of anticipated employment trends in major industry groups will provide a sense of relative magnitudes—a perspective. In Table VI-6, the percentage of total local employment engaged in each of sixteen major industry groups in 1960 is presented (column 2) along with the corresponding projected shares for 1975 (column 3). The projected level of total local employment in 1975 (1,700,000) was then multiplied by these projected shares to derive the expected number of workers in each of the sixteen

Table VI-6

DETROIT METROPOLITAN AREA EMPLOYMENT PROJECTIONS, 1975, BY INDUSTRY

Major Industry Group	Employment, 1960		Projected Employment, 1975		Projected Change, 1960-75	
	Number*	Per Cent	Per Cent	Number*	Number*	Percentage Increase
Agriculture, forestry, fisheries	7.5	0.56	0.44	7.5	0.0	0.0
Mining	1.0	0.07	0.06	1.0	0.0	0.0
Construction	53.6	4.03	4.60	78.2	24.6	45.9
Manufacturing	541.4	40.75	36.90	627.3	85.9	15.9
Durables	447.9	33.71	29.40	499.8	51.9	11.6
Nondurables	93.5	6.93	7.50	127.5	34.0	36.4
Transportation	43.5	3.27	3.27	55.6	12.1	27.8
Communication	16.6	1.25	1.27	21.6	5.0	30.1
Utilities and sanitary services	19.1	1.44	1.45	24.6	5.5	28.8
Wholesale trade	42.8	3.22	3.45	58.7	15.9	37.1
Retail trade	195.6	14.72	14.25	242.2	46.6	23.8
Finance, insurance, real estate	51.0	3.84	4.40	74.8	23.8	46.7
Business and repair services	35.5	2.67	2.95	50.2	14.7	41.4
Personal services	63.6	4.79	4.65	79.0	15.4	24.2
Entertainment and recreation services	10.0	0.75	0.75	12.8	2.8	28.0
Professional and related services	146.3	11.01	13.20	224.4	78.1	53.4
Public administration	49.8	3.75	4.50	76.5	26.7	53.6
Industry not reported	51.3	3.86	3.86	65.6	14.3	28.0
Total employment	1,328.6	100.00	100.00	1,700.0	371.4	28.0

*Figures in thousands.

industry groups (column 4). The fifteen-year change in employment both in absolute number (column 5) and as a rate of increase (column 6) was then derived. Table VI-6 is, in essence, the spelling-out of two basic assumptions: (1) The Detroit metropolitan area will experience a near-zero rate of migration over the next fifteen years; that is, it will grow at its natural rate of population increase; and (2) the Detroit area economy will steadily evolve toward an industrial structure typical of the large urban area of 1975.

Manufacturing is expected to account for only 86,000 additional jobs, or well under one-quarter of the total gain. This projected increase is divided between durables and nondurables in the ratio of about 3:2, as has already been stated. It is in the service sector that the major gains are expected. Professional services alone are projected to add 78,000 jobs (nine-tenths of the manufacturing gain), and wholesale and retail trade are projected to add another 62,500 jobs by 1975. Public administration, with an increase in employment of 26,700, and finance, insurance, and real estate, with 23,800, are the third and fourth largest service industry gainers.

These projected gains for service industry employment should be of especially great interest to the beleaguered central city, since service industries represent more promising sources of new employment at central city sites than manufacturing does. Even if the trend toward suburbanization of manufacturing and retail trade should continue, the industrial outlook for the central city is really quite bright, if the core area can retain its traditionally strong attraction for government, finance, and related professions, the most rapidly growing sectors of the Detroit area economy. And the collateral point can be made that the more successful the central city is in holding these key activities, the greater is the probability of luring the educated and affluent employees of these industries back into town to live. Just as central city contraction has been cumulative in the recent past, so success can beget success in the near future—with good planning and management in the local public sector.

Re-counting our mixed blessings

The economic implications of the coming transition of the Detroit area from a brash and dynamic industrial center to a full-blown metropolis are implicit throughout this paper. But a recapitulation here will make the major points more explicit.

As the Detroit area matures, its many growth and income characteristics will approach those of the average metropolis and the nation. The movement of more and more of our population to these giant urban areas will create a situation where the major metropolises almost are the nation. The "nationalization" of the performance characteristics of the Detroit area economy will not be an unmixed blessing. True, greater cyclical stability will be achieved as the area comes to depend less on motor vehicles and more on metropolitan services. But this area's per capita income, now above average, will probably exhibit a *relative* drop because it will rise less rapidly than that of other urban areas. Again, Detroit as the biggest factory town on earth has enjoyed a relatively low level of income inequality. The narrow range of occupations and the egalitarian influence of trade unions have combined to produce this effect. Now with the ascendancy of finance, entertainment, and various professional services, Detroit will assemble more and more of the very rich and very poor—corporate lawyers as well as messenger "boys." This means that the talented will find more opportunity, although the implications with respect to the unprepared are less favorable to general welfare.

The local growth rate, much faster than the nation's up to 1955 or so, has slowed and will probably approach the national rate of change. In population terms, the Detroit area growth rate will probably approach the local rate of natural increase, roughly that of other large metropolitan areas and ultimately that of the nation at large, as the nonmetropolitan areas are drained to minimum populations. But then slow, steady growth in population probably presents the optimum conditions under which to plan and develop an efficient and pleasant urban area.

All in all, I foresee a Detroit area large enough to offer the advantages which ensure its competitive position. As a metropolis it will therefore share, if no longer exceed, the general nationwide level of well-being and will grow steadily and exhibit greater cyclical stability. This rather rosy picture is dimmed a bit by the further expectation that a growing income inequality will demand of local leaders the closest attention and greatest skill. In common with all metropolitan areas, the Detroit area must, then, address itself to the growing problem of welfare and the development of human resources. "Detroiters" will have the money; they must also have the will.

VII

SOCIAL STRUCTURE OF THE MICHIGAN LABOR MARKET

Louis A. Ferman

What changes can we envision for Michigan's labor market over the next dozen years? What impact will technological change have on patterns of labor force participation and utilization? What role will less favored workers play in the labor market of the 1970's? These questions about the Michigan labor market, although of interest to every citizen of Michigan, cannot easily be answered. In most cases, the field research which would make even tentative answers possible has not yet been done. In the present state of knowledge, the best that the social scientist can do is to make some shrewd guesses and careful speculations based on his understanding and evaluation of current social and economic trends. These conjectures, if accepted with due caution and qualification, can give some idea of the *kinds* of problems that Michigan will face in the years ahead and can suggest some solutions to them.

An inquiry of this kind must necessarily be selective. The scope and content of this chapter have been dictated by two considerations: What will be the nature of the emerging industrial structures in Michigan, and what impact will these have on patterns of labor force participation and utilization in Michigan? The chapter is divided into three sections: (1) the emerging manpower trends in the Michigan labor market; (2) the participation of non-white workers in the Michigan labor force; and (3) the education and training of workers in Michigan.

Emerging Manpower Trends

Although there are some variations, the national patterns of employment, labor force participation, and unemployment have their counterparts in the Michigan labor market. This is not to say that *all* communities of Michigan share the problems of the national economy in the same way. For example, in the Upper Peninsula the major problem is the "aging" of the labor force, brought about by the out-migration of youthful workers who have failed to find any steady employment following the mass shut-downs of the mines. In southeastern Michigan we are faced with the problem of a labor force having to adjust to a marked shift from commodity to noncommodity employment and hence requiring new skills and new training for job opportunities. Although the following discussion will treat the Michigan labor market as a single, uniform entity, these local variations should be kept in mind.[1]

Industrial and occupational distribution

The labor market patterns of Michigan reflect an economy that is shifting from commodity production to noncommodity production, with relative declines in blue-collar employment and increases in opportunities for white-collar workers. The percentages of employment by industry are going to show relative declines in the commodity-producing industries—such as agriculture, mining, and manufacturing—and large increases in trade, services, and to a lesser extent construction and government employment. In 1960, 51.9 per cent of Michigan's civilian labor force were in noncommodity employment, and projections by the National Planning Association (N.P.A.) and the Bureau of Labor Statistics indicate that this proportion will increase to 54.4 per cent by 1970. The long-range N.P.A. estimates published in 1962 predicted that two out of every

[1]A detailed discussion of local labor market problems in Michigan will be found in Sigmund Nosow, *Vocational Curricula in Michigan,* Educational Research Series No. 17 (East Lansing, Mich.: Office of Research and Publications, College of Education, Michigan State Univ., Sept., 1963).

three workers in the Michigan labor force will be in noncommodity employment by 1976. The employment losses will be concentrated in Michigan's leading commodity industries: transportation equipment, primary metals, and nonelectrical machinery; while increases will occur in trade, services, construction, and government. The N.P.A. data are shown in Table VII-1.

These industrial shifts in employment may be attributed to a number of causes. First, labor-saving devices and technological change, especially the development of automated equipment, are achieving sizable reductions in manpower needs in the very industries that have been at the core of Michigan's industrial complex—the industries which manufacture durable goods. The productivity increases in the private sector of the economy have been achieved largely in agriculture and production-worker manufacturing. Second, Wilbur Thompson has noted that in Detroit, where a substantial proportion of Michigan employment is located, the industry mix is undergoing a change in the direction of noncommodity employment. The concentration of production industries in Detroit is giving way to a complex of service industries that are typical of a metropolitan center serving the trade and commercial needs of a large hinterland. Thirdly, although durable goods manufacturing will increase in the United States, Michigan has been unable to share in this increase by attracting durable goods industries with high growth potential (e.g., electrical machinery manufacturing). Finally, Michigan will probably continue to be subjected to the market forces that bring about geographical decentralization of the auto industry and its supplier firms. This is a trend that started in the postwar period; and, although the decline in Michigan of automotive manufacturing capacity appears to be leveling off, there is no indication that Michigan will receive the investment from this industry in the future that was typical prior to 1955.

These industry shifts have changed and will continue to change the occupational distribution and manpower needs of the Michigan labor market. The most striking change has been the growth of white-collar employment (Table VII-2). In 1940, 32 per cent of the Michigan labor force were in white-collar

Table VII-1
DISTRIBUTION OF MICHIGAN CIVILIAN EMPLOYMENT BY INDUSTRY, 1947 AND 1957, AND PROJECTIONS FOR 1976

Industry	Employment (In Thousands)			Percentage of State Civilian Employment		
	1947	1957	1976	1947	1957	1976
Commodity employment	1,277.9	1,258.4	1,215.3	52.0	44.3	34.2
Agriculture	220.0	193.0	157.2	9.0	6.8	4.4
Mining	17.1	14.2	12.5	0.6	0.5	0.4
Manufacturing*	1,040.8	1,051.2	1,045.6	42.4	37.0	29.4
Primary metals	99.3	86.7	80.0	4.0	3.0	2.3
Fabricated metals	92.8	107.6	105.0	3.8	3.8	2.9
Nonelectrical machinery	150.3	172.2	175.0	6.1	6.1	4.8
Transportation equipment	411.2	376.0	305.0	16.7	13.2	8.6
Noncommodity employment	1,178.6	1,585.1	2,336.1	48.0	55.7	65.8
Transportation, communication, and utilities	141.0	161.0	182.2	5.7	5.6	5.1
Trade	447.9	524.0	784.1	18.2	18.4	22.1
Service	264.8	443.7	739.0	10.8	15.6	20.8
Finance and real estate	54.7	81.2	97.3	2.2	2.9	2.7
Construction	99.2	138.2	204.4	4.1	4.9	5.8
Government	171.0	237.0	329.1	7.0	8.3	9.3
Total civilian employment	2,456.5	2,843.5	3,551.4	100.0	100.0	100.0
Total population	6,075	7,690	10,289			

*Only major Michigan manufacturing industries are shown.

Source: U. S. Bureau of Labor Statistics, *Projections to Years 1976 and 2000: Economic Growth, Population, Labor Force, Leisure, and Transportation,* a Report to the Outdoor Recreation Resource Review Commission, prepared by the National Planning Association (Washington: Government Printing Office, 1962), table F-9, p. 328.

Table VII-2

OCCUPATIONAL DISTRIBUTION OF THE LABOR FORCE, MICHIGAN—1940–60*

Major Occupational Group	1940			1950			1960		
	Total	Male	Female	Total	Male	Female	Total	Male	Female
Professional, technical, and kindred workers	141.8	86.1	55.7	202.0	126.0	76.0	312.6	200.9	111.7
Farmers and farm managers	144.2	141.0	3.2	113.3	110.3	3.0	60.1	57.1	2.9
Proprietors, managers, and officials (excluding farmers)	136.2	123.1	13.1	189.3	165.9	23.4	200.0	173.9	26.1
Clerical, sales, and kindred workers	305.1	173.7	131.4	462.1	221.1	241.0	582.0	251.4	330.6
Craftsmen, foremen, and kindred workers	281.6	276.1	5.6	392.3	382.1	10.2	420.1	410.1	10.0
Operatives and kindred workers	412.4	349.7	62.7	619.2	510.1	109.1	606.4	494.8	111.6
Domestic service workers	59.9	1.9	58.0	40.1	1.9	38.2	58.7	2.0	56.6
Service workers (excluding domestic)	129.4	76.4	53.0	181.9	98.7	83.2	236.4	106.6	129.9
Farm laborers (wage workers) and farm foremen	66.7	64.8	1.9	42.5	35.3	7.1	25.3	20.8	4.5
Laborers (excluding farm)	125.9	119.8	6.1	118.7	113.3	5.5	109.3	104.8	4.5
Total	1,821.4	1,423.9	397.5	2,391.9	1,784.8	607.1	2,726.9	1,898.0	828.8

*In thousands. Totals will not equal combined male and female totals because of rounding.

Source: U. S. Bureau of the Census, *Census of Population: 1960*.

employment. This proportion increased to 36 per cent in 1950 and to 40 per cent in 1960. We anticipate that this growth will continue in the remainder of this decade and into the 1970's in *at least* the same magnitude that characterized the 1950-60 period, when professional and technical employment increased by 54.7 per cent and clerical and sales employment increased by 25.9 per cent (see Table VII-3).[2] Although the demand for sales workers was strong in the 1950-60 period, the coming decade should bring a leveling off in this demand, largely because of new self-service principles of operation in the retail merchandising field.

Among blue-collar workers, we foresee a sizable increase only in service employment. In 1950-60 such employment increased by 30 per cent, and we fully expect it to do as well in 1960-70. The total blue-collar employment should increase slightly, but this increase will be almost entirely in crafts and maintenance. There should be a slight decrease in operative and kindred occupations, occasioned by new advances in machine technology. The number of laborers, both farm and nonfarm, will decline sharply, about 20 per cent for nonfarm labor and 48 per cent for farm labor. These last estimates are quite consistent with the long-run trends for unskilled workers and with the reduction in the need for such manpower because of labor-saving devices (Table VII-3).

Technology and the structure of jobs

The major force that will structure the job in the 1970's will be automation. Although the precise minimal job requirements for automated equipment are not yet known, there is every reason to believe that the demand for better-educated workers and workers who have some technical training will increase. This may not come simply from automation; requirements for all jobs in America will be generally stricter.

[2]Some idea of the remarkable growth in these occupations in the 1950-60 period is possible if we consider that the increase for total employment was 17 per cent.

Table VII-3

PERCENTAGE CHANGE IN EMPLOYMENT IN SELECTED OCCUPATIONAL CATEGORIES, MICHIGAN, SELECTED PERIODS

Occupation	1940–60*	1940–50	1950–60
Professional, technical, and kindred workers	48.6	42.4	54.7
Farmers and farm managers	-34.2	-21.4	-47.0
Proprietors, managers, and officials	47.7	39.0	5.6
Clerical, sales, and kindred workers	38.7	51.4	25.9
Craftsmen, foremen, and kindred workers	. . .†	39.3	7.1
Operatives and kindred workers	. . .†	50.1	- 2.1
Domestic service workers	. . .†	-33.1	46.2
Service workers (excluding domestic)	35.3	40.5	30.0
Farm laborers (wage workers) and farm foremen	-38.4	-36.3	-40.5
Laborers, excluding farm	- 6.8	- 5.7	- 8.0
Total	22.5	31.3	14.0

*Based on mean rates of change 1940–60.

†Trend changed direction between 1940–50 and 1950–60.

Source: U. S. Bureau of the Census, *Census of Population: 1960.*

Probably the most important determinant of the training required for these jobs will be the condition of the labor market; the requirements are likely to be higher in a surplus labor market. The following trends in technology and job content seem probable in the 1970's.

Automation is a component in the short-run and long-run picture for both employment and unemployment. Although it is true that the increase of automation in many companies has not reduced the number employed (or increased the number of unemployed) in these companies in the short run, there being a reassignment of personnel following the introduction of labor-saving equipment, it is clear that in many cases persons will not be replaced as they retire. Thus there is an attrition effect in the number of employed as a result of automation.

It should also be mentioned—and this will illustrate the complexity of the problem of assessing the effects of automation—that the work done after automation is not always work that was done earlier by operatives or clerks. In many cases it is altogether new work, work of a kind that could not be done at all prior to automation. Since the new technology is labor saving, it also has a downward influence on costs and this effect could expand markets in some sense. Therefore, automation can expand employment in some ways and yet contract it in others.

Where automated equipment is used in industry, there will be a reduction in the need for production workers and an increase in maintenance jobs. Operators and maintenance men for this equipment will certainly require new skills. The skills will not be *higher* but *different.* The emphasis in these new jobs will be on the observation and recording of data rather than on manual operations. The jobs should be less demanding physically but more demanding mentally.

Jobs in this technological area will be more intricate and require more of the worker's attention. Since automatic controls are an integrative technology, the worker will be responsible for a much wider range of operations on a single job. The physical surroundings at work should be better, with more space, cleaner equipment, and better lighting. There is every reason to believe that the job should be safer, in view of the large number of inspection and control mechanisms. While few of these jobs will be upgraded, there is little doubt that they will be better paid. On the other hand, the trend toward greater co-ordination and control of production through the use of this technology will mean that the worker will have less and less control over the pace of his work, a chronic source of worker's dissatisfaction in the past. In addition, supervision is bound to be much stricter, and fewer jobs and supervisory positions will mean less mobility among workers. Whether the gains in workers' satisfaction will outweigh the dissatisfaction from these sources is hard to predict at this time.

Although job dislocation and job displacement by technology have been felt disproportionately by blue-collar workers, the 1970's will extend these problems to many groups of white-collar workers. We can expect a substantial increase in the use of electronic data-processing equipment in the public as well as the private sector of the economy. About 11,000 electronic digital computers, valued at $4.5 billion, were in use in the United States in late 1962, little more than a decade after such computers had their first commercial application. Between 1960 and 1962, computers more than doubled in number and value.[3] In a special survey conducted by the Federal Reserve System in March, 1962, one-third of 972 commercial banks reported that they were using or planning to use electronic computers in their banking operations.[4]

This revolution in computer technology in the office will bring changes in the requirements for office jobs. Clerical workers with routine, unspecialized skills will decline in number and importance. Most office jobs will require some special training and preparation, probably for a longer period than has been typical in the past. There will be fewer opportunities for office workers to be mobile, excluding technical and administrative personnel, since the automated office of the 1970's will have fewer workers and fewer supervisory positions.

The pace of technological change should quicken in the 1970's. We base this estimate on current trends in research and development. First, the annual investment in the United States for research and development of new products and

[3]This estimate is based on a special report prepared for the U. S. Department of Labor by the Diebold Group, Inc.

[4]U. S. Department of Labor, "Manpower Report of the President and a Report on Manpower Requirements, Resources, and Training" (Washington: Government Printing Office, 1963), p. 55.

processes shows signs of steady growth. In the 1953-54 fiscal year the total investment was about $5 billion. By the 1961-62 fiscal year the sum was almost $15 billion. Even at a considerably reduced rate of growth, we should expect research and development expenditures in 1970 to be around $20 billion. Second, there have been some major breakthroughs in process development which in turn will become the basis for further technological change. One of these is numerical control—the use of tools which are automatically operated through pre-coded instructions built into the machine. At the present time only a small percentage of tools use numerical control, but it is estimated that in five to six years 50 per cent of all machine tools will use numerical control.[5] Finally, the increasing rationalization of research and development has created a well-organized industry of invention. This development assures more efficient allocation of scientific resources and manpower, which should in turn give a powerful impetus to new scientific discovery. Research and development work creates new jobs, but frequently these gains are at the expense of other jobs. The coal miner is not easily retrained for work in the oil refinery. The textile worker's economic security is certainly affected by the development of dacron produced in a chemical plant. Even if one new job were created for each one lost, there is no guarantee that the old job-holder could master the new work without extensive retraining. In many cases, the worker may not be able to adjust to the demands of the job and may find himself displaced.

In the above discussion of technology and job content, we indicated some probable trends for the 1970's. The changes they bring about will have an impact on the national as well as the Michigan labor market. One effect will be to decrease the proportion of opportunities for semiskilled and unskilled workers. Production workers in manufacturing will feel these changes disproportionately because their simple, repetitive jobs are the most easily automated.[6] Tools operated by numerical

[5] *Ibid.*, p. 56.

[6] Exceptions are the jobs involving sensory processes. For example, aesthetic judgments are not readily automated, but these are exceptions rather than the rule.

control may make some small inroads into the ranks of the skilled workers.

Among white-collar workers, there will be some reduction in the ranks of unskilled clerical workers. The new jobs which develop in the automated office should be more challenging, require greater training, and pay better. Opportunities in white-collar employment will greatly increase in proportion to other opportunities, especially among professional and technical workers.

Skilled and trained workers will be in greater demand than ever before. Training of the young entrants into the labor market will become a major necessity. Displaced workers will certainly need retraining to fit into the new job hierarchy. The major needs of the labor market will be for workers who have specialized education and training. The traditional view of what constitutes an adequate high school education will probably be changed. A high school program with a major emphasis on vocational training will be needed for substantial numbers of students. It is more than likely that a high school education will not be preparation enough and that further training, perhaps in junior colleges, will have to be offered.

Labor force participation

The growth in the size of the Michigan labor force is similar to that of the nation as a whole, but some patterns of labor force participation differ significantly from those of the national economy. The labor force participation rate in Michigan has increased steadily over the last three decades, and this growth compares favorably to national labor force growth. In 1940 the Michigan labor force participation rate was 52.7 per cent. Ten years later it had increased to 53.8 per cent, and in 1960 it reached 55 per cent. If this growth in participation continues, 56.7 per cent of our population over 14 years of age will be in the labor market by 1970, the highest rate of any peacetime period since the turn of the century.

Growth in labor force participation is not distributed uniformly through all segments of the population. The rates for groups vary with the demographic structure of the population, the availability of jobs, and their requirements. In Michigan some groups are now participating more than ever before, others less. These differences in participation are important for an understanding of the structure of the Michigan labor market in the 1970's.

Sex and age. The most striking long-term trend in the Michigan labor market is the increase in the participation of women, concurrent with a decline in the participation of men.[7] Between 1940 and 1960, the mean rate of increase for female employment was three times as high as for male employment (see Table VII-4). In 1940-50 the increase was twice as great, while more recently, in 1950-60, the increase was six times as great. This is considerably ahead of the national growth rate for female employment. Two basic factors should be mentioned: (1) the change in the industry mix in Michigan, and (2) the nature of new employment opportunities. The heavy concentration in durable goods manufacturing that has characterized the Michigan economy in the past afforded limited employment opportunities to women, except in times of labor shortage. The increase in noncommodity employment in Michigan, and particularly in Detroit, is developing opportunities that attract women and for which women have the necessary skills and training. In addition, many of the increasing job opportunities such as in clerical and sales work and in domestic and nondomestic service have been in areas traditionally assigned to women. This is true even in the professions, where more and more opportunities exist in nursing, teaching, social work, and counseling.[8] This may be viewed as a correction in the

[7]The participation rate for women has steadily increased. In 1940, 23.3 per cent of the women over fourteen years of age were in the Michigan labor force. In 1950, the rate was 27.5 per cent, and in 1960 it increased to 32.7 per cent.

[8]Between 1950 and 1960 there was a decline of 12,739 operative jobs, of 53,280 jobs for farmers and farm managers, of 17,203 jobs for farm laborers, and of 9,640 nonfarm laborer jobs. Most of these declines represent losses in male employment (see Table VII-2). During the same period, women gained 90,000 more jobs in clerical and sales work, 18,400 more jobs in domestic service, and 46,700 more in other service. Almost all of these jobs gained were in work where women are traditionally employed in preference to men.

Table VII-4

PERCENTAGE OF CHANGE IN EMPLOYMENT, MALES AND FEMALES, MICHIGAN, SELECTED PERIODS

Occupation*	Males			Females		
	1940–60	1940–50	1950–60	1940–60	1940–50	1950–60
Professional, technical, and kindred workers	52.9	46.2	59.5	41.8	36.6	46.9
Farmers and farm managers	-35.0	-21.7	-48.2	- 4.1	- 5.2	- 3.0
Proprietors, managers, and officials (excluding farm)	41.4	34.8	37.9	44.9	78.1	11.7
Clerical, sales, and kindred workers	20.5	27.2	13.7	60.3	83.4	37.2
Craftsmen, foremen, and kindred workers	22.9	38.4	7.3	. . .†	83.4	- 2.1
Operatives and kindred workers	. . .†	45.9	- 3.0	38.1	73.9	2.3
Domestic service workers	3.8	0.1	7.6	. . .†	-34.2	48.2
Service workers (excluding domestic)	18.6	29.1	8.0	56.5	57.0	56.0
Total	15.8	25.3	6.3	44.6	52.7	36.5

*Data for farm and nonfarm laborers are not included.
†Trend changed direction between 1940–50 and 1950–60.

Source: U. S. Bureau of the Census, *Census of Population: 1940*, *Census of Population: 1950*, and *Census of Population: 1960*.

labor market to bring Michigan patterns of participation by sexes more in line with those of the nation as a whole, since in the past women have had a lower rate of participation here than elsewhere in the United States. Male workers, especially those between 25 and 45 years of age, have had a higher participation rate, and their declining rate may also be considered a movement toward national labor market patterns.

The decline in the male participation rate is not explained solely by the change in employment opportunities. The data in Table VII-5 indicate that the decline in the male participation rate was accounted for substantially by the reduction of males over 65 and males between 14 and 24 years old. The older workers are in the group most subject to age discrimination in employment, and their chances for re-employment are slight if they are retired or displaced from their jobs. There has also been increasing pressure by younger workers for the older group to accept final retirement at age 65, instead of prolonging employment in a "phased-out" retirement. The younger workers without at least a high school diploma or specialized training have found a declining market for their services, hence the decrease in their participation in the labor market. The data in Table VII-5 also show that the large increase in female participation was in the 35-64 age group, although between 1950 and 1960 the participation rate increased in all of the age categories. Even female workers over 65 increased their participation, and this is the age group where the decline in male participation was most apparent.

The labor force profile for Michigan is being characterized more and more by younger workers. In 1960, 18.8 per cent of the labor force were in the 14-24 age category. By 1970 the percentage will increase to 24.4. This increase in young workers will be the major factor shaping the labor market of the 1970's. For the young males, the problem will be to find employment in a labor market where educational and training requirements for jobs will be higher and where the new opportunities, particularly in sales, clerical work, and services, favor females. The young females will undoubtedly need more training than has been given in high school, but they should find ample opportunities in the job market.

Table VII-5

LABOR FORCE PARTICIPATION PERCENTAGE RATES BY AGE AND SEX, MICHIGAN—1940, 1950, AND 1960

Age and Sex	1940	1950	1960
Both sexes:			
14+	52.7	53.7	55.0
14–24	44.5	46.1	44.4
25–34	62.4	60.2	62.9
35–44	60.8	63.1	67.3
45–64	55.9	58.4	64.8
65+	23.6	29.9	17.2
Male:			
14+	80.5	80.2	78.3
14–24	57.6	59.0	56.3
25–34	95.9	93.0	95.4
35–44	95.7	94.7	96.2
45–64	90.2	89.3	90.7
65+	42.2	42.0	26.2
Female:			
14+	23.3	27.5	32.7
14–24	31.3	33.6	35.5
25–34	28.7	29.3	33.2
35–44	22.8	31.8	40.5
45–64	16.5	25.4	40.1
65+	5.1	7.0	9.8

Source: U. S. Bureau of the Census, *Census of Population: 1960*, Final Report PC(1)-24C, *General Social and Economic Characteristics, Michigan* (Washington: Government Printing Office, 1962).

Race. Race is also a factor in labor force participation (see Table VII-6). The rate of participation for whites is higher than for non-whites among males over 14. Although the total male participation rate declined between 1950 and 1960, the decline for non-white males was 2.5 times greater than for white males. Lower participation rates among white males were apparent only in the age groups over 65, whereas lower participation rates for non-whites touched almost every age category, the most striking decline being in the 14-19 age group and the group over 60.[9] The decline in participation among the young non-white males is undoubtedly affected by their difficulties in finding jobs and their consequent decision to remain in school for a longer time. For the older non-white workers, lower participation can be traced to the difficulties these workers have in finding employment or re-employment in industrial work when they are faced with discrimination because of both age and race.

The pattern for non-white females is different. The participation rate is higher for non-white females, and it has been increasing at a faster rate than the rate for white females. The greatest participation increase for both white and non-white females has been in the group aged 45-55.

The following labor participation patterns for the 1970's seem indicated by these trends:

The competition from younger workers will reduce the participation rates for all male groups over 50 years of age, but non-white males at those ages will be particularly affected. There will be more pressure by unions for earlier retirement of older workers, and such retirements should increase. Voluntary withdrawals from the labor force of older workers who are displaced by automation and technological change should also increase.

[9]The decrease in participation in *all* age groups among non-whites suggests that job-seeking for these workers must be a frustrating experience, leading in many cases to prolonged unemployment and consequent withdrawal from the labor market. The unemployment rate, which represents only unemployment for people who stay attached to the labor market, probably understates the case for non-white males.

Table VII-6

LABOR FORCE PARTICIPATION PERCENTAGE RATES
BY RACE, AGE, AND SEX
MICHIGAN—1950-60

Age Category	1950		1960	
	White	Non-White	White	Non-White
Males:				
14-19	37.6	28.8	38.9	23.9
20-24	83.5	79.0	87.0	77.1
25-29	91.9	86.8	95.3	86.4
30-34	95.1	88.4	97.1	88.3
35-39	95.3	90.6	97.1	89.7
40-44	94.7	90.3	96.7	89.6
45-49	94.0	89.0	96.1	88.6
50-54	91.7	86.1	94.1	87.3
55-59	88.2	82.1	90.8	82.9
60-64	81.7	74.5	80.5	71.5
65-69	61.4	53.1	38.1	33.8
70-74	38.6	32.5	23.2	15.6
75+	17.5	10.8	13.0	11.2
Total	80.3	78.6	78.7	73.9
Females:				
14-19	25.9	12.5	27.5	14.0
20-24	43.7	30.0	.43.3	40.8
25-29	30.1	33.8	30.7	38.9
30-34	27.2	37.1	29.2	40.9
35-39	30.2	38.7	35.5	45.8
40-44	32.3	35.9	41.6	48.4
45-49	30.6	31.9	44.1	47.8
50-54	27.0	29.2	42.6	43.8
55-59	22.2	23.5	36.7	34.8
60-64	18.3	15.6	26.3	25.6
65-69	11.8	8.5	14.7	13.8
70-74	6.1	4.5	8.5	7.5
75+	2.2	1.5	4.0	2.3
Total	27.2	29.6	32.3	36.4

Source: U. S. Bureau of the Census, *Census of Population: 1960,* Final Report PC(1)-24C, *General Social and Economic Characteristics, Michigan* (Washington: Government Printing Office, 1962).

Current patterns of more participation by women in all age groups should continue. This trend is especially strong for non-white females. With respect to age groupings, females aged 14-24, both white and non-white, are expected to participate at a sharply increased rate because of economic factors associated with marriage. Whereas in the past early marriage took females in this age bracket out of the labor market, the lessening economic capabilities of males and declining labor force participation by males of comparable age may tend to postpone marriage. Any move away from the early marriage pattern will bring about more participation by younger females. The main growth in female rates, however, will still be in the groups beyond childbearing age.

There is a strong possibility that the trend toward decreased participation by non-white males in all age groups will continue. Since these workers are concentrated in jobs and industries where labor-saving devices have been reducing the need for manpower, they are likely to experience rather difficult problems in finding re-employment. Frequent and prolonged unemployment may weaken the attachment of these workers to the labor force. Civil rights legislation will give non-white males access to better jobs, but opportunities will be largely confined to the educated and trained workers. Although the interest in civil rights has resulted in a tendency to favor the employment of non-whites in some jobs, we do not feel that this development will affect the over-all employment for non-white males, especially for the older men. Past trends favor the employment of non-white females, particularly in technical, sales, and clerical work.

The participation rates for young people should continue to decline, since this group will increasingly seek post-secondary education and training. Their participation rate will be greatly influenced by the availability of higher education. By 1970 college enrollment will be almost double what it was in 1960. The resources needed for such expansion are enormous. For example, if we apply the student-faculty ratio of 15.3, the 1960 ratio for the state of Michigan, to the projected college enrollment of 1970, we would need 19,281 faculty members in

1970, an increase of 62.1 per cent over the 1960 faculty. We must add to this the cost of buildings, equipment, and administration. Any failure to provide these resources could add approximately 43,000 college-age youths to the labor market and make it necessary to provide a like number of jobs. This could prove to be a formidable task, since 500,000 jobs are already needed for other young people and for returnees to the labor force between 1960 and 1970.

The Structure of Unemployment

Important to understanding the Michigan labor market is the structure of unemployment in the state. The changes in employment opportunities, technology, and labor force participation will shape unemployment patterns in the 1970's. The structure of unemployment is never static. In Michigan, it has to a large extent paralleled regional and national unemployment patterns. In general we can make the following observations about Michigan as well as the nation:

The unemployment rate has been higher for blue-collar than for white-collar workers. Operatives and laborers have the highest rates of unemployment; craftsmen and foremen have also been hard hit. Low rates are found for white-collar workers, especially professional and technical workers. These differences stem from several causes. Blue-collar workers are concentrated in the commodity-producing industries where productivity gains and technological change have reduced the need for manpower. Although the service industries have been touched by these changes, there has been sufficient expansion in in other sectors of white-collar employment to offset these reductions in manpower.

The highest rates of unemployment are found in construction, mining, and the manufacture of durable goods. These are industries which have been operating at a diminished capacity and have disproportionate numbers of blue-collar workers. Technological change is most evident in these industries and has reduced the need for manpower.

Non-whites experience a higher rate of unemployment than whites. Most non-whites are blue-collar workers, and large numbers are in those industries that have been extending the use of labor-saving devices. Generally, the non-white worker has less education and less training, hence his re-employment after job displacement is more difficult. He is also less likely to be protected by seniority, and if he was the last hired he is the first fired. Finally, there are discriminatory barriers which limit his chances for employment and re-employment, especially in periods of labor surpluses.

The educated and trained workers are less likely to be among the unemployed than the less educated and the untrained workers. The importance of education to employment patterns in the labor market cannot be overstated. First, education is related to occupational status. A consistent shortage has been apparent in many professional and technical fields where a high degree of training is necessary, and workers in these fields experience relatively little unemployment. The labor market has also shown a marked tendency to increase the educational requirements for employment, and hence the median education of the employed workers has risen.[10]

Education does not confer an absolute advantage but rather one that is relative to a given time. While the median education of the employed has increased, so has the median education of the unemployed. More and more youths with a high school education are among the unemployed. This fact does not invalidate the high school education, but it does raise an important point about the traditional program in secondary schools. The increasing level of technological complexity in industry will probably favor least the youths who are high school drop-outs, and it will most favor those youths with special technical or vocational training.

The unemployment rate has been lower for women than for men. The reason is that the largest increase in employment

[10]The rationale for raising educational requirements by employers is usually that the better-educated workers have more flexibility in job assignments and more potential for mobility in the company.

opportunities has been in jobs which have traditionally been held by women. This is particularly obvious in the high demand for teachers, counselors, sales and clerical workers, and service personnel. Also, women are frequently second wage-earners in the family and hence have greater liberty to leave the labor market if a particular type of employment cannot be found. They are not counted as unemployed if they do not look for jobs.

The ranks of the unemployed have become increasingly dominated by young workers who have recently entered the labor force. One of the most important trends in the structure of unemployment is the steadily increasing number of unemployed youths in proportion to the total unemployment. Several factors explain this development. First, as a result of the population explosion in the postwar years, teen-age workers are entering the labor force in unprecedented numbers. As David Goldberg points out, this influx will be at its peak in the mid-1960's but should continue into the early 1970's. These youngsters should gain a greater share of employment in the market, but they will also be disproportionately represented among the unemployed. Second, the competition from these young people for jobs will probably occasion the voluntary withdrawal from the labor market of older workers who have been plagued by persistent unemployment. This decrease in the older segment of the unemployed will mean that unemployed youths will represent a higher proportion of total unemployment. Finally, these male youths are entering a labor market where requirements for jobs and the distribution of employment are changing. Unskilled and semiskilled jobs, which in the past have been the main source of employment for new entrants into the labor market, are disproportionately decreasing at the same time that jobs which require more education and specialized training are increasing. Of the 500,000 jobs needed by 1970 in Michigan, at least three-fifths will develop in service industries, with a large proportion in the clerical fields. These are jobs that favor females and require some degree of specialized training. The other 200,000 jobs will probably come from the commodity-producing industries, with an increasing emphasis on occupations which require specialized vocational training. These jobs will favor males who have some technical training beyond the traditional high school curriculum.

Some of these points about unemployed youth are even more disturbing when we consider the structure of long-term unemployment in the nation. In 1961 more than 46 per cent of the unemployed workers who had had no work during that year were aged 24 and younger.[11] In addition, this age group showed an increase of workers who had been unemployed for fifteen weeks or longer. The alarming aspect of current youth unemployment is that although past periods of unemployment for this group have usually been short they are becoming less so. The youth who enters the labor market of the late 1960's and early 1970's, especially if he lacks training, may not only fail to become employed but remain unemployed for a considerable time.

Unemployment in Michigan

Although the structure of unemployment in Michigan parallels the national structure of unemployment, certain local conditions intensify the problem: (1) The industrial mix, heavily concentrated in commodity production, will undergo more rapid change than national industry as a whole, with considerable revision in the requirements for employment; (2) the annual influx of 18-year-old youths into the labor market will be higher than the national rate; and (3) the opportunities for higher education and technical training will not be able to keep pace with the needs of the labor market and the number of youths that require training. These facts can be the basis of a pessimistic forecast. For example, Meier, in his evaluation of the Detroit labor market prospects, presents a pessimistic appraisal for the future.

[11]C. Rosenfeld, "Work Experience of the Population in 1961," *Monthly Labor Review*, LXXXV (December, 1962), 1358, Table 20.

> The prospects for the employment of youths have become poorer since 1960, when the data were collected. The number of places in college have not been expanded as rapidly as projected then, and the effects of accumulated unemployed 19-year-olds upon the employment of a new cohort of 18-year-olds had not been taken into account earlier. We estimate now that 60 per cent of the entrants to the labor force would remain unemployed in 1970 and four-fifths of these would be high school graduates.[12]

Some indication of the problems already being experienced by Michigan youths in finding employment is given by the United States Census data in Table VII-7. These data indicate that the unemployment rate was about twice as great for young males in the 14-24 age group than for males over 24. For males aged 16-19, the unemployment rate was three times higher than for all other males. The rate for non-white males is higher than for white males. The 17-year-old, non-white group had a higher rate than any other single group; about 43 per cent of this group were without jobs.

These data, together with our understanding of employment, technological, and participation trends, lead us to the following observations:

The unemployment problem for Michigan male youths in the next dozen years will be severe. Even assuming that the current economic picture remains bright, it will be difficult to provide opportunities for more than half of the 18-year-old, male job-seekers during the rest of the 1960's or early 1970's. At least 40 per cent of the unsuccessful job-seekers in this group will have a high school education. In making this estimate, we are assuming that (1) the current lag in educational and training facilities will continue, and there will be no dramatic increase in technical training capacity; (2) the pace of technological change in the industrial society will accelerate; and (3) state or federal youth employment and rehabilitation programs will have only a moderate effect on the labor market.

[12]Richard Meier *et al.*, *The Redeployment of Land, Water, and Human Resources*, Regional Development Studies II (Ann Arbor: Dept. of Conservation, School of Natural Resources, Univ. of Michigan, June, 1962), 40.

Table VII-7

UNEMPLOYMENT PERCENTAGE RATE FOR MALES BY AGE AND COLOR, MICHIGAN—1960

Age	Total	Whites	Non-Whites
14	5.7	5.0	18.6
15	8.0	7.2	23.9
16	14.6	13.9	28.5
17	15.9	14.4	42.5
18	17.6	16.2	35.6
19	15.8	14.3	33.4
14-19	14.6	13.3	33.2
20-24	11.1	9.6	25.5
25-29	6.8	5.6	17.1
30-34	5.8	4.7	16.2
35-39	5.6	4.4	16.1
40-44	5.4	4.3	15.7
45-49	5.6	4.6	14.8
50-54	5.6	4.8	14.9
55-59	5.9	5.3	12.3
60-64	6.1	5.7	12.1
65+	6.7	6.1	12.5

Source: U. S. Bureau of the Census, *Census of Population: 1960*, Final Report PC(1)-24C, *General Social and Economic Characteristics, Michigan* (Washington: Government Printing Office, 1962).

An investment in a public works program or a youth conservation corps could conceivably reduce this estimate by 10 or 15 per cent, but only a major investment would have this effect.

Barring a sharp improvement in non-white educational patterns, the bulk of unemployment will be more than ever among non-white males. Even if the number of non-white high school graduates increases, more than three-quarters of the non-white males will have difficulty in finding jobs. Paradoxically, these non-white youths will be better educated than any similar group in the history of the state. The non-white employment problem will be intensified by the higher training requirements for employment and the exclusion of non-whites from the opportunities for training offered by craft unions. This will undoubtedly result in more pressure from Negroes against local school boards and unions for access to better educational and training facilities.

Participation of Non-White Workers in the Labor Force

What progress have Negroes made over the years in the Michigan labor market, and what are their future prospects? As we have already noted, Negro male workers, especially the younger ones, have the highest unemployment rate in the labor market; the rate of labor market participation for Negro males in almost all age groups is declining. In contrast, Negro women are participating more. Although some Negro workers have made progress in Michigan, and especially in Detroit, Negroes as a group are still at a disadvantage with respect to opportunities for employment, income, and education. These differences are most apparent in the Detroit metropolitan area—Wayne, Oakland, and Macomb counties—where about three-quarters of the state's non-white labor force was located in 1960.

Employment

The United States Census data on Michigan in 1960 show that the bulk of non-white workers were concentrated in lower-skilled blue-collar and service employment (see Table VII-8). Among the employed males, 70.1 per cent of the non-whites were factory operatives, service workers, and laborers, while 36.1 per cent of the whites were so employed. Among the employed females, 55.2 per cent of the non-whites were in domestic or service jobs compared to 19.7 per cent of the whites. This distribution becomes all the more significant when we realize that it has taken two to three decades of Negro advancement in occupational opportunities to produce it.

Some long-run trends in non-white employment are discernible (see Table VII-8). To a large extent these shifts follow

Table VII-8

MAJOR OCCUPATION OF EMPLOYED NON-WHITES BY SEX, MICHIGAN—1940–60
(Percentage of Total Employees)

Occupation	Males			Females		
	1940	1950	1960*	1940	1950	1960
Professional, technical, and kindred workers	2.3	1.9	3.8	3.1	5.0	8.0
Farmers and farm managers	0.9	0.4	0.1	0.1	0.1	. . .
Proprietors, managers, and officials	2.4	2.4	2.1	1.3	1.7	1.3
Clerical and kindred workers	4.2†	3.8	5.4	4.9†	8.2	13.8
Sales workers		1.4	2.1		2.9	2.9
Craftsmen, foremen, and kindred workers	12.4	12.3	13.8	0.4	1.1	0.9
Operatives and kindred workers	26.8	42.6	42.0	7.4	19.5	14.1
Private household	1.6	0.5	0.4	56.0	30.5	25.9
Service (excluding household)	20.5	12.1	12.5	24.5	26.5	29.3
Farm laborers and foremen	1.3	0.6	0.5	0.2	0.3	0.2
Laborers (excluding farm and mine)	26.4	19.8	15.3	1.1	2.4	1.3
Occupation not reported	1.0	2.3	1.6	1.0	1.6	1.3

*10.0 per cent non-response in this year. This was distributed by assigning the mean average non-response rate for 1940–50 to the 1960 distribution and expanding each occupational category by .084.

†In 1940, clerical, sales, and kindred workers were combined.

Source: U. S. Bureau of the Census, *Census of Population: 1960,* Final Report PC(1)-24C, *General Social and Economic Characteristics, Michigan* (Washington: Government Printing Office, 1962).

the lines of changing occupational needs and opportunities in the labor market. Since 1940 there has been a decline in the percentage of non-white males employed in Michigan as laborers and service workers, and a concurrent increase in the percentage of non-whites employed as craftsmen, foremen, and operatives. The major shift occurred in the 1940's and was undoubtedly related to wartime opportunities. With respect to the non-white females, there has been a long-term decline in the percentage of these people employed in private household jobs and an increase in the percentage employed in clerical work and service. The proportion of professional and technical jobs increased among non-whites, the increase being greater for women than for men.

If we look at the Detroit metropolitan area between 1950 and 1960, some of the recent trends in non-white employment become readily apparent. The increase for non-white employment was 28.9 per cent compared to a total employment increase of 11.5 per cent. It is interesting to note that non-white males obtained only 4.9 per cent of all new white-collar jobs for men, and these jobs were mostly for unskilled clerical workers; in contrast, non-white females obtained 16.2 per cent of all new white-collar employment for women. In line with other patterns of labor force participation in Michigan, the increase in non-white employment was primarily an increase in female employment. There were 37,266 net additions to the non-white labor force, and two-thirds of these were women.

The changes in non-white employment between 1950 and 1960 parallel the employment trends for white workers; a gradual shifting from commodity to noncommodity employment (see Table VII-9). Thus in 1960 non-whites held a greater proportion of white-collar jobs than in 1950. To what extent did these changes narrow the differences in employment between whites and non-whites? Let us consider the male and female workers separately.

Among the non-white male workers, white-collar employment increased from 9.9 per cent of total non-white male employment in 1950 to 13.2 per cent in 1960. This gain should be compared, however, to the gain among white male workers, who increased their white-collar employment from 33.7 to 38.9

Table VII-9

MAJOR OCCUPATION OF EMPLOYED LABOR FORCE BY SEX AND RACE
DETROIT METROPOLITAN AREA—1950 AND 1960
(Percentage of Total Labor Force)

Occupation	White			Non-white		
	1950	1960	Difference	1950	1960	Difference
Males:						
Professional and technical	8.5	13.0	+4.5	1.8	3.4	+1.6
Managers and officials	10.3	9.9	-0.4	2.4	2.1	-0.3
Clerical	8.1	7.9	-0.2	4.3	5.6	+1.3
Sales	6.8	8.1	+1.3	1.4	2.1	+0.7
Craftsmen	24.5	23.5	-1.0	12.2	12.2	. . .
Operatives	29.3	23.9	-5.4	44.1	38.4	-5.7
Service	5.5	5.2	-0.3	11.1	11.2	-0.1
Laborers	4.8	4.2	-0.6	19.7	13.8	-5.9
Females:						
Professional and technical	11.9	13.4	+1.5	5.4	7.8	+2.4
Managers and officials	4.0	3.3	-0.7	1.7	1.2	-0.5
Clerical	36.5	37.8	+1.3	9.1	14.4	+5.3
Sales	11.0	10.7	-0.3	3.2	2.9	-0.3
Craft and trade	1.9	1.2	-0.7	1.1	0.8	-0.3
Operatives	17.4	11.6	-5.8	19.8	12.3	-7.5
Household	12.0	13.3	+1.3	25.4	24.6	-0.8
Service	0.8	0.4	-0.4	2.4	1.2	-1.2
Laborers	3.8	3.6	-0.2	30.3	23.8	-6.5

Source: U. S. Bureau of the Census, *Census of Population: 1950* and *Census of Population: 1960*.

per cent. Instead of narrowing the difference in white-collar employment, these changes actually *increased* the difference, as is illustrated below (numbers refer to white-collar employment as a percentage of total employment by color and sex).

	1950	1960
Males		
White	33.7	38.9
Non-white	9.9	13.2
Percentage difference	23.8	25.7
Females		
White	63.4	65.2
Non-white	19.4	24.3
Percentage difference	44.0	40.9

The data for non-white female workers show that their increase in white-collar employment narrowed the difference between white and non-white female workers. This showing is explained largely by the increased demand in the Detroit area for clerical, technical, service, and professional workers in jobs that favor the employment of females; examples of such workers are nurses, secretaries, typists, attendants, and teachers. This development has brought non-white females unprecedented opportunities in the job market and made it possible for them to narrow the occupational differences between white female workers and themselves. The opportunities for non-white males have been more circumscribed. White-collar jobs traditionally held by males--for example, medical technicians, engineers, doctors, and technical salesmen--require considerable training. The lower requirements for white-collar jobs available to women would favor more progress by the non-white females than by the non-white males.

In the choice blue-collar occupations, craftsmen and foremen, non-white male workers have slightly narrowed the difference, but only because of a decline in the proportion of whites who hold such jobs. Among operatives there was about the same proportional decline for whites as for non-whites, and the differential in employment remained the same. Non-white male workers, then, not only failed to keep pace with white male workers in white-collar employment, but also were unable to narrow the gap in blue-collar employment except as a result of white workers' withdrawal from blue-collar work.

Employment by industry

In 1960, a little more than one-half of the employed non-white males in Michigan were in manufacturing, and about one-third of the employed non-white females were in personal services (see Table VII-10). Some long-term shifts can be noted. As in the case of occupational shifts, industrial changes among non-whites follow the demands and needs of the labor market. Thus, between 1950 and 1960, the proportion of jobs for non-white males had declined in manufacturing, construction, and public utilities, but had increased in wholesale and retail trade, business and repair services, professional and related services, and public administration. Among non-white females, there was a decline in the proportion of jobs in manufacturing, wholesale and retail trade, finance and real estate, and personal services. The most marked changes in non-white employment have been caused by the continued decline in female employment in personal services and by an increase in female participation in professional services and public administration. In public administration, employment for non-white females increased by five times between 1940 and 1960.

The state trends are reflected in the Detroit metropolitan area. While non-whites were represented in most industries, they were substantially under-represented in machinery and chemical manufacturing, fabricated metals, the utilities, banking and finance, and business, legal, and engineering services. Non-whites accounted for 13.9 per cent of the Detroit area labor force but for less than 6 per cent of those working in these industries. Their greatest opportunities were to be found in public, professional, and personal services.

The industrial portrait for non-whites shows that the bulk of male employment in Michigan continues to be concentrated in

Table VII-10

INDUSTRY GROUP OF EMPLOYED NON-WHITES BY SEX, MICHIGAN—1940–60
(Percentage of Total Employed)

Industry Group	Males			Females		
	1940	1950	1960	1940	1950	1960
Agriculture, forests, and fisheries	2.5	1.0	1.1	0.3	0.4	0.3
Mining	...	...	...	...	...	...
Construction	5.0	6.2	5.9	0.1	0.3	0.3
Manufacturing	51.7	59.7	53.2	2.6	12.7	9.5
Transportation, communications, and other public utilities	4.6	6.3	5.7	0.2	1.5	1.7
Wholesale and retail trade	13.5	9.5	11.8	10.6	13.9	13.4
Finance, insurance, and real estate	2.1	1.2	1.3	2.3	2.2	1.7
Business and repair service	3.6	2.4	3.4	0.3	0.5	1.0
Personal services	9.7	5.1	4.2	74.8	48.2	38.4
Entertainment and recreational services	2.1	3.0	0.9	0.8	0.8	0.6
Professional and related services	2.1	3.0	6.6	5.3	14.0	26.2
Public administration	2.3	3.2	5.8	1.3	4.0	6.3
Industry not reported	1.1	1.4	1.0	1.2	1.3	1.0

Source: U. S. Bureau of the Census, *Census of Population: 1940*, *Census of Population: 1950*, and *Census of Population: 1960*.

manufacturing, especially in durable goods production, where there probably will be a decline in the number of jobs. Non-white female workers have shown considerably more progress in shifting to sectors of the economy that are less susceptible to labor-saving devices and technological change.

Education

Our observations on employment trends and technological change indicate that the job opportunities of the 1970's will require *more* and *better* education. This will be true in professional and technical jobs as well as in maintenance and crafts. Less favored workers in the labor market can improve their situation only to the extent that they have the education and training to meet the demands of the job market.

The educational achievement of non-whites is significantly below that of whites in Michigan (see Table VII-11).[13] Only 25.2 per cent of the non-whites 25 years old and over completed high school, compared to 42.4 per cent of the whites in this age group. Twice as many whites as non-whites have attended or completed college. Educational deficiency is most apparent in non-white males. Fifty-four per cent of all non-white males in the state did not go beyond the eighth grade of elementary school, while the comparable proportion for non-white females was 44.6 per cent. By way of contrast, only one-third of the whites in the 25-and-over age group failed to go beyond the eighth grade. In a labor market where emphasis on education is increasing, these data offer dramatic testimony to the disadvantages of the non-whites.

Although educational levels are rising for both whites and non-whites, the levels are rising faster for whites than for non-whites. The result is that the educational gap is widening, not narrowing, as indicated by the data in Table VII-12. These data are consistent with the data appearing in the tabulation on on page 269.

[13]This finding is not peculiar to Michigan but follows a national pattern.

Table VII-11

YEARS OF SCHOOL COMPLETED BY PERSONS 25 YEARS OLD AND OVER, MICHIGAN—1960
(Percentages by Color and Sex)

Color and Sex	Total 25 Years Old and Over	Years of School Completed							
		None	Elementary School			High School		College	
			1–4	5 and 6	7	8	1–3	4	1–3	4+
State	100.0	1.5	4.3	5.9	5.8	19.4	22.2	26.0	8.1	6.8
White	100.0	1.4	3.7	5.3	5.6	19.7	21.9	26.9	8.3	7.2
Non-white	100.0	2.2	10.9	11.9	8.3	16.1	25.4	16.8	5.5	2.9
Male	100.0	1.5	5.0	6.4	6.5	20.2	21.8	22.1	7.9	8.4
White	100.0	1.4	4.2	5.8	6.3	20.6	21.6	22.9	8.2	9.0
Non-white	100.0	2.7	13.5	13.1	8.6	16.3	23.5	14.2	5.0	3.0
Female	100.0	1.4	3.6	5.3	5.2	18.6	22.7	29.8	8.2	5.2
White	100.0	1.4	3.2	4.8	4.9	18.9	22.2	30.8	8.4	5.4
Non-white	100.0	1.8	8.3	10.8	8.0	15.8	27.2	19.4	6.0	2.8

Source: U. S. Bureau of the Census, *Census of Population: 1960*, Final Report PC(1)-24C, *General Social and Economic Characteristics, Michigan* (Washington: Government Printing Office, 1962), table 47.

Table VII-12

MEDIAN LEVEL IN YEARS OF EDUCATION FOR PERSONS 25 YEARS AND OLDER BY RACE, MICHIGAN—1940–60

	1940	1950	1960
Whites	9.0	10.0	11.0
Non-whites	8.4	8.5	9.1
Difference	+ .6	+ 1.5	+ 1.9

Source: U. S. Bureau of the Census, *Census of Population: 1940*, *Census of Population: 1950*, and *Census of Population: 1960*.

The educational outlook for non-whites, on the evidence of their present level of achievement and the long-range trend, is discouraging. To a large extent the future rests on the non-white youths still in high school. Concerted action has been taken in a number of communities to encourage young people to stay in school. The results of such action cannot be known for some time, but meanwhile we can judge from Table VII-13 whether non-white youths are dropping out of school as frequently as they were ten years ago.

The data in Table VII-13 indicate that the school drop-out rate has decreased in each age category both for whites and non-whites. The drop-out rate is, however, still too high for both groups. In 1970 these youths, who will then be between 28 and 34 years of age, will potentially represent the backbone of the labor force. This prospect seen in the light of Professor Goldberg's data on the out-migration of talented youth, discloses some alarming features of Michigan's situation with respect to the trained and educated labor force that will be needed in the state.

Although the drop-out rate for non-white youths decreased between 1950 and 1960, their employment prospects in 1960 were not greatly improved. We have said that the importance of education to the labor market can never be stated in absolute terms. The white youths also improved their educational level

Table VII-13

SCHOOL DROP-OUT RATES FOR MALES AGED 18-24, MICHIGAN-1950-60
(Percentage by Race)

Age Category	1950		1960	
	White Drop-outs	Non-white Drop-outs	White Drop-outs	Non-white Drop-outs
18	30.7	48.3	18.9	36.1
19	34.6	61.1	23.6	45.0
20	37.7	61.0	27.9	52.2
21	41.2	61.6	29.5	51.8
22	44.8	67.2	31.1	51.4
23	47.6	67.5	32.8	52.6
24	43.7	69.5	34.7	52.8

Source: U. S. Bureau of the Census, *Census of Population: 1950* and *Census of Population: 1960.*

and retained a relative advantage. The educational gap between the two groups was not appreciably narrowed; the drop-out rate in 1960 was still twice as high among the non-white youths in the 18-24 age category as among white youths in the same age category. One can readily see the problem that is posed for young non-whites. Any improvement in their educational achievement is likely to be matched by a like improvement among whites, leaving them as badly off as before. Added to this problem is the continuing disadvantage because of race.

What are the prospects for Negro progress in education? To some extent such progress hinges on the Detroit school system where Negro population is concentrated. A number of difficulties have beset this system and impaired its capacity to give high-quality education. The shift of industry and higher-income families from Detroit has reduced the tax revenue for the schools. At the same time an unprecedented demand has arisen to offer specialized training and broader education to greater and greater numbers of youths so that they can cope with the conditions of urban life. Unless the Detroit schools are able to increase their financial resources, prospects will be dim for a system that will meet the needs of underprivileged youths. At present the outlook for the Detroit schools in the 1970's does not warrant much optimism.

Income

The income inequality between whites and non-whites is worthy of note. Unfortunately, the data we have available do not permit us to make direct comparisons between incomes of white and non-white families. The best we can do at present is to compare non-white families with all families.

About 15 per cent of all families in Michigan had an income of $3,000 or less in 1959, compared to 33 per cent of the non-white families. At the other extreme, about 17 per cent of all families earned more than $10,000 in 1959, compared to 6 per cent of the non-white families. The differences in the city of Detroit were quite similar. On the state level, the median income of all families was $6,256; for non-white families it was $4,407. In the city of Detroit the difference in favor of whites is about $600 more. It is also interesting to note that even when education is equal non-whites are paid less than whites. As noted by the Detroit Commission on Community Relations:

> Such differentials can only serve to negate non-white educational efforts and aspirations. . . . Non-white college graduates receive incomes only $2,300 more than those with a minimum of elementary schooling and only $1,500 more than those with eight years of schooling. For whites, a college degree is worth $5,700 more than one to four years of education and $3,500 more than an eighth grade education.[14]

One further word about income inequality between whites and non-whites. The income difference between white and non-white families in Detroit increased between 1949 and 1959. In 1949 the difference in median income between white and non-white families was $990. In 1959 the difference had

[14]*Employment and Income. By Age, Sex, Color and Residence,* a Report prepared by the Detroit Commission on Community Relations, May, 1963, p. 18.

increased to $2,680, almost three times the difference in 1949. Although there was an improvement in both groups, the improvement for the whites was so much more marked that it made the income differential even greater.

Future prospects

What are the prospects for Negro employment in Michigan and Detroit over the next dozen years? Several factors should improve Negro employment opportunities. First, the Negro will have more legal guarantees of equal employment opportunities, since the passage of civil rights legislation. The growth of the urban Negro community into a political force, already apparent in Detroit, will encourage legal provisions giving Negroes greater access to jobs. Second, new technologies (e.g., automation) will create a greater need for skilled and competent workers, and job recruitment will emphasize personal capacity and ability, rather than race. As management is forced to become more and more selective, many of the artificial barriers to employment will fall. Third, certain occupational specialties will be in short supply, and we can expect Negro professionals and technicians to have unprecedented opportunities for employment. The most impressive Negro gains in jobs between 1950 and 1960 have been in these specialized occupations, and this trend should continue.

Although legal sanctions and labor shortages will increase job opportunities for some Negroes, there will continue to be strong impediments to the full utilization of the Negro labor force. The most serious handicap is the difference in education between whites and Negroes. It seems possible that even with more opportunities available to Negroes there will be no substantial increase in Negro employment because the Negroes who possess training are not numerous enough to fill the demand. We expect that only a small number of Negroes will gain the more desirable jobs, because the education requisite for these jobs would have had to be acquired in the mid- and late 1950's.

Another source of problems for the Negro worker is his

inaccessibility to apprenticeship training in craft unions. Although there have been some exceptions, Negroes have not gained the necessary access to craft union membership that entitles them to receive training for the skilled craft jobs in construction and maintenance. Little progress has been made toward giving the Negro legal access to this training, and we suspect that the immediate prospects in this area are not encouraging.

Another handicap to the full utilization of the Negro labor force is that positive motivation has been difficult to develop. A Negro youth, like any other, relates himself to the job market by determining what kinds of jobs are available and by feeling some assurance that training will make these jobs accessible to him. Such information and assurance generally come through "models," that is, members of the same group who have completed the training and found desirable jobs. The lack of models among Negroes--the result of a long heritage of discrimination—suggests that many Negro youths may hesitate to undertake training without definite assurances of jobs. The situation will undoubtedly become better as management moves to equalize job opportunities, but until a core of successful Negro professionals and technicians can be established to act as models, recruiting young Negroes to train for these jobs may be slow.

To sum up the prospects for Negro employment in the 1970's, opportunities in the professional and technical areas will be increased, but there will not be an adequate supply of trained Negroes to fill these jobs. Some gains will be made in opening trade jobs to Negroes, but progress will be slow. Negroes will probably make the greatest gains in white-collar clerical and sales jobs because these require a minimum of training. The bulk of the Negro labor force will continue to be concentrated at the lower end of the occupational hierarchy: in semiskilled, unskilled, and service jobs.

Unemployment will remain higher among Negroes than among whites, but this difference will be narrowed in the more skilled occupations. For Negroes, the impact of job displacement will continue to be stronger because their jobs will be in the segment of the economy where labor-saving devices and automation are most applicable. Retraining and training programs will still be needed by Negroes to a greater degree than by other groups in the labor market.

The differential between median incomes of Negroes and whites in the professions, technical trades, and skilled jobs is expected to be narrowed in the 1970's, largely because of the short supply of people in these occupational categories. The market value of a Negro worker may also increase because he may represent a public relations investment for the company. However, if job displacement should continue at a rather high level owing to impending technological changes, we feel that some Negroes will experience reduced incomes.

Education, Training, and Retraining of Workers

The need for a comprehensive vocational education and training program in the Michigan labor market is obvious. Such a program would have to be multipurpose: to prepare and train youths for jobs in the labor market, provide compensatory education and job training for less favored workers, permit employed workers to improve their skills, give a program of training in the mechanical and technical skills that are in short supply, and train unemployed workers so that they can adjust to changing job demands. Although some of these goals may be overlapping, the labor market of the 1970's will clearly demand that all be recognized and implemented.

Reimbursement by government

The future of vocational education in Michigan is tied to (1) a revision in the reimbursement practices for vocational training by the state and federal governments, and (2) the willingness and ability of local communities to diversify their investment in education. The present structure of vocational education in the state is not geared to the needs of the labor market or the emerging world of work in the 1970's. Unless there is a marked change in current trends, a viable system of vocational education will not become a reality.

Table VII-14

REIMBURSED VOCATIONAL EDUCATION ENROLLMENTS IN MICHIGAN SCHOOLS BY SERVICE—1961–62

Service	In-School Students	Out-of-School Youths and Adults	Total Enrollments
All services	67,505	78,481	145,986
Agriculture	12,455	4,310	16,765
Distributive and office	6,051	13,827	19,878
Homemaking	40,443	20,430	60,873
Trade and industrial	6,317	34,631	40,948
Practical nursing	. . .	1,828	1,828
Area technical programs	2,239	3,455	5,694

Source: Michigan, Board of Control for Vocational Education, *Annual Descriptive Report for the Fiscal Year Ended June 30, 1962*, p. 1.

Most of the vocational education in Michigan is offered through a number of programs under which institutions that give certain kinds of training in vocational education are reimbursed from state and federal funds.[15] In 1961-62 reimbursed vocational education programs in Michigan provided training for 67,505 high school youths, slightly less than 20 per cent of the total number enrolled in high school and 25 per cent of those who need a salable skill when they leave high school. In addition, 78,481 out-of-school youths and adults attended the programs.[16] The vocational offerings are in the four fields of

[15]Vocational education programs in agriculture, homemaking, trade and industry, and distributive occupations are reimbursed under the Smith-Hughes and George-Bardon acts. Under Title VIII of the National Defense Education Act of 1958, vocational-technical training in post-secondary institutions is reimbursed

[16]Harold T. Smith, *Education and Training for the World of Work: A Vocational Education Program for the State of Michigan* (Kalamazoo, Mich.: W. E. Upjohn Institute for Employment Research, July, 1963), p. 13.

agriculture, homemaking, trade and industry, and distributive occupations. The distribution of enrollment in the 1961-62 school year is presented in Table VII-14.

These data show that among high school students about two-thirds of the enrollments are in homemaking courses. These students, together with those in agricultural courses, account for three-quarters of all enrollments. There is a heavier enrollment in the trade and industrial courses among out-of-school youths and adults, but *over half of the enrollees in vocational education were concentrated in homemaking and agricultural courses*. In considering this distribution of enrollment one must also remember that enrollment in agricultural and homemaking courses has decreased since 1959 and that enrollment in trade and industry courses has increased.

The incongruity between the needs of the labor market and the actual offerings in vocational education is more apparent if we note the following facts. In June, 1962, Michigan had 537 high school districts. Of these 43 per cent offered courses in agriculture, 63 per cent in home economics, 17 per cent in sales or office work, and 17 per cent in trade and industrial subjects. Only 12 of the districts offered programs in all four fields. A few of the large high schools had classes for technicians.[17] Many districts were too small and did not have the resources to offer anything but the most elementary training in any of these fields.

This distribution of offerings is influenced by the force of tradition. Many of the homemaking and agricultural courses were started in the first quarter of the century for a population whose needs were different from ours. The decline in agricultural employment and the increased participation of women in the labor force would lead one to question the wisdom of placing such heavy emphasis on agriculture and homemaking courses today. Moreover, most of these courses aim to prepare the student primarily for the needs of a local labor market. Agricultural training is given to the youths in the farm community. But is this realistic? If current trends persist, we shall see a continued decline in rural employment. By 1970,

[17] *Ibid.*

Table VII-15

AVERAGE RATES OF REIMBURSEMENT FOR VOCATIONAL EDUCATION IN MICHIGAN SCHOOLS BY SERVICE

Service	Peak 5-Year Period	Average Percentage of Reimbursement of Costs		Reduction in Average Percentage of Reimbursement
		In Peak Period	In 1958–62 Period	
Agriculture	1938–42	67.2	38.0	29.2
Homemaking	1934–38	55.2	20.0	35.2
All-day trade and industrial	1936–40	58.8	20.6*	38.2
Co-operative trade and industrial	1941–45	68.0	27.0	41.0
Co-operative—distributive	1938–42	75.0	27.0	48.0
Co-operative—office	1941–45	68.2	27.0	41.2

*20 per cent for the last 4 years.

Source: Michigan, Board of Control for Vocational Education, *Annual Descriptive Report for the Fiscal Year Ended June 30, 1962,* pp. 59-64.

almost 76 per cent of the state's population will be in urban centers, and the majority of the labor force will be seeking urban employment. In addition, about 6 per cent of the state's population moves annually to another community, the mobility being especially pronounced among younger people. It is likely, then, that training aimed only at the needs of a local labor market will never be used.

Another reason for the heavy emphasis on agricultural and home economics courses is the pattern of reimbursement for vocational education by the federal and state governments. As Smith has noted, the reimbursement patterns in the fields of agriculture, home economics, and trade and industry have continued with little change for forty-five years, and reimbursement in business courses has not changed in twenty years.[18] These patterns are most favorable to courses in agriculture and homemaking (see Table VII-15).

The data in Table VII-15 show that the greatest reduction in reimbursement for courses has been in the occupations most in demand in the labor market--trade and industrial, distributive, and office. This differential has undoubtedly been one reason why training in these crucial occupations has not been expanded and why training continues to the same extent in the occupations and skills that are becoming obsolete. The future of vocational education in Michigan is tied to some revision in the present reimbursement formula.

Local diversification of educational investment

Changes in reimbursement patterns in vocational education are necessary, but the major factor in the development of a strong vocational education system is the willingness and capacity of local communities to establish and pay for such education. Almost thirty years ago a sociologist, A. B. Hollingshead, noted that in developing the curriculum local school boards often neglected the need for special training of high school youths.[19] The tendency, undoubtedly based on the class interests and experiences of the local school board members, was to commit the bulk of resources to general education and pay scant heed to the needs of the community for technical and trade education.

The case for vocational education in Michigan is not helped by the practice of depending largely on local tax resources to support such education. Under this system the willingness and capacity of a school district to diversify its educational investment become largely a matter of local priorities and economics. The critical problem is that the same school system must serve the needs of many diverse groups: the

[18]*Ibid.*, p. 34.

[19]A. B. Hollingshead, *Elmstown's Youth* (New York: John Wiley and Sons, Inc., 1949).

underprivileged, the college-bound, the employment-bound, and the handicapped. An overinvestment for one group means a denial of resources for another. The heavy demands currently placed on local community resources for the education of unprecedented numbers of elementary and high school students do not create a suitable climate for establishing a comprehensive vocational education program such as that needed by the labor market. It is difficult to see how such a program can be established without massive support from the state and federal government.

It is also apparent that the local community program of vocational education has a number of inherent defects. The students are usually prepared for jobs in the particular community; little attention is paid to the needs of the larger labor market. Frequently, such training becomes useless if the worker migrates to another community where the labor demands are radically different. Another difficulty with this system is that, since the quality and range of training depend on local resources, vocational education will vary considerably from community to community. In a small community, the variety and quality of vocational education is likely to be more circumscribed than in a larger community with more resources.

The complexity of the problem can be seen in Detroit. Nowhere in Michigan is the need for a comprehensive system of vocational education more pressing than in the city of Detroit, and nowhere are the prospects so bleak. If Detroit had retained its temporary millage increase in the election of November, 1962, the educational investment could have provided more diversified technical education. The failure to approve the millage proposal meant that such education could be offered only at the expense of other vital services.

The system of local community responsibility for developing vocational education presents further difficulties in Detroit. The tax base of Detroit has been decreasing, largely as a result of industrial decentralization, over-aged housing, and the exodus to the suburbs by higher-income groups. Nevertheless the school enrollment continues to increase. This means a further reduction in the funds that can be invested in the education of a single individual. Of the 43 school districts in Wayne County in 1959, Detroit ranked thirteenth in valuations per resident school child (i.e., the total assessed valuation of property divided by the total school enrollment). By way of contrast, River Rouge ranked third. In dollars and cents, Detroit's valuation per resident school child was $19,016, while that of River Rouge was $46,803. Detroit is thus at a disadvantage in the availability of financial resources for education. We must also note that the per capita cost of education in Detroit is higher than in other Michigan communities because the children of less favored families frequently require a sizable investment in compensatory education. These conditions have made it difficult for Detroit to invest in a comprehensive vocational education program, although such an investment is urgently demanded by the changing needs of the labor market and the labor force.

In retraining the unemployed in Michigan the major effort has been conducted under subsidies provided by two federal programs, the Area Redevelopment Act of 1961 and the Manpower Development and Training Act of 1962. As Smith notes, the programs are emergency measures, directed at particular jobs; they are in no way a substitute for a comprehensive program of vocational education.[20] There are two major differences between the programs. The ARA Retraining Program is restricted to training the unemployed in economically depressed areas so that they may fill jobs in existing or new industries, and the trainee is reimbursed for a period of sixteen weeks. On the other hand, the training of the unemployed under the MDTA program is not restricted to an economically depressed area, and reimbursement may last for fifty-two weeks. The cost of the latter program was borne completely by the federal government until June, 1964; since that date the cost of the program has been shared jointly by the state and federal governments.

Table VII-16 shows that 5,893 trainees were enrolled in these programs up to March 1, 1964. A total of 212 different courses was offered in 339 classes. About four-fifths of the trainees who completed the course obtained employment, and of

[20]Smith, p. 35.

Table VII-16

TRAINING PROGRAMS IN MICHIGAN UNDER THE AREA REDEVELOPMENT ACT AND THE MANPOWER DEVELOPMENT TRAINING ACT
(As Reported on February 29, 1964)

Location	Number of Courses	Number of Enrollees	Presently in Training	Completed Training	Drop-outs	Obtained Employment		
						Total	Related to Training	Not Related to Training
State	212	5,893	2,083	3,182	628	2,562	2,197	365
Detroit area*	80	2,766	1,219	1,343	204	1,052	912	140
Lower Peninsula	91	2,181	543	1,289	349	1,037	897	140
Upper Peninsula	41	946	321	550	75	473	388	85

*Includes city of Detroit, Mt. Clemens area, Pontiac area, and Royal Oak area.

Source: Michigan Employment Security Commission data.

this number 82 per cent were in jobs related to their training. These are commendable accomplishments, but the total number of trainees is a small fraction of the state's unemployed. How much can these programs do to solve the problems of mass retraining that will be encountered in the labor market of the 1970's? We will first consider the question of costs and then turn to the question of resources.

The average cost per trainee under the MDTA program was about $1,500; one-fifth of the cost was administrative and the remainder was divided between subsistence and training. The ARA program costs less, about $700 per trainee, because the period of training is shorter. If estimates are based on these figures, the cost of retraining unemployed workers under the MDTA program would be $7.5 million for 5,000 workers, and $30 million for 20,000 workers. The comparable sums under the ARA program would be $3.5 million and $14 million, but this training would be less intense and shorter.[21] When we consider the many thousands of unemployed workers who may require training in the next decade, the financial costs alone become staggering. We must also remember that these estimates do not cover the testing and placement of workers after they are trained.

Even if such financial resources were available, and that is doubtful, the question of training facilities and instructional staff still remains. One of the key problems facing these programs is dependence on local community resources for instructional staff and training facilities. All too often co-operation has not been forthcoming because community leaders felt that an investment in these programs would mean curtailment of some existing community education program. In some cases adequate instructional personnel and facilities were not

[21]It may be argued that $1,500 per student is unrealistic in the future, since the cost will be reduced after the training facilities have been established and the initial curricula developed. However, the $1,500 estimate is based on a 52-week maximum of training, and intensive technical training may need a longer period. Furthermore, as training reaches the chronically unemployed—a group relatively untouched so far—there will have to be an added investment in literacy training. These factors may actually *raise* the cost of training.

available in a given area. Unlike states with a long history in vocational education, Michigan does not have *at present* the curricula, the experienced personnel, and the facilities to sustain programs of vocational retraining on a mass scale. As a result, such retraining is too often conducted on an *ad hoc*, improvised basis, and its value is reduced accordingly. At present funds are sufficient for a considerably expanded program if the personnel and facilities were available. Although some progress has been made, Michigan is still far from possessing the resources to meet the exigencies of retraining the unemployed in the next dozen years.

Prospects for vocational education

The discussion of vocational education and retraining of the unemployed in Michigan leads us to the following observations for the 1970's:

Current practices in Michigan regarding reimbursement and responsibility for vocational education do not give grounds for optimism about the near future. Some revision in these practices is necessary if a comprehensive program is to be developed. The present reimbursement policies favor agricultural and home economics training, and although such programs may be useful they do not prepare youths for participation in the labor force. The decentralized responsibility for vocational education poses the problem that training under local systems may be too restrictive for the needs of the larger labor market.

It is more than likely that the next step in Michigan must be to establish vocational education systems to serve a broad geographic area, such as the training center at Northern Michigan University in Marquette. Such centralization makes possible the following advantages: (a) a greater concentration of training facilities and personnel than would be possible in a single school district, (b) a spreading of costs over a wide area, and (c) a continuity of instruction in certain technical specialties. Although it is not completely clear at this time, the basic unit in such a system may be the community college.

The vocational education system in Michigan will undoubtedly be helped by the recent federal legislation that has broadened the scope of federally supported vocational education. The Morse-Perkins act, approved by President Johnson in December, 1963, provides for progressive boosts of federal aid for vocational education over the next four years. The 1963 federal contribution for traditional vocational education was $55 million. Congress authorized that this sum be more than doubled by 1965. By 1967, and thereafter, the federal government will contribute $225 million annually. Under the new law, funds are also provided for building facilities and for the training of underprivileged youth. Of special importance are the provisions that favor reimbursement to states based on their need for funds to provide training for skills presently required in the labor market. This latter provision de-emphasizes the traditional support that has been given to agricultural and home economics training.

The retraining of unemployed workers will continue to be conducted under the ARA and MDTA programs. These programs are largely emergency measures, and their true value may be as catalysts toward developing state and local community manpower programs. The costs and structure of these programs indicate that they will be able to offer training for only a limited number of the unemployed.

In the early development of these programs, the trainees selected were not really representative of the Michigan unemployed. They were better educated and younger than the general population of the unemployed. There has already been some correction of this tendency, and we may expect more concentration on the chronically unemployed and on underprivileged youths. The amendments to the Manpower Development and Training Act in December, 1963, provide compensation to more youths during training, literacy training, and experimental programs to encourage geographical mobility for the trainees. These amendments should change the structure and composition of the program significantly. We do not expect, however, that there will be a dramatic increase in the training capacity of the number of trainees under MDTA or ARA programs.

The training and retraining concept has become an accepted part of a broad-gauged manpower utilization plan. It would be dangerous, however, to think that the complex problems of the next ten years can be resolved simply by more retraining. Retraining programs can have meaning only if more job opportunities are developed and sound practices in employment security are established.

Summing Up

The Michigan economy is currently adjusting to a new set of social and economic forces that will affect the utilization and participation of human resources in the labor market for the next dozen years. We have entered a new phase of government spending, particularly in weapons, that will have profound effects on the Michigan economy. A major technological revolution is in progress, changing the requirements for employment as well as the content of jobs. The demographic structure of the work force is feeling the impact of the high postwar birth rates and the continuing emancipation of women from time-consuming household chores. There is also the steady pressure from non-whites for equal employment opportunities with whites. All of these forces are shaping the Michigan labor market of the 1970's.

In the 1970's, if present trends persist, the labor force will be much better trained than the work force of preceding years. It will comprise more young people and more women. A greater share of the 1970 labor force will be engaged in services and similar activities rather than in producing goods, constructing buildings, extracting minerals, or growing food. The central expectation about the 1970's is that most occupations will demand more and better training than they do in this decade.

These circumstances will raise a number of problems for Michigan. It is not our intention, nor would it be possible, to name and discuss these problems in detail, but some of the more important ones deserve mention.

Considering employment prospects in the aggregate, we find some cause for sustained concern. In the 1970's there will be an unprecedented demand for professional, technical, and skilled workers to serve the needs of new technologies and the growing metropolitan character of Detroit. The inadequacy of the present structure of vocational training in the state, the failure to plan for sufficient expansion of higher education, and the drain of talent described by David Goldberg do not augur well for the fulfillment of needs of the labor market in the 1970's. This bottleneck in trained personnel will also mean that new productive enterprises requiring such personnel will not locate in the state and thus will not help provide the 500,000 new jobs necessary for the added labor force.

The unprecedented numbers of youths entering the labor force will create another problem. The new technologies of the 1970's will mean that these young people will require more training than has been necessary in previous generations. In addition, these young workers will bring greater pressure to bear on older workers, especially on those displaced from work, and will compound their re-employment problems. Earlier retirement may be the solution for the older workers, but the structure and financial support for such retirement are problems that must be solved by both young and old in the work force.

Competition for jobs will increase not only between young and old workers but also between men and women. Training for jobs traditionally open to men will increasingly be extended to women. It is also possible that as the number of jobs in fields traditionally occupied by women increases male job-seekers will be under strong pressure to undertake training in these specialties. Predicted shortages in such fields as nursing, social work, and teaching may be filled through the greater utilization of males in these occupations. This will involve the serious problem of changing the image of these occupations to stimulate the recruitment of males.

Another problem that will receive increasing attention is the employment of non-white persons. Given the gap in educational and job opportunities that has existed between whites and non-whites, what is the most expeditious way of narrowing these differences? It is quite apparent from the data we have cited that the gap will not be closed without special efforts by whites and non-whites. The need to remove artificial barriers to employment will demand special programs of aid to the less favored. The very emotional responses that this problem evokes will make it one of the most difficult to solve.

Needless to say, other problems could be cited. How, for example, do we encourage displaced workers with obsolete skills to seek retraining? How do we increase the number of jobs that will be needed for our labor force? It should be apparent that we cannot rely on the labor market to make self-regulating adjustments to furnish the solution. The problems will be too complex. More than ever before, the 1970's will demand the planning and application of long-range policies to assure the efficient functioning of the labor market.